120G

N
d

Secular
Wholeness

Secular Wholeness

A skeptic's paths to a richer life

David E. Cortesi

Cover design by Dany Galgani.
http://www.galgani.com
Galaxy image courtesy Space Telescope Science Institute and NASA.

This book has a home page!
For updates, extra material, reader dialogue and more, see
http://www.tassos-oak.com

National Library of Canada Cataloguing in Publication Data

Cortesi, David E.
    Secular wholeness : a skeptic's paths to a richer life

Includes index.
ISBN 1-55369-175-X

    1. Secularism. I. Title.

BL2747.8.C67 2002   211'.6   C2002-900115-3

TRAFFORD

This book was published *on-demand* in cooperation with Trafford Publishing.
On-demand publishing is a unique process and service of making a book available for retail sale to the public taking advantage of on-demand manufacturing and Internet marketing.
On-demand publishing includes promotions, retail sales, manufacturing, order fulfilment, accounting and collecting royalties on behalf of the author.

Suite 6E, 2333 Government St., Victoria, B.C. V8T 4P4, CANADA

Phone	250-383-6864	Toll-free	1-888-232-4444 (Canada & US)
Fax	250-383-6804	E-mail	sales@trafford.com
Web site	www.trafford.com	TRAFFORD PUBLISHING IS A DIVISION OF TRAFFORD HOLDINGS LTD.	
Trafford Catalogue #01-0577		www.trafford.com/robots/01-0577.html	

10   9   8   7   6   5   4   3

Contents

Introduction

This book is a long answer to a short question. Here's the question: Can you build a vital, fulfilling life experience using methods and ideas that are purely secular, not based in religious doctrine?

If that seems like a pointless question to you, you are probably one of the majority of Americans who profess a religious belief. You naturally assume that when you need an answer to one of life's big questions, you'll find it in that belief — and probably you will. But some of us do not find any religion satisfactory, and I am one. Although I am content with my choice, when I watch people who diligently practice a religion, I see their practice yielding important benefits. I had to ask: are those benefits uniquely "religious" and so unavailable to people like me? Or do they have secular sources? Are all the routes to wholeness, to an integrated life practice, exclusively religious? Or can a *secular life practice* lead to a meaningful, satisfying life?

This book is my answer, to be shared with others who want to deepen their lives and who find religious ideas unhelpful.

If you *are* comfortable in a religious belief, understand that this book is about finding secular sources for things that your religious practice ought to be giving you. If you aren't getting them, I respectfully suggest you look deeper into your own faith. But you are certainly welcome to walk along with the rest of us on our quest!

The goods of religious practice

When I observe the life-styles of devout people, I see their religious practice delivering these important values:

- The philosophical comfort of existential validity — in plain language, assurance that one is not an accident but an intentional creation, with a role in a great story.

- The social and material support of a congregation of like-minded people.

- The psychological benefits of contemplative prayer and meditation.

- The emotional comfort of ritual.

- For a few, the bliss of ecstatic union with the All.

- Constant challenge to be a better person, to transcend one's limits.

- The use of a predefined ethical system.

- Fearless awareness of death and comfort in bereavement.

These are the benefits for which I hope to find secular sources. As a skeptic by inclination and training, I have been quite selective in my search. I only tell you about things I have personally tried, or things that are documented in respected scientific journals, or things that, like the philosophy of Epicurus, are both satisfying to common sense and visibly harmless.

Chapter summary

Here is what follows this Introduction:

- Chapter 1 elaborates on the good things any religious practice should give to those who devotedly practice it.

- Chapter 2 explores the philosophical and emotional implications of being a "mere accident" and shows how contingency can be turned into triumph.

- Chapter 3 reviews the research that shows how crucial human contacts are to your life and health, and points out many techniques to improve them.

- Chapter 4 introduces a single model incorporating meditation, contemplation, and prayer, and introduces simple meditation practices whose benefits have been documented.

- Chapter 5 shows how pervasive ritual is in everyone's life, and suggests ways to take control of the rituals in your life.

- Chapter 6 surveys the literature on the mystical experience, showing that it is probably a real, though rare, state of brain function; then takes up the tough question of whether the experience is worth pursuing.

- Chapter 7 proposes that we cannot be taught heroes but have to discover them, each of us in an idiosyncratic way; but then says there are plenty of them to be discovered.

- Chapter 8 tackles the problem of defining and justifying a personal ethical code, drawing elements from a wide range of traditions.

- Chapter 9 urges the importance of facing up to death and bereavement, and shows ways to prepare for one and deal with the other.

- Chapter 10 surveys the research on what makes people happy, and covers a number of strategies for becoming more happy.

- Chapter 11 is about four radical techniques for making oneself more resilient in the face of disaster.

Notes and References

A numbered reference like this[1] refers to one of the notes that begin on page 201. Some notes only give a citation for a quote or statement, but others expand on the main text, or shed a sidelight on it, or take off at a wild tangent to it. Your rule can be: if you want to know more about the sentence with the note, turn to the note; if not, skip it.

On page 231 you'll find a list of books that can take you deeper into any of the subjects I touch on. A bibliography of print and internet references follows it.

Acknowledgements

The following people made constructive or challenging comments on early drafts: Marian Cortesi, Gloria Gatlin, Katie Hover, Nancy Howe, Thane Plambeck, Pam Sogard, Jon Thompson. The book is far better for their input.

I was very fortunate to be able to wander amid the amazing riches of the Green Library at Stanford University; without it, I could never have finished this work.

1. Benefits of a Religious Practice

Even a perfunctory religious practice takes time, energy, and money. If a middle-class family only goes to church every Sunday, that still costs a few hours a week and a few hundred dollars a year — time and money for which any family could easily find other uses. A devout person's practice can dominate life with activities like prayer five times a day, or daily attendance at mass or temple. It takes as much as a tenth of one's income, and fills the remaining free time with voluntary activities such as being a reader or a deacon.

Why are people willing to donate so much of their precious time and wealth? The simplest explanation is that a religious practice returns immediate, practical benefits that amply repay the believer's investment. Any religion, whatever else it may be, can be viewed as a kind of mutual-aid society, set up and maintained by its community of believers, with a mission of delivering important social, psychological, and material benefits.

Religions are so effective at this part of what they do that we can fall into the habit of assuming that the benefits they dispense are uniquely religious in nature, unavailable from any other source. I don't think that's so; but let's look in detail at what I believe are the important benefits that a religious practice delivers.

Existential validity

This dry philosopher's phrase is the vital center of what most people mean when they talk about "the meaning of life." Every religion supplies answers to the questions like "why am I here?"

and "how am I to live?" According to a standard psychology text, the feeling that you have answers to such questions "lowers anxiety and promotes resiliency, hope and peace."[1]

Noncontingency

A Jewish, Christian, or Moslem believer gains the comfort of an assured place in the scheme of things as a "child of God," created by God intentionally for some purpose. The purpose may not be clear, but it can be sought.

As a Hindu, you know that you're the current embodiment of a spark, an *atman*, that has existed for immeasurable time. As a Buddhist you can take comfort in knowing that your nature and your birth situation were determined by *kamma* accumulated in past lives, and that with effort in this life, you can improve the circumstances of your future lives, eventually escaping the wheel of suffering entirely.

In philosophical terms, a believer is assured that he or she is *noncontingent*; in other words, not an accident. If you aren't an accident, it follows that your personality, your features, your talents and shortcomings, your birthplace and parents — your whole inheritance — are not accidental either. In philosopher-speak, your "nature is determined" by a supernatural plan.

The opposite view is that each of us is the expression of a random shuffle of the deck of human DNA, so the only possible answer to "why am I here?" is, "You just are, OK?" That idea is usually presented as profoundly scary. However, we need to pass through the fear and find the clarity on the other side.

A role in the great war of good and evil

Some doctrines offer the believer a role in a cosmic drama of good against evil. The believer is not merely a non-accident, but an actor in an engrossing drama.

In many Christian denominations, members are encouraged to think of themselves as "peculiar people"[2] whom God has set apart from mundane society. Other religions encourage the sense of uniqueness by emphasizing the constant need to be vigilant against the infidel, the godless, the material world, against the temptations of everything outside the faith. At its most vivid, among some

Christian Fundamentalist denominations, this attitude encourages believers to think they are under daily assault by evil spirits sent by Satan. Here's a recent example of this kind of thinking. After a deranged man shot up a prayer meeting in Fort Worth, Texas, one student at Southwestern Baptist Theological Seminary told the New York times,

> It is the enemy, conducting spiritual warfare. It's an attack on Christianity in general, on christians, and it's Satan trying to stop God's work on Earth. He'll use whoever he wants, whoever he can. The guy who did this was obviously angry. Satan uses anger.[3]

You might suppose that thinking this way would lead to fear, even paranoia. On the contrary, and I speak from personal observation, it salts an otherwise-drab life with drama, and gives believers frequent feelings of triumph. They enjoy testifying about resisting the wiles of the devil, saying things like "I said, 'Get thee behind me, Satan,' and I just walked right out of there"[4]; and they enjoy giving credit for all successful outcomes to God: "I just yelled 'Jesus, help me' and hung on to the wheel, and He helped me pull that car right out of that skid, praise His name."

A belief like this is a great gift to those who can hold it. It doesn't matter how humble or wretched mundane life might be; the believer can think: I have a vast unseen dimension; I can defy and outwit the very Antichrist; I can call upon God Almighty whenever I need him. I cannot offer an exact secular substitute, but just the same, a person who grasps the scientific world view is able to bestride the world in a different way. We'll see how in Chapter 2.

Community

Denominations differ in the degree of community they create, but any time "two or three are gathered together" for worship[5], a community of like-minded people is formed. It is a powerful psychological benefit to be accepted as member of any group of people. To be a part of a group of people who all hold opinions like yours on important subjects is even better. In Chapter 3 we will look at comparable alternatives.

Community-building

The act of meeting regularly for worship services holds each congregation together. At the assembly on Friday, Saturday or Sunday the members see each other, become familiar with each other's faces, and keep up to date on each other's life passages — new babies, children moved away or come home again, people ill or recovered. And they note each other's needs. ("Poor old Johnson, he can hardly walk since that stroke." "Well, at least he's on his feet again. I think I'll stop by and see if his wife needs any help.")

A wonderful feature of the modern Catholic mass is the "kiss of peace," when everyone hugs or shakes hands with everyone else within reach. Some Protestant denominations emphasize and intensify the congregational spirit with an "us versus them" mindset, call each other Brother and Sister, and label nonbelievers as "worldly" or "unsanctified." Similarly, the Quran reminds believers they are "the best community" among mankind[6].

Professional advisor and arbiter

Every church, mosque, and synagogue comes equipped with a full-time, trained counselor, arbiter, and personal advisor: its pastor, priest, rabbi, imam, roshi, or whoever. Free access to a sympathetic, confidential advisor is a benefit that the congregation gives to itself.

Mutual aid

The Latter-Day Saints have a particularly strong mutual aid organization. A Mormon in trouble anywhere in the USA can find willing help at any local Stake. But in all churches, membership is a link to a circle of people that can be called upon for help in time of trouble, for job contacts, or just for sympathy.

In many churches on Sunday morning there is a public announcement of communicants in need: "Let us pray for Brother Smith, who is in the hospital with heart trouble, and let us pray for Sister Jones, who has family problems."

It has been well documented[7] that people who are active church members gain health benefits. For example, active church members have a significantly lower post-operative mortality rate than those who are not. The percentage of non-members who die in the days following a major operation is nearly double the percentage of church-goers who die. We'll consider some of the many possible explanations in Chapter 3.

Like minds

There is comfort in being part of a group of people that you can trust to think the way you do on key issues[8]. It's relaxing to be with people among whom you will not have to defend or justify your opinions. Conversely, it is stressful to be among people who, however nice they might be otherwise, are likely to challenge your convictions if you voice them.

This trust is a great stress-reducer for a parent. Believers with children expect, rightly or wrongly, that other children in the church community are better playmates and potential mates for their own kids. I was a child of devout parents and, remembering well what hellions I and my peers were, I would say this is a pathetic mirage! But true or false, the expectation itself reduces stress.

Contemplation and tranquility

Most religions encourage some form of contemplation. Imagine kneeling in the tranquil dimness of a Catholic church; fixing your gaze on the illuminated crucifix over the altar or on the twinkling votive candles; letting the rosary beads slip through your fingers as you whisper simple, patterned prayers. Whatever else it may be, this is meditation, and its real, physiological benefits have been well-documented in the literature[9].

The believer comes to prayer with a list of worries — family problems, financial problems, concerns for the world at large — and, in the quiet of the prayer, organizes these worries, considering each one and putting it into a context of the eternal. The believer who prays properly can't avoid getting up with a clearer, more settled mind and a more positive attitude.

We'll explore some of the psychological results of these things in Chapter 4. There are secular routes to contemplation, tranquility, and clarity.

Ritual and pageantry

Rituals are immensely comforting. They bring stability to life. They help us process shock, trauma, and uncertainty. We can use rituals to motivate and program our own minds in positive or negative ways.

A religion provides its followers with a variety of satisfying rites and celebrations for major life transitions. In addition, church rituals provide esthetic experience. From the grandeur of a Papal mass to the gripping psychodrama of a revival meeting, churches "make show"[10] to the satisfaction of the congregation. Isaiah Berlin has said,

> I am not religious, but I place high value on the religious experience of believers. I am moved by religious services — those of the synagogue, but also of churches and mosques. I think that those who do not understand what it is to be religious, do not understand what human beings live by. That is why dry atheists seem to me blind and deaf to some forms of profound human experiences, perhaps the inner life: it is like being aesthetically blind.[11]

In Chapter 5 I urge you to examine the place of ritual in your secular life. Every person and family develops rituals; but are yours healthy and supportive? (I leave it to you to find your own esthetic satisfaction.)

Mystical ecstasy

A few people have the fortune to be visited by a mystical experience of life-changing force. A central feature of such experiences is a blissful sense of losing the self in a greater All. For example,

> ...all at once, as it were out of the intensity of the consciousness of individuality, individuality itself seemed to dissolve and fade away into boundless being, and this not a confused state but the clearest, the surest of the surest, utterly beyond words — where death was an almost laughable impossibility — the loss of personality (if so it were) seeming no extinction, but the only true life. I am ashamed of my feeble description. Have I not said the state is utterly beyond words?
>
> – Alfred, Lord Tennyson[12]

The mystical experience has usually been pursued in a religious context, and when it is achieved in that context, it is interpreted in religious terms. However, mystical experience can be sought in other contexts. In Chapter 6 I adopt the view that this, like every other experience anyone can have, is in the last analysis a state of the brain. The question is, how to induce that state, and is it worth the effort?

Self-transcendence

Every religion constantly urges its members to be better people, to transcend their mundane lives, to achieve more, give more, challenge themselves to be more. A cynic might snap that most people manage to ignore the challenge, but nevertheless, some do take it up and transcend themselves in the religious context. Whether it's the young woman later known as Mother Theresa, first seeing Christ in the faces of the poor, or the alcoholic who stays sober through AA's semi-religious program, or the Buddhist who diligently practices compassion for all sentient beings, some challenges to self-transcendence do work, do inspire people to become heroically better.

Outside of religion, inspirational models and heroes are said to be rare in American culture. In Chapter 7 we consider where we can look for inspiration, and end up considering the meaning of Quality.

Ethical structure

Every religion has an asset that is the labor of many lifetimes: the careful work of its theologians in crafting an ethical system. Not just the Torah, but the labor of uncounted rabbinical scholars; not just the Bible but the work of untold theologians; not merely the Quran, or *Science and Health*, or the Pali canon, or the *Bhagavad Gita*, but all the countless volumes of interpretation based on them.

These generations of commentators were not stupid! From an unbeliever's standpoint, some began their work from bizarre basic assumptions, and as a result the ethical systems they derive may seem bizarre (for example, the aspect of the Islamic ethical system that sanctions the *fatwa*, or death sentence, on Salman Rushdie can seem bizarre to non-Muslims). But within the context of each doctrine, these thinkers have created a self-consistent code that is available to every member without further effort.

In *The Brothers Karamazov*, Dostoevsky has Ivan Karamazov say "If God does not exist, everything is permitted"[13]. Ivan expresses an attitude that is still common today. Four percent of believers choose "Without God there is no morality" as their top reason for believing[14]. Pop philosopher Dennis Prager has said "if there is no God, there is no good and evil — there are only opinions about good and evil."[15]

Statements like these are initially gripping because they set up a frightening choice: you either accept a religious moral code or face the awful prospect of having the whole burden of designing and justifying a moral code dumped on *you*. And how are *you* going to select between differing "opinions about good and evil?" Possibly by — oh, I don't know — *thinking*? In Chapter 8 I will show that thinking about ethics is not only possibly but quite doable.

Comfort facing death and loss

When someone you know dies, it tears a hole in the fabric of your life. There's a deep need to think that the missing person is somewhere still; the concept of "just gone" is really difficult to form, as well as unpalatable. Here is Douglas Hofstadter, a rationalist if there ever was one, writing of his wife who, tragically, died young:

> And these days, when I'm running that same old Bryan Park loop and I come to that same old spot, every once in a while I'll still softly yell out, *ciao bella*!, half-hoping to catch that merry wink and to hear her echo my call. I don't know why I do it. I just wish she could hear me. And — who knows? — maybe, dashing on in miniature, safely ensconced in the recesses of my faithful heart, she still can. *Magari*.[16]

If it is hard to accept that a loved one is gone, it is just about impossible to imagine that of your own sweet self! Religions offer help to justify death, to integrate it into life. The congregation offers emotional and practical support. There is the promise of an afterlife that may or may not make death easier to face.

In this area, the advantages are not all on the side of religious practice. The downside to believing in an afterlife is that the dead are never truly buried. They hang around in your imagination, watching and criticizing your progress through life. Yet they cannot learn, adapt, or grow, as your own life evolves. Their imaginary presence remains a dead hand of the past on life.

Also, the promise of an afterlife is conditional; afterlife is held as a hostage to good behavior in the now. This make a believer's conscience to some degree an involuntary captive of the religious doctrine. It also makes the approach of death even more traumatic than it naturally would be. Not only are you going to die, but immediately afterward you are going to face some kind of judgment on the quality of your life — a judgment with dire consequences and no appeal.

There's another, less noble reason for the popularity of belief in the afterlife: vengeance! It's comforting, for a powerless person, to believe that every unpunished scoundrel will eventually scream in agony and remorse.[17]

We who don't practice religion have to live without these comforts, as the late Carl Sagan knew:

> I would love to believe that when I die I will live again, that some thinking, feeling, remembering part of me will continue. But as much as I want to believe that, and despite the ancient and worldwide cultural traditions that assert an afterlife, I know of nothing to suggest that it is more than wishful thinking.[18]

In Chapter 9 we'll discuss how it is still possible to come to terms with death, use it as a motivator, and even learn to celebrate it.

Summary

Completely aside from the truth or value of its doctrines, a religion is a social structure: a fraternity, a mutual aid society, and the source of a wide variety of psychological supports and comforts to its members. In the following chapters we will search for ways to claim the same benefits from secular sources.

2. Finding Validity

In Chapter 1, I noted that conventional religion offers its practitioners the comfort of a cosmic story that accounts for their existence, nature, and purpose in life. We who cannot subscribe to these great stories must find a way to be comfortable with the belief that we are *contingent*: the result of a lucky combination of genetic units — what some might call "a mere accident." What difference should that make in life?

On being no "mere" accident

The first thing I want to do is to drive a stake through that adjective "mere"! If we are accidents, it is in the same sense that a snowflake is an accident. Folklore has it that every snowflake is unique. Well, consider that there are astronomically more ways of combining DNA codons than there are ways of crystallizing plain water molecules. So we are each an accident that is uncountably more rare, more intricate, more unlikely than any snowflake that ever fell in all of Earth's history.

Many billions of people have lived and died and are dust. The mathematically-possible combinations of human DNA are nearly uncountable. Only an infinitesimal fraction of those possibilities — that is, people! — have every existed. Only the tiniest fraction ever will exist. Yet here we are! We made it! What incredible good fortune! Why are we not celebrating?

Existential dread

The choice between being an accident or being an intentional creation is a fundamental issue in philosophy. The choice is between contingency and noncontingency; that is, between seeing the universe as a network of causes leading to effects, each effect contingent on many causes before it, and seeing everything as somehow planned and proceeding in a way that a supernatural intelligence intends.

Camus, Sartre and the rest of the Existentialists were the first thinkers to face up formally to contingency: if there is no central plan or planner, the universe and all beings in it must be determined only by circumstances, without preplanned nature or essence. What then follows? How should people order their lives in the cold light of that idea?

When you first absorb the thought of contingency, it is profoundly unsettling. We have been taught to expect that there is an explanation for every event and a purpose behind every action. We start asking "why?" at age 2 and never stop, even after we learn that there is often no meaningful answer. It is upsetting to think that there is no simple, direct explanation for our own existence (other than a boring mechanical one about a sperm and egg getting together) and no purpose behind our birth (other than our parents' possibly casual plans for the size of their family). Somehow, it seems a betrayal. Where do we fit? Who stole the instructions?

Pascal said that man found himself "suspended in the material body that nature has given him, between the two abysses of infinity and nothingness." The Existentialist writers liked to revel in the scariness of it all, as when Camus opened a famous essay with the lines

> There is but one truly serious philosophical problem, and that is suicide. Judging whether life is or is not worth living amounts to answering the fundamental question of philosophy... And if it is true, as Nietzsche claims, that a philosopher, to deserve respect, must preach by example, you can appreciate the importance of that reply...[1]

The scariness of contingency has been noted by psychologists such as Abraham Maslow:

> Many orthodoxly religious people would be so frightened by giving up the notion that the universe has integration, unity, and therefore meaningfulness (which is given to it by the fact that was all created by God or ruled by God or *is* God) that the only alternative for them would be to see the universe as a totally unintegrated chaos.[2]

Yet in my opinion, the alternative — a nature determined by a supernatural plan — turns out to be just as scary in its way; while the contingent universe is not at all chaotic and anything but unintegrated.

Consequences of a predetermined nature

We have solid evidence from biology that both our bodies and the deepest tendencies of our personalities are the expression of our genetic inheritance. From psychology and sociology we have strong evidence that almost everything else about us is the result of our interactions with our environment, parents, family and peers in our early years.

All this evidence fits perfectly with the idea that each of us is a wonderful accident, a random selection of DNA[3] that then expresses itself amid the pressures and influences of a unique family, and culture, and moment in history. These are what "determine our natures" in any practical sense.

If we are all this and yet our natures are also somehow determined by a plan, the only way it could happen is that some agent determined our basic structure by controlled the mating choices of our parents down to the exact choice of sperm and egg at the moment of conception. More; to finish the job, the same agent had to control all the defining experiences of our formative years. To make *every* person, not only you, non-accidental and preplanned, this agent would have to intervene undetected in every one of the billions of conceptions, as well as every personality-forming event of every childhood around the world.

Dark side of a divine plan

It seems to me that if we are noncontingent — if, as some people like to say, "everything happens for a purpose" — some very uncomfortable conclusions have to follow. For one, we would have to acknowledge that the same plan that produces splendid specimens like us also mandates children with Down Syndrome, spina bifida, and neonatal cancers, to mention only three of many tragic possibilities. And, in order to give some people their natures, the plan requires that their formative experiences should include disaster, privation, and physical and emotional abuse.

It seems to me that this idea alone is a good deal less comfortable to live with than existential dread. I would much rather think that things like birth defects, diseases, and child abuse are the outcome of contingent circumstances, than think that some supernatural being plans them.

Incompatibility with free will

A second problem with noncontingency is a side effect of all the billions of interventions that are needed to produce every person to a plan. Each of the things that determined *your* nature — your parent's mating choices, and every childhood interaction you had with another person — was also an event in *other* peoples' lives. In order to produce a particular nature in any one person, there has to be control and alteration of the lives of countless other people, some in major ways. People are dying from seemingly-random causes — landslides and floods and drive-by shootings — every second. Presumably at least some, perhaps all, of these deaths are required by the plan for the purpose of forming the natures of the people who are affected by them.

In short, the idea of a predetermined human nature cannot help but require predestination of most events in every life, possibly all events. In order to accept that consequence you would have to pretty much give up the idea of free will[4], and accept that much of your life experience is stage-managed for the purpose of molding other people's natures. That conclusion also seems to me a high price to pay only to avoid existential dread.

Fill the abyss with light

Very well, we must settle for being contingent, each of us another amazingly unlikely intersection between a random shake of the DNA dice and a moment in history. And that forces us to peer into Pascal's abyss, a scene that a modern cosmologist summarized this way:

> One of the strong and pervasive images of the twentieth century western world is that man is alone in an alien universe, absurd in his inability to participate in the vast schemes of the cosmos, a fluke, a mistake, perhaps even a cosmic joke... A stranger and a tourist in the physical universe, we contribute little other than our refuse and receive little other than an earth upon which to stand.[5]

Before you take too seriously this image of fragile, naked humankind, huddling below the cold, black emptiness of space, you should ask yourself who benefits from spreading it.

Like every mythic image, it survives because it serves someone's needs. It was shaped by nineteenth-century astronomers to emphasize the grandeur of the sky and the power of their telescopes. It was reinforced by NASA to underline the bravery of the astronauts and the cleverness of the engineers. It pleases religious proselytizers because it makes the alternatives to belief so scary. And it flatters anyone who, for any reason, likes to think of humankind as especially privileged in the scheme of things. When you view people as brave, lonely representatives of consciousness, you can forgive them almost anything in their struggle to survive in the face of a cold, inimical universe.

It's also an image that, when properly considered, is almost perfectly contrary to observation! People who spend their lives looking closely at nature come to see this. Here is naturalist Bernd Heinrich, observing beech tree reproduction in the Maine woods:

> Each seed contains a tree embryo, the *information* to make a tree, which can become expressed if it becomes implanted in the earthen womb ... A tree's life is an extraordinary achievement against incredible odds, from an individualistic perspective. From the perspective of nature, on the other hand, there is assurance that each tree will produce, on the average, just one other reproducing tree ... to a tree, and to most other organisms, life itself is the very ideal of the "luck

of the draw." ... The world we inhabit is built on chaos rather than on a predetermined order. And that is precisely what I find to be uplifting, and food for joyful optimism.[6]

When Heinrich writes "chaos," I think he means the mathematical chaos: results that are unpredictable because they are exquisitely dependent on the fine details of the initial conditions. He does not find hope in the conventional idea of "without form, and void," but rather in a world in which every natural process displays the dizzying combination of long-term stability with short-term unpredictability that is characteristic of chaotic math.

Universal Fecundity

This fecund chaos is found everywhere we look. The universe is *not* cold, empty, and dark; it bubbles with form and structure at every scale of measure that we can observe. At the shortest meaningful lengths (the Planck length) the vacuum seethes with energy, throwing up matching pairs of particles and annihilating them in literally inconceivable quantities — as if the universe was effervescent with the urge to create.

At molecular scales, great swathes of "empty" space are filled with clouds of dust and gas within which a myriad of chemical reactions proceed — at a stately pace owing to low temperatures, granted, but the universe has plenty of time. Astronomers have observed molecular clouds containing sugars, amino acids, and other chemicals of life, cooked up on dust grains by the light of new stars.

At stellar scales, the more we learn about stars, the more structure and variety we find. At galactic scales, stars and gas organize themselves into a zoo of interacting dynamic structures. At cosmic scales, herds of galaxies stream in gravitationally-bound clouds.

The more closely we look at *anything*, the more structure and form the universe reveals. Among the planetary bodies of our own solar system (which only a few decades ago were tiny dots of pastel-colored light) we have yet to find a boring object. Each planet and moon is stunningly unique, and each one has been as impossible to predict from first principles as a human personality. No geologist or science-fiction writer could ever have dreamed that the universe is able, using only rock, ice and time, to make something like the terrain of Jupiter's satellite, Europa:

– Courtesy NASA/JPL/Caltech (Web NASA)

Or the South Pole of Mars:

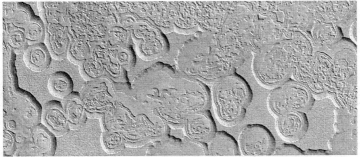

– Courtesy NASA/JPL/Caltech (Web NASA)

Far from being cold and empty, the universe *sparkles* with radiation, *bubbles* with form.[7]

The Dance of Maya

The Vedanta branch of Hinduism takes the view that the essence of the universe is *play* — the universe is at exuberant play with itself, dancing a vast private dance in which each interchange of energy is a step, each structure a graceful gesture[8]. The more carefully scientists look, the more their observations support this grand metaphor: *the universe drives toward structure at every scale of measurement*, any structure at all, filling out every possibility.

At the level of biochemistry, the universe likes to ramify branching structures, whether tree roots or blood vessels in the eye. We carry the most elaborate branching structures ever made inside our heads — our brains. However (lest we get cocky), our foliage is pathetic, and we couldn't filter plankton through our teeth at any price. In other words, we are only another gesture in the great dance of form.

In this view, we do indeed have a right to exist, but only the same right as any other arrangement of matter and energy: the right to continue to exist until transformed into something else. And the universe has no special interest in when that happens. After all, it is no less invested in the "something else" that we will become (and in what that becomes, *ad infinitum*) than it is in ourselves.

Try to replace Pascal's "abysses of infinity and nothingness" with this image of an exuberant, light-filled universe, bursting out into forms and living species as readily as an ocean bursts out in waves and sea-foam, and reabsorbing them just as readily. When you do, two nice consequences follow.

First, any "problem of evil" disappears. This universe regards the murder of one human by another exactly the way it regards an avalanche falling on a human, or a virus infecting one: with sublime indifference. Avalanches fall; viruses infect; mammals prey on one another — it's what they *do*. Now, this absolutely does not mean that *we* should be indifferent! On the contrary, desiring to be moral, trying to be compassionate, and urging other people to be moral and compassionate, are also things that we *do*, quite as naturally and with better outcomes for our own survival. However, when the virus infects or the avalanche or blow falls, we no longer have to torment ourselves trying to invent explanations why, or trying to see how such awful things can fit into a plan.

Second, the light-filled universe makes it easier to know why you are here, and what you should do with your existence. Why are we here? Because each of us is one tiny "yip" of pleasure from a careless, tap-dancing infinity. In that sense, you and I are exactly as important as the same number of eagles, or oak trees.

We have no choice but to be part of Infinity's dance. We do have a choice of what kind of partners we will be! How, then, should we live? There can only be one answer: emulate the universe. Ramify! Burgeon! Dance!

Revelation without end

The account of the world that is contained in the doctrines of a religion helps to explain where the world came from, paints grand dramas of good and evil, and supplies metaphors for life. Useful as it is, this canon of wisdom is fixed in extent. Those outside of religion have access to a canon, as well; and it is infinite and ever-unfolding. Too few know this or celebrate it.

Fixed extent of human revelation

Each great religion is based on the revelation perceived by one founding master and teacher — Moses, the Buddha, Jesus, the Prophet, or in recent history, George Fox, Joseph Smith, Mary Baker Eddy. Once the master has gone, it falls to the disciples to preserve what they can of the master's teachings.

Two things follow from this. First, the most that current believers can receive of the master's insights is that fraction which the master was able to convey by word and example. We can never know the breadth and depth of the original revelation as it formed in the master's mind; what is left to us is what the master could communicate. Buddhists are specific about this; one of the most often-quoted teachings of the Buddha is this one:

> Once the Blessed One was staying at Kosambi in the Simsapa forest. Then, picking up a few Simsapa leaves with his hand, he asked the monks, "How do you construe this, monks: Which are more numerous, the few Simsapa leaves in my hand or those overhead in the Simsapa forest?"

> "The leaves in the hand of the Blessed One are few in number, lord. Those overhead in the forest are far more numerous."

> "In the same way, monks, those things that I have known with direct knowledge but have not taught are far more numerous [than what I have taught]. "
> – Samyutta Nikaya LVI.31

Beyond what the master was able to teach, the canon as received today is only that fraction that the disciples could accurately remember and pass on. Accurate preservation is essential. After all, people do not ask, "What do you, Peter or Ananda, think?" They expect Peter or Ananda to tell them what the master thought.

The second result of a preserved canon is that it cannot, of itself, adapt to changing circumstances. Anything less than complete, accurate preservation of everything in the canon of teachings is unthinkable; yet that inevitably means that the sweeping spotlight of passing centuries will pick out bits that now seem nothing less than embarrassing[9], while the passage of time also raises new issues that the master had no reason to address — for example, the social consequences of genetic engineering or cheap birth-control.

Beyond preservation, the disciples' main task is interpretation and re-interpretation of the canon to deal with changing circumstances. Dedicated, intelligent people in every creed have selflessly spent their lives working out how to do this, in the process inventing marvels of intellectual agility from exegesis[10] to Kabbalism[11].

Endless extent of natural revelation

At first glance, it might seem that outside of a religion there is no canon of revelation at all, but that is not true. In *Age of Reason*, Thomas Paine begins with a mordant critique of human-written revelation, but then, roaring in capital letters to mark the central point of his credo, he describes the true revelation. Read this passage aloud, as if from a pulpit:

> The WORD OF GOD IS THE CREATION WE BEHOLD and it is in this word, which no human invention can counterfeit or alter, that God speaketh universally to man. ... It is an ever-existing original, which every man can read. It cannot be forged; it cannot be counterfeited; it cannot be lost; it cannot be altered; it cannot be suppressed. ...In fine, do we want to know what God is? Search not the book called the Scripture, which any human hand might make, but the Scripture called the Creation.

> ...That which is now called natural philosophy, embracing the whole circle of science, of which astronomy occupies the chief place, is the study of the works of God, and of the power and wisdom of God in his works, and is the true theology.[12]

Our secular canon is the whole magnificent physical universe! It is a book of teachings that is infinite not only in breadth, but in depth: the closer we look at any detail, the more structure unfolds to be seen. It requires as many years of a scholar's career to fully grasp the life-cycle of a virus, of a rhinoceros, of a forest, of a hurricane, or of a star.

This revelation far exceeds the extent of any one teacher's lifetime output, and when new questions arise, it extends itself in surprising new ways to answer them.

True, the canon of creation needs interpretation, but that is a world-wide cooperative undertaking in which anyone can participate, with results available to any mind to use or to contradict, and there is a public system for constant revision and correction.

The revelations of most religions contain human dramas, parables, and great metaphors. Is the canon of science bloodless and abstract, lacking in human interest? Certainly the conventional language of scientific papers makes a fetish of abstraction and passivity. Because science findings are conveyed in an arcane, specialist vocabulary and supported by mathematics, they are far less accessible than one of the Buddha's earthy metaphors or a vivid Biblical drama.

The opaque language of professional science — and the fact that a lot of science consists of mountains of detail that are stunningly boring to everyone but the specialists who make a career of those particular details — explains why so many nonscientists think science is not only dull but the very enemy of poetry, excitement, and possibility.

But the *results* of scientific discovery shake the foundations of society. Try to imagine what your world would be like today without — and name any of a thousand discoveries that were unknown when your grandmother was born. The modest and often anonymous people who work on exegesis of the physical universe remake human society over and over. Which had the greater impact on lives today: any Biblical parable, or cell phones?

Bestriding the world

And those who make the effort to absorb the scientific world-view find that it equips their minds with a marvelous zoom lens of the imagination. You and a poet look at a rainbow: you see exactly the same beauty that a poet sees; but you can also, in imagination, zoom into the rainbow and see it as an uncountable number of water droplets, each a tiny, perfect, crystal ball, each spraying the image of the sun back toward you in a spectrum, so that the billions of drops

along one precise arc in space reflect back only violet to you, while
the drops along a different, concentric, arc reflect back only indigo
to you (but violet to someone a few yards away). You look into a
clear night sky and see the same blaze of stars Van Gogh painted;
but you can also see into the depth of both space and time, and
know the stars, not merely as diamond chips on a jet sphere, but as a
swirling cloud, with three-dimensional flows and swirls like sparks
from a campfire; only these sparks are suns, many immensely
grander than our own sun, each with a life span, a story from birth
to a chilly or an explosive death.

Price of Knowledge

This endless vision comes at a price: Although the universe is
stupendously rich and full of endless wonder, and a great deal of it
is knowable, we have so far learned only a tiny fraction of what
there is to know. From this it follows quite inexorably that we have
to be willing to live with "Just don't know (yet)" as the answer to
many questions, even big ones. As Arthur C. Clarke puts it,

> ...men have debated the problems of existence for thousands
> of years — and that is precisely why I am skeptical about
> most of the answers. One of the great lessons of modern
> science is that millennia are only moments. It is not likely that
> ultimate questions will be settled in such short periods of
> time, or that we will really know much about the universe
> while we are still crawling around in the playpen of the Solar
> system.[13]

Like contingency itself, our lack of knowledge is not a catastrophe,
just a condition of life. Richard Feynman accepted it:

> I think it's much more interesting to live not knowing than to
> have answers which might be wrong... there are many things
> I don't know anything about, such as whether it means
> anything to ask why we're here ... but I don't have to know
> an answer, I don't feel frightened by not knowing things, by
> being lost in a mysterious universe without having any
> purpose, which is the way it really is, so far as I can tell.[14]

Despite our limitations and the immaturity of our civilization, we
have done marvelously well. Picture mayflies swarming happily
over a sunlit pond. To a mayfly, the leaves on the alder tree are as
eternal as the pole star is to us. Our lives, compared to the stars, are

tinier than a mayfly's life compared to the alder tree's. Yet we can describe the birth and death of stars! This is quite as remarkable as it would be if we found that mayflies knew about the budding and the fall of alder leaves.

Being more than a spear-carrier

And the great drama of Good versus Evil, in which some believers think they participate? If you envy the color and excitement this gives them, and would like to be more than a spear-carrier in some great contest, consider substituting the eternal battle of Truth versus Error, of Seeing versus Denial. These are genuine conflicts that are being fought on many fronts every day. For example, I drafted this chapter in the month in which the State of Kansas decided to expunge the word "evolution" from its textbooks. Do you understand the arguments in this dispute? If challenged at a party, could you defend the idea of evolution against charges it is "just a theory," or defend yourself against a charge of being a "blind materialist"? You may (if you wish) take part in the real battle between those who want to know and those who prefer to close their eyes to the canon of creation[15].

Summary

When you do not subscribe to a religious account of the world, you cannot derive existential validity from a claim of being a specially-planned creation; but when you closely examine the idea of having such a determined nature, it turns out to have consequences that are quite unpalatable. Far better to celebrate being an astronomically unlikely accident within a fertile, effervescent universe. One help in that task is to deepen your appreciation of the infinite, open "revelation" of the natural universe, so much richer and more accessible than any prophet's teachings.

3. Finding Community

There's ample medical research to justify saying that the more human relationships you have, the longer you will live, the healthier you will be, and the more contented you will be with life. Conversely, the fewer and weaker your relationships, the more likely you are to be sick, to die prematurely, and to be unhappy in the meantime. Psychologist Maslow put it this way:

> ...basic human needs can be fulfilled only by and through other human beings, i.e. society. The need for community (belongingness, contact, groupiness) is itself a basic need. Loneliness, isolation, ostracism, rejection by the group — these are not only painful but also pathogenic as well.[1]

Here are some examples. Cohen tells how they swabbed the virus of the common cold in the nostrils of 276 brave volunteers, and found that those "with many social ties were less likely to develop a cold, shed less virus and produced less mucus"[2]. Williams writes

> People with poor social support whether it is defined by the number of social contacts, the satisfaction derived from them, or some combination of the two have a higher risk of dying from all causes. The effects of isolation are even more dramatic in chronic illnesses. People with coronary artery disease who lack both a spouse and a confidant have a 50% death rate over a five-year period. For those less isolated, the death rate is under 20%.

> Psychological and social conditions that impair social ties also result in higher death rates. People in their 20s with

hostile personalities... have four to six times the average
chance of dying before age 50.[3]

It is not only the old and middle-aged who are affected. Resnick,
reviewing a longitudinal study on adolescent well-being, said that

Specifically, we find consistent evidence that perceived
caring and connectedness to others is important in
understanding the health of young people today.[4]

Whatever sources you check, the story is the same: forming and
maintaining social ties is not just a matter of fun or general comfort.
It is basic to quality of life and to plain survival.

Effects of community

There are numerous causes for the effect of social ties on health,
many of them interrelated, many of them poorly understood in any
scientific way. People with more social ties have generally lower
levels of stress hormones. And yet, it is stressful to maintain a social
life (just ask any adolescent, or remember your own teen years).
People with more social contacts generally have more active
immune systems. Is that because they challenge their immune
systems by exposing them to a wider variety of germs and viruses?
Or because they have lower levels of stress hormones? Or because
some genetic combination that produces better immune systems
also encourages gregarity? And how could these influences ever be
untangled?

Some possible causes leap to mind. For example, it makes intuitive
good sense that people who have frequent social contact will, on the
average, take care of themselves more sensibly. They have occasions
to talk to other people about their problems, and those people are
going to say sensible things like "Well, have you had that checked
out by a doctor?" or say encouraging things like "Oh, sure, you can
exercise, my cousin does and she's a 70-year-old diabetic."

One commonsense explanation that would be hard to document
scientifically is the psychological and practical support that we
receive from friends when we are ill or in trouble. It isn't only the
visits, flowers, and encouragement, nor the practical assistance to
the family members, although these things surely help during a
health crisis. The magic that really works to keep a sick (or
depressed) person alive is an inner assurance that there are other

people who want you to recover and who would mourn if you were to die. Connections of responsibility — to pets, to family, to a job — have the same effect. Even the care of a potted plant can do it: when elderly people in a nursing home were told it was their responsibility to keep a plant watered and healthy, they died at *one-half the rate* of a control group who were told the staff would care for the plant[5]. People who don't feel wanted and useful die easily; people who do, cling more tenaciously to breath. This subtle inner motivation can have a dramatic effect in a crisis.

Confession good for the body

A recent experiment explored the effect of writing on patients suffering from asthma and arthritis[6]. Some patients for several days wrote down, anonymously, their "deepest thoughts" about the most stressful event in their lives — typically a death or a childhood incident. The control group spent the same amount of time writing down plans for that day. The patients who wrote honestly and deeply about stressful things displayed improvements in their disease symptoms that lasted for months. Half the experimental group improved over four months, against 25% of the controls; 20% of the controls got worse but only 5% of the experimental group worsened.

What could be going on here? Presumably it was not the physical act of writing that made the difference. It had to be the mental act of organizing and then verbalizing honest thoughts about serious life events. The experimental group deposited their anonymous writings in a sealed box, from which the experimenters retrieved them. We can only wonder if the benefits would have been the same if the participants had kept their writings, or if the writings had been ceremonially burned without being read. In other words, did it make a difference that they knew that someone would read their stories?

In any event, we know that this same mental act — honestly recalling and verbalizing stressful events — goes on in two other contexts:

• When two intimate friends talk.

• When a believer prays.

We'll talk about the matter of prayer in Chapter 4. For our purposes here, it seems clear that having someone you can confide in, someone to whom you can tell stories about the worst things that happen to you, can have a significant effect on your health.

Effects of religious community

Many studies have focussed on the health benefits of being an active churchgoer[7], but we can choose to think that being part of a religious congregation is simply a very convenient way of forming social ties. When a believer practices the religion and takes active part in the life of the congregation, plenty of social ties, and a sense of being useful and wanted, will result automatically.

Does that mean people who don't practice religion must shrivel in lonely isolation? Of course not; but we may need to reach farther and work harder for connectedness. My purpose in this chapter is to urge you to improve your life by going out and cultivating your social ties, increasing the number and richness of your connections to other people. A confession: I am urging myself right along with you, because this is an area of my own life that needs work.

Although the reason for doing this is self-interest — we want to improve our own prospects for health and long life — it is not a cynical or selfish exercise. To have value, social relationships must involve *mutual* support. Our connections to other people are not one-way; we have to spend a great deal of time and effort in supporting others in order to receive support in return. And, because of the general cussedness of human beings, there will be times when we will wonder whether connectedness really yields a longer life, or only a life that seems longer.

Not who you know, but who they know

Let's use "your community" loosely to mean the set of people who recognize your name and face. But it seems to me that an effective community has a special form. The important fact is not the number of people who know you; it is the degree to which those people also know each other. In other words, you need more than a well-stuffed address book to gain the benefits of community or to help create those benefits for others. To be truly supportive, your community should have, in the terms of graph theory, a high degree of connectivity.

Let's say you are a Willy Loman business type, perhaps a salesman or a personal trainer. You know a hundred or more people well enough to greet them by first name and be greeted in return. However, these people are in different places around the city or the state and the only connection among them is that they know you. A map of your community would resemble a daisy or a giant asterisk:

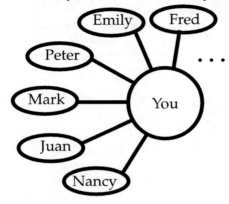

What happens if you come to need help, support, or encouragement? The only members of this community who will know about your needs are the ones whom you tell. They won't hear it from someone else, because they don't know anyone else who knows you. Let's say that one of them, Emily, does find out that (to choose an example that I hope is imaginary) one of your children has been diagnosed with leukemia. Emily mentions that to some third party: "I heard the saddest thing today. My personal trainer's kid has leukemia." The response will probably be along the lines of, "That's too bad. Say, did you hear Sosa had another two-homer game?"

This account is a bit of a cheat because it leaves out your kinship connections. Let's add them to the picture, as follows.

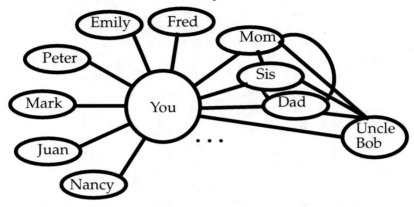

There's an obvious difference between your business connections and your kin: your kinfolk know each other as well as knowing you. A map of these connections looks more like a spiderweb than an asterisk. If your sister hears about your problem, Mom and Uncle Bob will know about it in short order.

The effectiveness of your community is multiplied many times when the people who know you also know each other. There are three reasons for this. First, people are motivated to talk about their mutual acquaintances, but they waste little breath talking about third parties that their hearers don't know. When you have news about a mutual acquaintance, it makes an interesting and enjoyable item for conversation. "Say, did you hear Merton's kid has leukemia?" "Oh, gosh, Elmer Merton from the gym? That's awful, I better call him." In other words, the better-connected your community, the more likely it is that news of your need will travel to the ear of someone who has the time and willingness to help in some way — even to simply call you up to express sympathy.

Second, people perceive more significance, more importance, more psychological reality in the needs of a mutual acquaintance, as compared to the need of a person that only they know. At least, it seems intuitively clear to me that someone's troubles will seem more moving when that same someone is also an acquaintance of two or three of your friends.

Third, people are more likely to offer practical help to mutual acquaintances. The reason, rarely expressed, is natural self-interest. Because the needy person is known to the volunteer's friends, the friends will hear about any help they render. "You hear about Merton's kid?" "Yes, isn't it too bad? They take him to this special clinic, it's hours of driving. Janelle Peters has been minding their other kids for them when they go."

The imaginary Janelle is undoubtedly helping the Mertons out of genuine concern. Just the same, she is gaining status as a selfless person in *her* community, and building credit against a time when she might need the community's aid. That wouldn't happen if none of her other friends knew the Mertons.

Opportunities for community

Edward Hallowell's *Connect*[8] is a psychologist's hymn to the critical importance of connectedness. Hallowell lists the kinds of social connections and urges us to reexamine each one in our lives. The following paragraphs are my own interpretation and extension of these sources. We need to look at each of the following areas to see how it could yield new, revived, or improved connections:

- Our intimate family
- Our extended family and ancestors
- Our friends
- Our neighbors
- Our interests
- Our community
- Our electronic connections

Intimate family

The most important connections in your life are your spouse (life partner, significant other, whatever) and any other people with whom you share your home and daily life. These are the people who are most important in sustaining your own life (Remember the sentences quoted earlier: "People with coronary artery disease who lack both a spouse and a confidant have a 50% death rate over a five-year period. For those less isolated, the death rate is under

20%.") But don't forget, these relationships are reciprocal. These intimates are people whose lives *you* help to improve and lengthen by your companionship.

Consider this. Simply by virtue of living intimately with this person or persons, you have allowed them to permanently mark your life. Even if you eventually separate, you will never be able to forget them, nor they you. So, without getting all soppy about it, is there anything you can do to remove an irritation or otherwise deepen and improve these relationships? These people are permanently part of you; you need them, and they need you.

Roots

Take a few minutes to write down the names of all your blood relatives that are still alive, plus any family friends that meant something to you in childhood. With how many of these people are you now in contact? Do you at least know their addresses?

I'm not saying you should run out and organize a huge family reunion, or make peace with a relative with whom you've been feuding for years. But you could make a habit of telephoning or emailing these people often enough that they remember you.

Consider taking up the genealogy hobby, at least in a small way[9]. Constructing a family tree is a fine way to increase your own sense of a foundation in time and in society — a reminder that you have a heritage and a valid place in history. Also, it creates a good excuse to call up people you haven't talked to in years, and gives you things to talk about when you do call them. If making a family tree doesn't excite you, consider a family recipe book, a family historical website, or any other project that involves historical research.

Friends

How many friendships have you had and since abandoned? We all do it. We change our interests, or our schools or jobs, or our marital status, and somehow we see that person less and less often. Then it's only Christmas cards; and then silence.

Hallowell uses a strong phrase for this: "Letting go of friends is like dumping money in the river." Perhaps. Yet not every friendship is worth preserving. We allow some of them to wither because, for whatever reason, it cost us more in time or stress to keep the friend than we got back in companionship.

But there are probably at least a few people you can name whose society you *do* enjoy, but with whom you do not stay close. Why? Time pressure, perhaps. It's just too much trouble to set up a date, to schedule a sitter, or to deal with some other logistic problem that comes up when two busy people try to make time for each other.

But remember, you need friends for your own survival (and they need you). Think: can any of these connections be revitalized? One way around the logistic problems and phone-tag games is to set up a regular meeting: a regular date to run or cycle together; a date to try out a new restaurant for lunch once per quarter, the choice of restaurant alternating between you; a monthly family dinner held alternately at each other's house; or, for parents of small children, a regular play-date at a playground halfway between you. There are thousands of activities and interests to share; use your imagination.

When you meet only occasionally, you have to go through scheduling hassles every time. That raises a barrier to keeping in touch and lowers the perceived value of the connection. When you meet on a regular schedule, you can plan your dates far in advance, making it much easier to integrate friendship into a busy schedule. In addition, a regular meeting can become a ritual (see Chapter 5).

Neighbors

You don't really choose your neighbors. Like plumbing, they come along with your house or apartment; or they wander in later for their own reasons. As a result, it's good luck if you can make genuine friends of your neighbors — but you need to be on good terms in any case. Because of where they live, they are perfectly placed either to do you a lot of good, or to cause you endless aggravation (and of course, you them).

Here's one way to think about your neighbors. Collectively, they constitute an ideal community, if you can cultivate it: they are a bunch of people with at least one common interest (the neighborhood), who all know each other as well as knowing you. Here's another way to see it: you could spend many thousands of dollars on locks and alarm systems for your suburban home — or you could invest a few hours a month making yourself agreeable to your neighbors, with probably a greater improvement in the security of your property.

Again, as with your relatives, I do not advise you to try the big gesture, organizing a block party or a round of pot-luck suppers. All that you need to do is to make a point of *talking* to people. When are your neighbors likely to be out and about, in the front yard, sidewalk, or stoop? You make an unobtrusive point of being out around at that same time.

Take the trouble to learn your neighbors' names, and use them. (If, like me, you have trouble remembering names for thirty seconds after you learn them, admit this debility and compensate for it. There's no shame in running into the house to jot down a newly-learned name. You can pretend you heard the telephone.) Besides their names, remember people's concerns and ills, and ask after them. This is really all it takes to be well regarded by your neighbors. It doesn't hurt to invite people over to visit, to volunteer to help with whatever needs doing, and so on; but the foundation of being a neighbor is simply being present and paying attention.

Hobbies and interests

Your interests, hobbies, avocations can be the basis for increased human connection. Obviously if you pursue an interest alone — work alone on your models or your macramé, go alone to a concert or a gallery, sailboard or hike or roller blade alone — you gain nothing in human terms, however satisfying the activity might be.

However, for almost any interest there is an affinity group. You can meet with other makers of models or macramé; join a group who view art or hear music and then discuss it; or you can sail, hike, or 'blade in a group. Being part of an affinity group will also improve your skill at the group's common pursuit, whether that is breeding persian cats, skydiving, playing softball, writing fiction, birding, or caring for an aged parent. Being in the group puts you in touch with people who know more about the common pursuit than you do, helps you to organize what you know about the pursuit, and motivates you to take the pursuit more seriously.

However, for the purposes of this chapter, the really important thing about any affinity group is that it makes you part of one of those ideal communities: a group of people with a common interest who know each other as well as knowing you. Of course, it isn't enough to be only a dues-paying member. You need to give time as well, helping to organize meetings or doing whatever is needed to make the group work. It is this participation in the creation and maintenance of the group, not your mute presence, that makes you known to and well-regarded by the other people.

Work

If you have a daily job, you are a member of a special kind of affinity group: your company. Superficially your work group might appear to be the right kind of community, a bunch of people who know each other as well as knowing you. However, must of us keep an emotional distance from our work-mates. We didn't choose to know these people; they were thrust on us. Work-mates are chosen for us by the company for reasons that have nothing to do with compatibility or shared interests. For this reason we are naturally cautious about forming connections with them. It takes long enough to find out if they are a help or an impediment to our work, let alone finding out if they are people we want as friends.

Moreover, the company can and often does take workmates away, moving them to other divisions or offices or simply firing them. In my milieu of Silicon Valley, people are always ready to change jobs. Every position is seen as a temporary stop on a career path, so it would be emotionally wasteful to form more than superficial ties to people who will probably soon move on. Recently, I met for a dinner with the cohesive and compatible bunch of people that I worked with two years ago. Only one person was still employed at the same company where we'd all been workmates, and she was planning to leave. Updating each other on our new email addresses was an important feature of the gathering.

So we can't depend on stability in work relationships, and as a result we are quite reasonably reluctant to involve ourselves in the lives of our workmates. In addition, there are practical reasons for making sure that we keep our personal affairs away from work. We avoid talking about financial, emotional, or health problems with co-workers, because if problems of that sort become known, it can affect the way our company sees our fitness for employment.

Some professions foster a high morale and strong sense of community. The public-safety professions do this: members of the firefighters, the police, and the emergency medical techs all enjoy a group bond because they see themselves as guardians of the community, people who can deal with terrible experiences that the rest of us don't know how to handle. The military services also see themselves as guardians and encourage close bonds within the profession.

In ordinary jobs, it is still sometimes possible to find emotional community at work. This can occur when the work group feels like a team that is tackling and overcoming a worthwhile challenge. It's a great feeling to be part of such a team effort, and it leaves good memories to look back upon. Ask yourself: is your job likely ever to produce that kind of group satisfaction? If not, consider changing jobs, or even careers.

Volunteering

Yet another way of adding to your community is to donate your time to any worthwhile cause. It's all very well to donate money, either directly to causes you favor or indirectly by donating to United Way, but this has no effect on you directly and it does nothing to enlarge your community.

When you donate your presence, your time, and your labor, you come face to face with other people who believe in that cause. It's the right kind of community: you become known to a group of people who know each other as well as you. It's an easy kind of community to join: the only membership requirement is a willingness to help. You always have things to talk about with the other volunteers, which makes it easy for people who aren't good mixers. And your time and skills probably have more real value to the cause than the sum of money you would be willing to donate.

The range of organizations that need volunteer help is amazingly wide; you will find a dozen opportunities in even a small community, and hundreds in an city. Whatever public good you approve of has a volunteer organization supporting it. You don't have to work in a soup kitchen (but hey, why not?). You can be a museum docent, a classroom aid, build trails in a park, and so on endlessly.

If your work gives you membership in a professional body, you can become a delegate, an officer, a board member, or help to publish the newsletter or journal, or help organize the annual convention. Robert Fulghum calls professional associations "secular churches" because of the strong sense of community among their inner circles, and opines that the municipal convention centers where associations meet for their annual conventions are "the basilicas of secular religion."[10]

Imaginary friends

Some people would say that you can form an electronic community by spending time in internet chat rooms, Usenet news groups, or on email lists. And it may be true that some of the benefits of social connection can be realized online. After all, if arthritis patients improve after writing their deep thoughts on paper (page 31), would they not also improve if they wrote them in an email, or posted them in the *alt.deep.thoughts* news group?

Bandwidth is one good reason for thinking that electronic communications can't possibly be as beneficial as "f2f." What is the effective bandwidth of face-to-face contact, with its nuances of tone of voice, facial expression and body language? Surely it's greater than an HDTV signal, an order of magnitude greater than that dream of all web surfers, a dedicated T1 line. Online communications are necessarily slow, shallow, and lacking in nuance. And the conventional styles of online forums work against meaningful connection. After all, except for private, one-to-one email, online forums are all public. You can't let your hair down; you have to always think about how your words will look to a crowd of strangers. True intimacy, truly honest communication, is only occasional on the internet.

Just the same, in more than a decade of daily internet use, I have twice had the luck to see a genuine community form. The first formed around the "cold fusion" sensation of 1987-9. The *alt.fusion* news group was the focus of an extraordinary group of people who argued about the theory of nuclear fusion at a sophisticated level, and who also performed cutting-edge experiments in their basements and reported the results as they occurred, online. The excitement level was electric and remained so for months.

The second community formed on an email list. When the American Basketball League (a professional women's league) folded in December, 1998, it was a devastating shock not only to the players but to the fans. As charter season ticket holders, my wife and I could not have been more shocked by the death of a close friend. The fans of the San Jose, California ABL team, the Lasers, had created an email list months earlier. In the aftermath of the ABL's collapse, fan after fan would post a long, heartfelt account of what the ABL had meant, or a memory of a special game or an interaction with a player. Reading the email each day had all the teary joy of attending a wake for a much-loved person and sharing memories with other mourners. Eventually the fans used the email list to organize a celebratory dinner and later, a memorial game.

In each of these cases, there was an extraordinary event that caused a profound emotional shock among a select group of people. The internet enabled those people to come together to share their reactions, quickly and cheaply. The connections were true and honest because the people participating badly needed to be able to say what was on their minds, and because the seriousness of the event validated honesty and openness.

This combination of circumstances is rare. If it happens, treasure it. But, by and large, you are better off looking for communication in the physical world.

Obstacles to community

The big problem with getting close to people is... that you end up so close to so many people. Speaking as a lifelong nonmixer, I can attest that the emotional barriers to increased human contact are steep, sometimes insurmountable.

Shyness

How to find me at a party: look for the guy standing forlornly on the fringe of a group of chattering people, trying to look as I was part of the conversation when I'm really not. No, don't look for me at a party; I probably went home early.

My wife (another lifelong nonmixer) and I have discussed this — actually, agonized over it — more than once. What's *wrong* with us? Other people clearly enjoy socializing; why can't we? "What do they find to talk about?" she asks. I think I know: themselves and each other. Somehow, the majority of people draw real pleasure from talking about themselves and other people, to other people. They find other people *interesting*: interesting to be with; interesting to listen to; interesting to engage with in an exchange of social gestures. And we don't. It's as simple as being tone-deaf at a musicale. But it makes life hard at a party, because unless we can find the rare conversation that really exchanges information about an interesting subject, we're both at a loss as to how to participate, and bored.

Some other people have the worse problem of being, not merely bored and uncomfortable, but actually frightened, truly panicked by the prospect of talking to strangers, or even to neighbors.

Both problems — genuine shyness, or our social tone-deafness — are potentially life-threatening. They create the social isolation that can literally shorten your life. They are worth fighting and worth getting help for.

A few of the sources of community I've listed are free from these problems. Your intimate family and your extended family already know you, accept you, and are pretty much obliged to socialize with you. And in an affinity group or a volunteer organization you have the external activity to focus on. You have a common, neutral subject to talk about with the others, and activities to do when your conversation fails.

Reluctance

Hallowell notes an important, paradoxical reason why some people are reluctant to make a new connection: they fear they might meet a positive response! If you reach out to another person, that person might respond with embarrassing eagerness or — the real disaster — with *need*. You could end up stuck in some time-consuming round of helping, and have to give up some of the solitude and autonomy that you treasure. Worse, you could end up with some degree of *responsibility* for another person's well-being.

Reviewing the sources mentioned above, this isn't a realistic worry among your intimate family (you're already committed to supporting them), or your friends (you don't make them friends unless you're pretty sure they are self-sufficient), or in your work, affinity, or volunteer groups. The fear of stepping unaware into an emotional swamp might be realistic when you open communications with a relative or a neighbor.

But look: you are a competent person and you know your own limits. It is quite unlikely that a relative or neighbor should turn out to be some kind of leech, and if they do, you can deal with it. In the slightly more likely event that you should uncover a genuine need — for example, an elderly relative who, you realize with dismay, is inadequately cared for, or a neighbor who, you slowly come to realize, is drowning in family responsibilities and really needs help coping — you can see it as an opportunity. If you help such people even a little bit, you do so within a community of people who know that person as well as knowing you. And that builds your own credibility and standing in that community — valuable credit that you might need to draw on someday.

Time and money

There's a practical reason why we (or at least, I) don't do more to develop community: the expense in time and money. Although semi-retired and childless, I still don't seem to have as much time as I need for the writing and other solitary activities I want to pursue. How do my neighbors with three small boys, or the other neighbor couple who have two sets of children and grandchildren, ever find time to take a breath? And yet, I have to admit that both pairs of neighbors have numerous friends and voluntary activities, more of both than I have. Could it be that I'm kidding myself about the demands of time?

The demands of work and other time commitments make a dandy excuse to defer starting the community-building activities I've outlined. But if I'm honest with myself, I recognize the truth of this insight from my wife's bottomless store of wisdom: everyone finds time for what they really want to do. Whenever someone tells you they mean to do something — write a novel, learn to hang-glide — after they retire and have more time, you just smile pleasantly and think to yourself, "baloney." If they really wanted to do that thing, they'd find the time now; and if they haven't started now, they won't then. People find time for what truly engages them.

We are not talking about a huge commitment of time. Oh, if you need a reason to kill the idea, you can blow it up to frightening proportions: "Well, if I invite all the neighbors in for dinner, that'll take days to plan and cost a fortune just to buy enough good wine to serve them, let alone the 12-pound crown roast..." But that's not the program.

What is the program *is*, is to find ways to invest an hour or two each week in community-building activities selected from the wide array that I've sketched and that your imagination can enlarge upon. And these needn't be unpleasant hours, either. Each of the things I've suggested has inherent satisfactions and rewards of its own. Many can be overlapped with existing time-slots. For example, if you jog regularly, you can set up a regular appointment to jog with a friend, and get that connection time at no cost.

I know that my life offers an hour a week of slack and more. It could be that your life is so hectic you haven't got even that much discretionary time. If you feel that you don't, there are plenty of books to advise you on time management.

Summary

Social connectivity is not just a nice idea, it's a way of staying healthier and living longer and, reciprocally, a way of bestowing health and longer life on other people. I've suggested looking for more and better social ties in several areas:

- Your intimate family
- Your extended family and its history
- Your friends
- Your neighbors
- Your avocations and the affinity groups they lead you to
- Your work
- Volunteer services
- Online communities

You can find endless cogent reasons for not making this effort: you don't really enjoy socializing or you actively fear it; the cost of time and money; the chance of having your autonomy reduced. But these reasons all evaporate or become small if you can accept that the end result is an improved, longer life for both you and the people you touch.

4. Practicing Contemplation and Tranquility

Until recent years, two mental arts had been left almost entirely in the domain of religions: the practice of tranquility and the pursuit of mystical experience. Today, we know that we can explore both in a secular context. In this chapter we look at the practice of tranquility, which has many practical benefits. These arts are sometimes used as springboards to the mystical experience, which we examine in Chapter 6.

The practice of tranquility

It seems to me there is a spectrum of mental practices that are all founded on one skill: *deliberate control of the focus of the mind's attention*. The various practices differ in their purposes, and they differ in the target on which the attention is focussed. Here are some activities that illustrate the range of this spectrum:

- To *daydream* is to focus your attention on an engaging fantasy. The purpose is amusement and emotional satisfaction.

- To *contemplate* is to focus your attention on a single thought or a connected series of thoughts. The purpose is to gain deeper understanding or to solve a problem.

- *Autohypnosis* is to focus your attention on a message you want to send to your subconscious. The purpose is to repattern your own habits or attitudes.

- To *meditate* is to focus your attention on a non-verbal object such as the physical sensation of your breath. The purpose is to achieve a state of serenity and, in some disciplines, to gain insight into the workings of your mind.

What varies as we move across this spectrum is the quality of the mental content we permit into our minds. Each practice differs in how much, how varied, and how tightly structured is the flow of thoughts and images we allow. In daydreaming, we allow a wide range of content and impose little structure, letting one passing image associate to the next. At the opposite end of the spectrum, a meditator avoids verbal content entirely, or focusses on a single word. This one model, a spectrum of mental disciplines that differ only in the variety of content that each allows into the attention, unites a wide area of practices.

In pure contemplation, Christian religious contemplatives spend many hours focussing their attention on on a single scripture or on an image such as the blood of Christ[1]. Zen contemplatives spend hours focussing on the unanswerable questions called koans.

Successful writers, composers, programmers and artists all enter a contemplative trance while composing new work. This state falls between daydreaming and religious contemplation on the spectrum: the attention is focussed on more than a single idea, but the thinker carefully controls the sequence of thoughts, methodically following out the connections between them.

Between autohypnosis and meditation on the spectrum, athletes spend hours visualizing athletic performances, replaying key moves and skills in their mind, in the hope of patterning automatic responses into their nerves.

Control of the mind's attention

Each of us learns to control our attention to some degree, to bend and focus the mind upon a single issue for an extended time. Almost everyone has had the experience of being so involved in a task or a daydream that they failed to hear the doorbell, the telephone, or their own name being called. Successful athletes, especially, can block out a stadium filled with hysterical fans to focus totally on the next pitch, pass, or free-throw. Less dramatic, but just as essential to success, are the composition-trance of the writer or artist and the study-trance of the scholar in the library.

Concentration is so useful in so many occupations that it is strange that schools don't teach it as a specific skill. People who can do it well are admired for their ability to "focus," while people who can't do it are called "scatterbrained." Uncontrollable concentration on inappropriate objects is a feature of autism and some types of mental illness. Loss of the ability to concentrate is one of the symptoms of clinical depression. When we are tired, drunk, or in emotional turmoil we "just can't think." These physical connections may explain why people assume that concentration is an inborn talent, like an ear for music. But the experience of the meditators is that concentration can be taught, practiced, and improved.

Everyone learns daydreaming for themselves. And there are many books that teach autohypnosis and athletic visualization. Here we will look at contemplation and meditation, two skills that are normally mentioned only in a religious or semi-religious context. These are arts that anyone can practice and benefit from.

Meditation

Three thousand years ago, give or take a few centuries, someone in the Indus Valley first formalized meditation as an intentional practice, as part of the bundle of ascetic practices that are today called yoga. The Indus Valley people always portrayed divine figures as seated in yogin posture, with heels touching[2]. Around 1500 B.C.E. the Indus Valley civilization was overrun by the Vedic culture of the tribes called Aryans, and the new mix of cultures created a fertile medium from which grew three great religions (Hinduism, Jainism, Buddhism) that give a central place to meditative practices.

Buddhism had the greatest early success, spreading north, south, and east from India, taking on the language, dress and artistry of each culture that it entered, but retaining meditation as its principle activity everywhere it went. In the Twentieth century, teachings in meditative techniques reached our European cultures through several traditions: from Zen Buddhism (originally Chinese, but coming to us from Japan), from Tibetan Buddhism, from Theravadan Buddhism out of Cambodia and Sri Lanka, and direct from India in numerous Yogic schools both ancient and modern. Yet all of these traditions trace their roots back to the Indus Valley culture of about 1500 BCE.

The antiquity of a practice tells us nothing about its efficacy or value. There are plenty of venerable delusions and evils still current among us. What we can say, based on the long history of meditation, is that it is a *benign* practice. If it had bad side-effects, we'd know by now. On the contrary, meditation does not increase fear, anger, or any other kind of distress; and it doesn't inspire its practitioners to do bad things. For example, I know of only one instance in history when someone was murdered in the name of Buddhism[3]. Thus the worst result of experimenting with meditation is that you might waste some time.

Meditation does have practical, measurable benefits in several areas, notably stress reduction and pain control[4]. At a minimum, a regular meditation practice is a way to practice and improve your ability to quickly focus on any subject or task. Once you master the state of relaxed attentiveness that meditation fosters you have a convenient gateway to other activities such as contemplation, autohypnosis or visualization.

Sitting meditation

You can find books that make something complicated and subtle out of meditation. However, if it could be perfected 3,000 years ago, it is safe to assume it is not rocket science. Here is the basic technique.

- Go to a comfortable place where there is no intrusive noise and where you won't be interrupted by a person, phone or beeper. Set a timer for ten to fifteen minutes.

- Sit in a posture that is comfortable but dignified: not stiff, not slouching, but calmly erect, a posture that reflects your status as a competent, dignified person. Leave your hands loose in your lap.

- Allow your eyelids to relax half-closed or completely closed, whichever is more comfortable.

- Spend a few moments reminding yourself that here, for this time, you have no enemies, no threats, and no deadlines — in short, you have no reason to be fearful, defensive, or rushed. Allow your muscles and your heart to soften.

- Begin paying attention to the sensations of breathing: the touch of air in your nostrils, the slight motion of your abdomen against your clothing. Do not narrate or analyze; simply watch these sensations like a cat watching a mouse-hole.

- After a brief time (ridiculously brief, at first) you will realize that some other thought has arisen and you are no longer attending to your breath. Without judgment or emotion, recognize what has happened and return your attention to your breath.

- Repeat the preceding step until the timer goes off.

There's a straightforward reason for everything in this procedure. Sitting erect, you are less likely to fall asleep than if you slumped or reclined. You focus on a nonverbal thing because the point is to practice controlling your mind's attention apart from your usual interests. You focus on something physical so that you know you aren't asleep or daydreaming — as long as you can perceive your breath, you know you aren't asleep! You focus on the breathing process because it is convenient and contains a variety of sensations.

The preceding routine is the first steps in a standard Buddhist method called *vipassana* (a word usually translated "insight"). Gradually, over repeated sessions, you cannot help but gain an understanding of how skittish and shallow your thinking processes are. This is only the first of the insights to be gained.

The meditative attitude

A particular attitude is needed for success in any attention-based practice, an attitude that includes delicacy, non-judgment, patience and non-striving, and self-compassion.

You need delicacy because the mind does not respond to forceful control. You cannot maintain a focus by strength or by will-power, only by a sort of balance — you balance your attention on its object the way you balance a pencil on its point on your fingertip.

Non-judgment means that, at least during meditation, you suspend the habit of judging events as good or bad, smart or stupid, or along any other scale. For example, when you discover that your mind, for the two-hundredth time in a sitting, has run away to thoughts of sex or systems administration, you don't judge that as bad, or boring, or put it into any other category. It simply *is*. Observe it, and refocus your attention. (We examine non-judgment as a general life strategy in Chapter 11.)

You need patience because none of these practices produce quick results; they work by a slow repatterning of habitual responses[6]. Non-striving is the attitude that you are pursuing the practice for its own sake, for what it feels like right now, without straining toward any imagined goal. Patience and non-striving reinforce each other.

Self-compassion means having an attitude of sympathy toward yourself, an attitude of fondness and respect toward your own efforts — almost a parental attitude of tolerance and concern toward your own difficulties and failings.

To summon the combination of these attitudes is really to summon The Adult within you, to treat yourself with the patience, generosity, grace and tolerance of a wise adult. And who is more deserving of your very wisest attitudes, if not yourself?

Visual field meditation

Here is a second form of meditation that you can practice when sitting is not convenient, for example when walking, jogging, or driving. The game is simply to *perceive* everything that your eyes can *see*.

There is a lot more visual data falling on your retinas than you normally take into your mind. If you have normal eyes, your visual field spans only a little less than 180 degrees: from just in front of one shoulder to just in front of the other, and vertically from your eyebrows to just forward of your knees. Most of the time, you discard all that, except a patch in your zone of sharpest focus and a few degrees around it. In this exercise, you try to perceive the entire field at once.

- As you walk along a street or corridor, focus your gaze easily at a point some distance ahead of you. You may need to slightly defocus your gaze.

- Without changing the direction of your gaze, begin to take in as much of the visual field as you can, especially the objects far out on the periphery.

- Continue to walk and to perceive everything that falls on your retinas. When you realize that your mind is occupied by a thought and you've stopped perceiving, calmly return to perceiving.

If you do this while walking or jogging, you should be able to perceive the motion of your hands as they swing forward alternately, and the flash of each alternate toe as it swings forward in your stride. If you are driving, you should be able to perceive everything from your passenger's knees on one side to your own elbow on the window-sill on the other; and be able to perceive motion in both the inside and outside mirrors at the same time. Walking or driving, you'll notice how passing objects move slowly near the center of the visual field, but stream away rapidly at the edges.

If you become proficient at perceiving all you see, you can try to bring in other perceptions as well. Let your attention fill with the physical sensations of walking, the rhythmic pressures and frictions of motion.

Effects of meditative practice over time

Meditation practice is a way of developing a skill: the skill of calm concentration. From personal experience I can say that if you can practice sitting meditation 20 minutes a day, five days a week, for a year, you will observe a slight but definite change. The length of time before your mind wanders from the breath will gradually lengthen, until on a good day it reaches several seconds.

With time you may find yourself treated to moments of concentrated serenity. (We look at what is known about effects like these in Chapter 6.) Moments of "single-pointed concentration" might make occasional, brief, unpredictable appearances in sitting meditation after some months of practice. Other effects can occur. You might sometimes find yourself observing lights, colors, or other visual phenomena that have the characteristics of hypnogogic illusions[7]. Although such phenomena can be entertaining, they are only products of your imagination, and they are dismissed as unimportant in all Buddhist traditions.

The first reward of a basic meditation practice is that "watching the breath" becomes a habitual, easy way to induce concentration on any task. It becomes a way of quickly gathering your mind to focus on the demand of the present moment, whatever that may be. For a trivial example, I use it on bicycle rides, to bring myself into the moment before starting a fast descent. Following my breath helps to keep my mind concentrated on the instantaneous physical demands of the bike and the road surface. But the same technique lets you bring yourself fully into any demanding or important moment.

A second reward is a practiced ability to recover emotional stability. With a moment of breath-awareness you can put on the tranquil mind of the meditation session like a garment, together with its patient, non-judgmental attitude. In this regard, meditation can be a help in dealing with grief (see "First-person grieving" on page 152).

A third reward is the ability to bring a concentrated awareness to bear on contemplation, athletic visualization, and auto-suggestion.

Contemplative practices

When you turn your attention away from the pure physical reality of the breath and begin to entertain ideas, images and words, you cease to meditate and begin to contemplate[8]. There is an infinite number of ways to contemplate, because there is an infinity of subjects and end-purposes.

I want to emphasize that no kind of contemplation can substitute for meditation, because once you allow your attention to turn to *anything* other than an immediate physical object such as the breath, you leave the realm of the mindful present and enter the realm of imagination. The "relaxation response" documented for meditation[9], which is the source of many of its benefits, is most likely to arise when your mind's focus is the unadorned physical present. When your mind's focus is a thought, a plan, or a desire, or indeed anything that has emotional content, then every sort of internal stress can arise, just as if you were discussing the same topic with another person.

Self-help gurus and inspirational speakers present all sorts of contemplative methods for visualization, motivation, and self-programming, and no doubt every such scheme will work for someone[10]. I want to point out two contemplative practices that emerge from religious tradition, but which can be beneficial for anyone: the Buddhist practice of *metta*; and a secular approach to the efficacy of prayer.

Cultivating a limitless heart

Buddhist writers often use the Pali word *metta*. It is usually translated "good will" or "loving-kindness." However, the sense of metta is very close to that of the Greek word *agape* (ah-gah-pay), used throughout the New Testament to describe the attitude of God toward humankind and the proper attitude of one Christian toward another: the attitude of love or charity.

> He that loveth not, knoweth not God; for God is love [agape].
> — 1 John 4:8

> And the Lord make you to increase and abound in love [agape] one toward another, and toward all...
> — 1 Thess. 3:12

> Let all your things be done with charity [agape].
> — 1 Cor. 16:14

Metta is a key concept in Buddhist practice, one of four sublime states to be cultivated[11]. The Pali Canon[12] contains many exhortations to develop metta:

> As a mother would risk her life to protect her child,
>   her only child,
> even so should one cultivate a limitless heart
>   with regard to all beings.
> With good will for the entire cosmos,
>   cultivate a limitless heart:
> Above, below, & all around, unobstructed,
>   without hostility or hate.
> — *Sutta Nipata* I.8

There are practical, mundane reasons to develop metta. The Buddha taught that when one develops and cultivates metta,

> One sleeps easily, wakes easily, dreams no evil dreams.
> One is dear to human beings, dear to non-human beings.
> The devas protect one.
> Neither fire, poison, nor weapons can touch one.
> One's mind gains concentration quickly.
> One's complexion is bright.
> One dies unconfused...
> — *Anguttara Nikaya* XI.16

These are worthwhile goals: dreamless sleep, the affection of all, a bright complexion, an unconfused death. How do you cultivate such good will? Through contemplation.

Metta practice

Here is a simple metta formula, easy to remember, fitting well to the relaxed breath rhythm of meditation:

> May *name* be well.
> May *pronoun* be content.
> May *pronoun* have strength
> to meet what comes.

Sit in your usual meditation posture and find your breath. When you are calm, begin to let the formula pass through your mind, starting with good will for yourself:

> May I be well.
> May I be content.
> May I have strength
> to meet what comes.

After a few repetitions, change the name and pronoun to the person dearest to you. In my case, that's

> May Marian be well.
> May she be content.
> May she have strength
> to meet what comes.

Gradually move on to other people you care about; then to other people you know; and then (although this may be hard to do at first) to people you fear or dislike.

Effects of metta practice

As with any other kind of autohypnosis, the purpose of metta practice is to gently reprogram your own attitudes and unthinking reactions.

You begin with yourself because it isn't possible to feel good will toward anyone or anything until you feel it toward yourself. It is reasonable and healthy to wish yourself well; after all, if you are not "well," how can you be of any use to yourself or anyone else?

Your aim in wishing good to others is to gradually school your own habits in the direction of greater generosity and tolerance. After you have wished someone wellness and contentment a few dozen times in your mind, it becomes more difficult to do or say something hurtful to or about that person in real life.

Metta practice gently and gradually modifies your attitudes so that it becomes easier for you to react to other people with kindness, and less easy for you to react with hostility, anger, or sarcasm. It should be obvious how, after such a change takes place to even a small degree, it will be more true that "One sleeps easily, wakes easily, dreams no evil dreams..." It has been shown that a habit of hostility and anger damages the coronary arteries[13]. Metta practice aims to cultivate the precise opposite of that deadly frame of mind.

The efficacy of prayer

Although the metta formula uses the syntax of a request — "may I be well, may I be content," etc. — it is not a prayer. If we don't imagine a supernatural being hears our thoughts, we don't expect one will act on our wishes. We skeptics assume that anything that happens inside the mind has no effect outside of it, except — and this is an important exception — that what happens in our minds can modify our own attitudes and actions.

A prayer, as a request for help, is not going to produce any result unless some human being hears and acts on it. But there is one human being who always hears your internal dialogue: you. For example, the metta formula expresses a fact: you do indeed sincerely wish yourself and other people to be well. It is satisfying to express that wish, to form it into words and to listen to them in the quiet of your own mind. The words *do* have an effect outside your mind: they modify your own subsequent actions. Prayer, as internal dialogue, can be very effective in changing the behavior of the one who prays.

Prayer for believers

A person who prays forms an organized, sincere expression of his or her greatest needs and desires. A religious believer feels that this internal speech is heard by someone else: God, Jesus, the Virgin. That belief has three important effects.

First, it is crucial that the believer has great respect for the imagined listener — respect to the point of awe. When you respect the person you are talking to, you takes pains to organize your thoughts. You make an effort to be clear, to stick to the point, and above all, to be honest. Who would want to waste Jesus's time? Who dares lie or equivocate or waffle, to God? But this act of forming a terse, honest account of one's troubles is often enough to reveal solutions[14].

Second, when you feel you have a sympathetic listener, it is easier to express yourself. It is easier to bring out true feelings and verbalize them, and through verbalizing, to discover and acknowledge them.

And third, it is a great emotional relief to unload these deep thoughts and have them heard. We all feel better when we have said what we think and feel we've been understood. And it has been shown that this kind of catharsis has physical benefits as well as emotional ones (see "Confession good for the body" on page 31).

For these three reasons, a believer's prayer has genuine healing power: it makes you tell the truth about yourself *to* yourself; it makes you organize your thoughts; and then it bestows the physical and emotional relief of feeling you were heard. It has the likely side-benefit that the believer gets up with a much clearer understanding of the problem, perhaps a new idea of how to deal with the issue or else the perspective needed to accept it.

In short, prayer for a believer is likely to be very effective indeed: it can relieve emotional distress, clarify the mind, and generate creative ideas and positive attitudes.

A prayerful consultation

The benefits of prayer, for a believer, depend on a belief that the prayer is heard by a respected, superior being. If you don't share that belief, are the benefits of prayer out of reach?

The benefits of prayer come from expressing yourself as if to a sympathetic, knowledgeable, and respected other person. If you are very lucky, you might actually know someone like that. Even a person who is merely sympathetic and knowledgeable would be sufficient. Buy that person lunch and express yourself!

Few of us are lucky enough to have a mentor of this kind, and anyway, the mentor isn't always available when we need to talk. But you could create an imaginary mentor. In your imagination, write the bio of your ideal counsellor — a knowledgeable, empathic, highly admirable figure that you would consult if you only knew him or her. Lets see... in youth, she followed up her Rhodes scholarship with a stint in the Peace Corps before entering a distinguished career as an economist and labor negotiator, during which she did the work that later won her a Nobel prize; now in nominal retirement, she does research in psychology and publishes papers on medical ethics... No need to think small when selecting an imaginary counsellor, is there? Modify these *vitae* to suit your own preferences: what imaginary person would you truly respect? Or what historic figure would you consult if you could?

Go to your meditation place and find your breath and tranquility. Imagine you are about to have a short appointment with that imagined counsellor. In a little while, he or she is going to make a brief stop in your room, shake your hand, sit down and listen to you. Organize the story you are going to tell and then, in imagination, tell it. Make it concise; make it detached in tone; make it complete; and make it brutally honest — your counsellor is unshockable and very knowledgeable of human nature.

As you are telling the story to your wise, tranquil, sympathetic, imaginary counsellor, listen to it yourself. Hear it with the deep perspective of the person you've imagined. Ask the questions your counsellor might ask: Did you try that? Why not? That was a bit cowardly, wasn't it? What's an acceptable long-term outcome? Well, what's a first step toward that?

Do remain aware that whatever comes out of this counselling session is coming from your own mind. It is really an exercise in unleashing your own best instincts. Preparing and telling the story helps you review the facts and the options, find fresh approaches. Listening to your own story with the ear of the most adult, most civilized person you contain within you is a way of mustering your own experience, knowledge, and good sense — what the Buddhists call your Buddha nature.

Summary

Many religious and semi-religious practices are based on one skill: deliberate control of the mind's focus of attention. So also are the kinds of concentration that are essential to success in sports, scholarship, and the arts. You can arrange these practices on a spectrum based on the amount of verbal content and structure they allow, from daydreaming at one extreme, to meditation on a physical sensation at the other.

Meditation is an ancient practice that has well-documented benefits when done consistently over time, and is the basis for many other attention-control practices. A basic meditation practice is easy to begin (although less easy to maintain over the long term) and needs no religious context for success.

When thoughts and imagined images are brought to mind, meditation becomes contemplation. The Buddhist practice of *metta* is a contemplative method of developing a "wider heart," that is, a habitual attitude of trust and generosity that has practical benefits.

For a believer, the psychology of devout prayer can bring relief and mental clarity, but anyone can get some of the same good effects by creating and summoning an imaginary counsellor.

5. Using Ritual

Let's define a ritual as any activity that we perform at least as much for its *symbolic and emotional value* as for its practical value. We perform a ritual because the act in itself has meaning, or because doing it make us feel better about ourselves, or both.

Our American culture provides us with a whole repertoire of standard rituals: standing for the national anthem before a sports event; singing "Happy Birthday" and blowing out birthday candles; sharing a meal at Thanksgiving; wearing caps and gowns at graduations; the complex ceremonies of weddings and funerals.

Our consumer economy exploits (some would say, parasitizes) our culture to direct us toward rituals of consumption: buying lots of gifts at Christmas; overeating on all holidays; distributing gobs of candy to children at Halloween; remembering that "a diamond is forever." The advertising industry works hard to load every purchase with symbolic and emotional value, for good reason: we are culturally (perhaps, biologically) programmed to enjoy doing things that have symbolic and emotional value, and to not count their cost too carefully.

A religious practice supplies a believer with a wide vocabulary of rituals: daily, weekly, and seasonal rituals to structure the year, and powerful ceremonies to mark the major life transitions of birth, adulthood, marriage and death.

Besides these standard rituals, every family and every individual develops private rituals: things that we do in a certain way because the doing expresses how we feel about ourselves, and reassures us that we are still in control of our lives.

Since *any* action is a ritual if we do it at least in part for its symbolic and emotional value, the whole field of human activity can be exploited as ritual. The aim of this chapter is to get you to inventory your personal selection of rituals, possibly discard some old ones, and perhaps adopt or invent some new ones.

Awareness and assent

There's a hazy boundary between the words "ritual," "habit," and "custom." I think the difference between a ritual act and a habitual one lies in *awareness* and *assent*. An act becomes a ritual for you when you perform it with conscious awareness of its symbolic and emotional meaning, and with willing assent to those meanings. Unless you act with both awareness and assent, your act is merely a habit (if it is unique to you) or a custom (if you share it with others).

Religious practice is full of activities that are meant to have symbolic and emotional value, but which can slip into mere custom owing to our very natural tendency to let awareness and assent fade with time:

> I know thy works, that thou art neither cold nor hot: I would thou wert cold or hot. So then because thou art lukewarm, and neither cold nor hot, I will spue thee out of my mouth.
> – Revelations 3:15-16

> ...in the course of the future there will be monks who won't listen when discourses that are words of the Tathagata [Buddha] are being recited. They won't lend ear, won't set their hearts on knowing them, won't regard these teachings as worth grasping or mastering. ...In this way the disappearance of the discourses that are words of the Tathagata...will come about.
> – Samyutta Nikaya XX.7

Awareness and intention are personal qualities that can exist only in your own mind. They cannot be coerced. Nobody can force you to pay attention to the symbolic meaning of an act. And in particular, nobody can force your assent to the meaning of a ritual. As I well know, because I can remember myself as an adolescent, being required to attend my parents' church in which I no longer believed.

y body was present at the rituals; my willing assent was most
finitely and defiantly not.

rivate ritual

e positive side of ritual is that you can invest *any* act with
hatever symbolic and emotional value you want; and this, too, is a
rsonal act that takes place in your head. Just as nobody can coerce
ur assent to a rite, nobody can prevent you from pouring
eaning into any act you choose.

at means that any act you want can become a personal ritual.
ke that regular Tuesday noon jogging date with your friend Alex.
t's just a run and a pleasant chat, it's a habit and no more.
owever, occasions like these can *become* rituals if you make the
nscious decision to be mindful of their implications: what they
nd for, what they imply, how they represent your status and
ndition of life. Suppose that while you are lacing your running
oes, you think: "At this time I am going to connect with the
tdoor air, with the weather and the season. I'm going to be aware
my body, its strength and limits, how it feels to get tired and to
over. And I'm going to attend to Alex, who is a friend." And you
uld consciously try to bring awareness of these points into the
nt of your mind several times during the run.

uld this kind of mental activity make your jogging date any
tter? Well, at the very least, it can't *lessen* the experience. The
ernal, practical activity of meeting Alex, running, talking, and
rting would be no different. The only difference would be the
rely internal activity of attending to, and assenting to, symbolic
lues.

any of us have habit/rituals that center around the Sunday
wspaper. My wife and I have a habit of going out for coffee on
nday morning, instead of eating breakfast and reading the paper
our kitchen at home as we do the other six days of the week. We
lattés and read the paper at a neighborhood bookstore. For us,
s routine just barely crosses the line from habit into ritual. We do
not so much because we like lattés and pastry, but because we
nt to mark the turning of the week. Going out makes Sunday into
elimiter that divides the previous week from the next one. The
nbolic and emotional content of our outing is this: a week has
ned; we are still alive and healthy; we are preparing ourselves to

plunge into the next week. We don't give special attention to this content, although if we did, the coffee would undoubtedly taste better.

Should you make the effort to invest habitual activities with ritual value? Possibly yes, because rituals have uses that rise above the details of their practice.

Uses of ritual

It seems to me that ritual acts have four main uses.

- They give time-structure to our lives on the daily, weekly, and annual levels.

- They assist and encourage the formation of trust and community between people.

- They give shape to public expressions of powerful emotions: expressions of grief, as at funerals; and of joy, as at weddings, graduations, birthdays and anniversaries.

- They help to reorient and stabilize our own feelings when we need to comprehend and cope with crucial life passages.

Let's consider each of these uses and the conventional rituals for them. Keep in mind that although I separate the four uses here, a ritual often serves more than one purpose.

Structuring life

Any repeated activity — your jog with Alex, our Sunday coffee outing — acts to stabilize the tempo of life, just as the beat of a metronome stabilizes music. We gain immense reassurance from this chronic stability. The time has rolled around and here we are, still able to meet the time with the right behavior: thus do we show that we are masters of our lives. We are *efficacious*; that is, we are able to control the circumstances of our lives. We prove our efficacy to ourselves over and over by doing expected things at appointed intervals. The feeling that we are efficacious is one of the most important feelings we can have; it's one of the foundations of a happy life, as we will see in Chapter 10.

There's a wealth of sources for ritual time-structures. Think how many people build their week around the television schedule; or who build their year around the school term, the baseball season, or the hunting season. Religions provide a rich seasonal cycle of rituals, from Easter to Passover to Ramadan. For those without a religious practice, our consumer society is eager to step in with seasonal occasions for consumption. Anyone can benefit by examining this aspect of life, and making a thoughtful choice of season rituals.

Helping people bond

A primary use of rituals is to give people, especially families, occasions to bond with each other. The ritual occasion creates a kind of emotional neutral ground where, by common consent, we permit ourselves to express emotions that we wouldn't be comfortable expressing at other times. You might not go around showing affection for your father (mother, sibling, aunt, cousin...); but you do join in caroling "Happy Birthday," or give hugs when you meet at Thanksgiving. If we didn't have these occasions, we'd be much more isolated.

In fact, plenty of us do *not* have these occasions, and *are* emotionally isolated as a result. Sometimes it's because we have moved out of reach of family. Equally often, the conventional family rituals like Christmas have lost their meaning for us; or worse, we have withdrawn our assent from them because the rituals have been poisoned by disappointment and bad memories.

A lack of occasions for bonding allows family ties to weaken and friendships to thin. But it's possible to create new rituals for this purpose.

Expressing and confirming emotion

Intense emotions beg to be shared. It is comforting to take part in a formal, public demonstration of a grief, a loss, or a triumph. If you have to deal with either tragedy or triumph silently, unshared, the emotional burden can be choking. Public rituals give us a way to externalize emotion, express it, and so finish with it. When you share its expression with others and see it expressed in other peoples' faces and voices, you can begin to release the emotion in yourself.

It seems to me that one purpose of a public ritual is to make an event psychologically real (make it, literally, undeniable) to the participants. Yes, this person has actually died and is gone; I know this because I stood with these other people and actually witnessed the coffin going into the ground, or into the crematorium. From this come two emotional conclusions. First, the grief I feel is legitimate because it is shared by others. Second, the loss is real, there is no point looking for ways around it, the only direction now is forward.

Internalizing transitions

In other cases, like weddings and graduations, the public ritual makes a life transition socially undeniable, and so irrevocable. Yes, I am now an adult; or yes, they are really married; it must be true because so many other people witnessed it along with me.

Religious practice is especially good at providing rituals for two common transitions: weddings and funerals. If you, a non-churchgoer, want to celebrate a marriage, where can you turn for ideas? Perhaps an awkward visit to the local Unitarian minister, who will be very gracious about helping you. If we don't practice a religion, going to a religious institution to get a ritual done has a certain hint of hypocrisy about it. In any case, religious custom does not cover every occasion of strong emotion in modern life. We need to be able to find, or invent, new rituals. This is not too difficult, if you have some imagination and you know the elements.

Elements of ritual

On the whole, we shouldn't be too self-aware, too calculating, in creating new rituals. For rituals that structure life and help to bond family and friends, it's enough to find any excuse to meet other people on a regular basis in comfortable surroundings. And we have time to plan these occasions. However, the need for a ritual to express emotion or transition can come up unexpectedly; and these occasions seem to ask for more formality. Thinking about the elements of ritual in a more analytic way can help us to be ready. Let's begin with ritual objects and spaces.

Ritual objects

If a ritual act is one that we perform for its symbolic and emotional value, we can apply the same qualifier to spaces and objects. A ritual *object* is something we keep because of its symbolic and emotional value, not because it is useful. You own many ritual objects, although you probably call them souvenirs, mementos, keepsakes, snapshots, and old-stuff-I-can't-bear-to-throw-away.

Just like ritual acts, ritual objects have value only to the extent that you bestow that value with your mind. Only you know why you would run back into a burning house to rescue a photo album. Nobody else would endanger themselves to save your mementos.

Ritual objects get their benign power over us in three ways. As mementos, they are tidy portable reminders of the good things we have known. Second, they often *signify*, as clearly as a neon sign. A ritual object can capture a whole complex of meanings and present that meaning to other people in a way that is clear and yet, because nonverbal, subtle. The picture of husband and child on the desk of that attractive woman at work is no doubt a fond reminder to her of her loved ones. However, it also quietly advertises her marital status to anyone who comes into her workspace.

Finally, no matter how rational we try to be, we all have a trace of the shaman in our hearts, especially an instinctive belief in the second law of sympathetic magic:

> Sympathetic magic has two "laws." ... The second law is the "law of contagion," which states that two things that have once been in contact retain some occult connection one with the other. Hence, if the magician obtains a fingernail paring or a hair cutting, he can affect the former owner thereof by working magic on that small part of him. On this principle, the "hair of the dog that bit you" was a serious dog-bite remedy.[1]

We almost can't avoid believing in some form of the second law of sympathetic magic. A picture of your child at age 1 reminds you of that time, but it is almost impossible to avoid the unstated assumption that there is some connection between the picture and the actual child[2].

Ritual spaces

A ritual *space* is one we reserve for ritual acts. In religion, the mosque, temple or church is the ritual space. The nature of a religious ritual space is always acknowledged by a ritual act on entry and exit: removing the shoes, or putting on a veil, shawl, or special cap[3]. Catholics use a whole set of little ritual acts to mark the church as a ritual space: crossing themselves on entry, genuflecting when crossing before the altar, etc.

You probably have another kind of ritual space, a much smaller one, devoted to displaying ritual objects. Such a space is properly called a shrine.

> Sometimes these items are put in a special place in an organized fashion — usually on a dresser top at home or a desktop or shelf at work. Little framed photographs, a rock or two, something a kid made in school, a key, a bronzed baby shoe, a little jar of dried flower petals and — well, you know. Shrines, altars. These are not accidental assemblages of sentimental detritus. They are the physical evidence of the ritual of remembrance.[4]

Walk around your workplace and look over your workmates' desks and computer monitors. How many shrines can you spot? The plastic toys on top of the computer monitor; the framed photos of spouses or lovers, of kids, of shiny vehicles; the collection of coffee mugs from trade shows of the past; the carefully-curated gallery of *Dilbert* or *Farside* cartoons — count them all, and don't skip the one(s) in your own cubicle or office. These are ritual spaces by our definition: they are devoted to storing and displaying ritual objects. The spaces aren't being used for anything practical; they haven't any functional value. They are reserved, prepared, and kept because of the symbolic and emotional value of the objects in them.

Conventional ritual elements

Just as any act is a ritual if you decide to invest it with meaning, any object becomes a ritual object and any space becomes a ritual space when you decide to make them so. However, we've all absorbed a vocabulary of familiar symbols from our culture. When we create new ritual, we might as well take advantage of the symbolic weight of these familiar elements. A table set for a meal is just a table. A table set *with candles* is a ritual space: we don't need candles for light any more, they have only symbolic and emotional value.

Here are some familiar ritual objects. As you read this list, think of the times you've seen these items used in ritual: Candles and lamps; banners; clean, crisp cloths; fire, and ashes; seasonal flowers, fruits, and foliage; bread, salt, alcoholic drink; water, soap, aromatic herbs; rings, necklaces, shawls; bowls, goblets, boxes.

Unmaking rituals

Now that you are a little more aware of the prevalence of rituals, you can take an inventory of your own rituals. Ask yourself if there are rituals in your life that are unhealthy. (For example, I heard one person complain they were stuck with a family Christmas ritual of getting drunk and having a fight.) Or perhaps the meaning has drained out of a ritual, leaving only a husk of custom or habit. That can happen when other participants grow older or move away, or it can happen when you grow away from the origin of the practice.

If you identify a ritual that is diseased or dead, you could simply drop out of it. But it might be worth asking: what value did it once have, or should it have had? Maybe you can replace the old ritual with a better one.

Making rituals

A ritual is anything you want it to be. And it turns out that Americans are amazingly creative at devising new rituals to adapt to the pressures on their changing lives. In the following paragraphs I sketch just a few of the possibilities, in order to encourage you to apply your own creativity.

Personal rituals

You surely have developed a personal set of daily, weekly, and seasonal habits that give structure to the progression of time. Make a list of these. Do you always start your workdays the same way? Your weekend days? Do you end every day the same way? Do you treat Super Bowl Sunday as a holy day of obligation (to use a Catholic term)? Or the weekend of the NCAA Basketball Final Four?

Having made the list, consider whether you would enjoy adding symbolic depth to one or more of these habits so as to make a ritual of it. Robert Fulghum writes eloquently about the benefits of making rituals out of your getting-up and going-to-bed times[4]. He says we reconnect to our own faces and bodies each morning in the mirror. A couple can make a ritual based on the old saying "never go to bed on your anger," agreeing to make at least a truce, if not a complete resolution, of any quarrel before turning out the light. People of either gender can profitably make a ritual of a weekly self-exam for cancer (your doctor can surely give you a pamphlet showing how).

Perhaps you take a shower every morning before dressing. What if your shower could wash away not only odor and dandruff, but stupidity, or clumsiness, or some other personal quality you'd like to have less of? It can't really do that, but there's a part of our subconscious that reacts to *intention* as if it was *action*. So, as you wash yourself, you could think: "May it be that my stupidity (or whatever weakness) washes away with these soapsuds, and that clarity (or whatever good quality) soaks in with this water." And see if you don't feel better about yourself and the upcoming day after a ritual shower[5].

Any regular occasion to get outdoors can become a ritual of connecting to the round of the seasons: the smell and feel of the air and the look of the sky and the trees or streets. Such occasions include daily dog-walks, runs, or bike rides.

And be sure to look over those seasonal occasions that advertisers are so eager to have you participate in. Do these holidays have little meaning for you? Get together with your family and friends and design a holiday that does have meaning, a holiday that has a genuine claim on your assent. There are plenty of resources in print and on the internet to give you ideas on how to create a simpler, more frugal, and perhaps more meaningful Christmas[6]. The tiny minority of people who are into pagan and Wiccan revivals have begun to create celebrations around the winter solstice; and this is too good an idea to leave only to them.

The four corners of the Solar year — the longest night on December 21st, the longest day on June 21st[7], and the equinoxes on March 20 and September 21 — can be the anchors for new family celebrations that substitute for worn-out, commercialized occasions. You could create a Yule celebration for December 21st, one that need not include the exchange of gifts. You could inaugurate an annual Long Twilight Picnic for midsummer. And the equinoxes are the times to celebrate winter's end and summer's end.

One good use for such new, equinoctial celebrations would be to replace and revitalize the worn-out custom of making new-year's resolutions. Instead of making resolutions once a year, you could make more limited resolutions specifically for the summer ahead (at Wintersend, March 20th) or for the winter ahead (at Summersend,

September 21). It is much more likely that a resolution you make for the six months of a season will actually be carried out, don't you think? You could make it a part of each of these celebrations that you recall the resolution you made at the last one, and celebrate whatever success you had with it. These times are nicely coordinated to the school year, so they might work well for families.

Rituals of family and friends

Rituals lubricate the awkwardness of coming together with friends, family, and community. First of all, the mere fact that a ritual repeats — whether it's Family Sit-Down Sunday Dinner or Monday Night Football At The Sports Bar — eliminates a host of logistic problems. Everyone involved knows the meeting time and place, and knows that they are expected. There is no need for telephone messages and comparing datebooks and saying "no, that isn't good for me, can we do it Wednesday?" It isn't easy to get a regular event established, but once it is established, the event owns its slot on every participant's day planner or electronic organizer. (The major holidays already own their calendar spots.)

Second, the ritual gives everyone a role to play and something to do. This removes a lot of stress. Nothing is emotionally tougher than walking into an ill-defined group where you have to invent your role on the fly. Take the hypothetical Family Sit-Down Dinner (which needn't be held on Sunday; you can designate any meal of the week as a special time at which everyone must show up and sit down to eat). Whatever else it may be, it is a meal, and there is the shared activity of serving and eating. Even if you are in a total adolescent snit, there is at least something to do (eat) and something to look at besides the other people (your plate)[8]. In the standard Christmas ritual, the giving and opening of presents serve much the same function: giving everyone involved defined roles to play.

All that said, the standard rituals fail some of us. Maybe you are geographically isolated from, or estranged from, or grown beyond, the people you used to meet with. Maybe your family has been disrupted by death or divorce. Or maybe the ritual occasions have simply lost meaning for you.

Very well: Invent some new ones. I can do no better for you than to recommend Susan Lieberman's *New Traditions* (Lieberman 1991), a delightful collection of things that real people have done to invent

new rituals of bonding between themselves and their families and
friends. Here are a few of the creative ideas Lieberman recorded
from real people:

- The great neighborhood flag football game: neighbors of all
  ages meet at the school playground Thanksgiving morning (it
  could as well be New Year's day or Super Bowl Sunday) to play
  a magnificently disorganized game of football. Everyone gets to
  play, even toddlers; those not playing, cheer. The organizing
  families bring doughnuts and cider; then everyone goes home
  red-cheeked and panting to their own celebrations.

- Single Mothers' Day Picnic: a group of single mothers (could
  equally be single fathers on Fathers' Day) feel they, too, deserve
  a celebration (damn it), so they organize and host their own
  Mothers' Day picnic (could as well be a brunch or any other sort
  of get-together), featuring games, food, shared kid-minding.

- Singles eating together: like the wonderfully-named ROMEO
  (Retired Old Men Eating Out) club, or the group of thirty-
  somethings who meet for breakfast in a diner before work one
  day a week, any collection of single friends can stay in touch by
  scheduling a regular meal together.

- Breakfast Out With Daddy: in a family with several kids
  competing for attention, father sets up the custom of taking
  each child in turn out to a restaurant for breakfast on Sunday
  morning. Child gets father's undivided attention for a couple of
  hours; father stays in touch with each child as a person.

- Family Circular Letter: reviving a very old custom, a family
  keeps an envelope moving around a circle of geographically-
  separated members. Rules: must not hold the letter more than
  ten days; must add a sheet of your current news. (Don't even
  think there could be an email equivalent!)

In these and other examples, a person who feels a need for
companionship or community establishes a simple, enjoyable,
repeated occasion. The emotional atmosphere of such a ritual need
not be solemn. For all but rituals of grief, it's perfectly fine to be
light-hearted, even giddy. And there's no reason to be ashamed of
any particular social status; in fact, if you are divorced, or
unmarried, or retired, you can make that a theme of the occasion.

Rituals of grief and loss

Conventional funerals deal fairly well with the occasion of the death of an adult, and mortuaries and funeral homes are ready and willing to help you organize one, for a price. But there are other occasions of loss that demand to be recognized in some way.

For example, there is no conventional funeral ceremony for a pregnancy that ends early, although this is a common tragedy[9]. A newspaper article[10] describes the way several families formalized their grief on these occasions. One couple ceremoniously planted trees to represent the children that weren't born. One couple began lighting a candle each day, at first "to light the darkness" they felt; but as they continued the daily ritual they began to see it as something "lighting their way forward."

Again, there is no conventional ritual to help us externalize our grief at the termination of a marriage or love affair — or indeed the end of any other process that fails, after having involved us deeply for a long time. I can remember the dismal, inconclusive ending of a software project that had consumed me and my coworkers for more than a year: it was wound up and unceremoniously shelved without being shipped, and we all moved on to other jobs.

Barbara Biziou spells out recipes for some rituals of termination and loss[11]. There are several common features to these rituals:

- Assemble ritual objects that strongly represent the failed relationship. (Be sensible, use pictures of valuables and copies of legal documents, not the originals.)

- With ceremony and formality, bring to mind the best features of the relationship and express them; for example, by writing a letter to the lost love, or by standing in front of a picture and reciting aloud the good things that you want to remember.

- Bring the ritual objects together and ceremonially destroy them: burn them (in a suitably fire-safe container), bury them (in a nice box, it's dreary to just drop things in a hole), or cast them into the sea (again, in a box, weighted to sink quickly).

- Ceremonially separate yourself from grief: wash your hands, as Jews do when leaving a cemetery; or shed a garment, or extinguish a candle, or move to another part of the ritual space.

- If others are taking part, share food and drink to celebrate the start of a new chapter.

From this meta-recipe you can compile a private or group ritual to formalize grief over almost any loss. For example, here's how my old programming group might have mourned our cancelled project.

The group would have been instructed to meet at a local picnic area, each bringing a sheet or two of paper that symbolized their best work on the project: the prologue of a module of code, cover of a test plan, a beta-test announcement. The project manager would have preceded them and built a good fire in a fireplace (defining the ritual space). After welcoming the group and having them assemble on one side of the fire, the manager would have invited each person in turn to step forward and say a few words about what he or she had learned from the project. Then each person would consign their symbolic paper to the flames and step to the other side of the space. The manager would go last, saying gracious words about what a wonderful group they'd been, and burning a copy of the organization chart. Then all would retire to a restaurant for lunch to talk about employment opportunities.

A special form of grief is personal regret over evils done — grief at having cruelly, or selfishly, or stupidly, harmed someone else. You could use this same meta-recipe to construct a private ritual of expiation — a ceremony in which you privately, but aloud, confess the damage you did and commit to whatever you plan to do to atone or amend.

Rituals of transition

Life transitions are happy/sad moments: an old life dies, and deserves to be mourned; simultaneously a new life starts, and its possibilities need to be brought to mind and celebrated. There are conventional rituals of transition; the most common are graduation ceremonies and weddings. There's not much to be done about graduation ceremonies, except to apply the imagination of family and friends to find ways to supplement them with a meaningful celebration. (At Stanford, taking part in the Wacky Walk means more to a lot of graduates than all the speeches.) Fulghum's chapter on weddings[4] makes very clear the pitfalls and rewards of designing your own wedding ceremony.

There are many other transitions that deserve celebration. Barbara Kato details some of the homemade rituals mothers and daughters have designed to honor a girl's first menstruation[12]. Beck and Metrick describe a simple and affecting family ritual that would serve to honor puberty in an adolescent of either gender[13]. The teen spends time alone, sorting possessions into three boxes: old things no longer needed; old things that are keepsakes; and things that represent his or her future self. Meanwhile, other family members select gifts for the third box. When ready, the teen invites the family into his or her room, and shows and describes the things in each box. The family offer their own additions to the third box and verbal good wishes. All retire to the kitchen for celebratory ice cream (or whatever).

Susan Lieberman makes the point that when someone leaves home — to go to school, to move into an apartment, to join the military, even to go to summer camp — the occasion needs to be marked with more ceremony than the usual awkward handshakes and sniffly hugs.

Robert Fulghum describes a nice ceremony for a transition that is rarely marked in our culture: bringing a new baby home to the neighborhood. After all, the neighbors will have more direct influence on this child's formation than will its blood relatives that live far away, so the neighbors might as well be formally introduced. However, new parents are usually not up to the task of planning and hosting any kind of party, so this is something that needs to be set up by the neighbors. Fulghum's ritual centers on a "treasure box," a box of symbolic gifts to be sealed and put away until the new child is 18, or 21, or old enough to leave home. The neighbors bring pictures, notes, or whatever they like to be sealed up in the box. The baby and mother are formally welcomed by all, and food is shared.

Summary

Ritual acts permeate our private and our public lives. We use ritual to assuage our grief, to help us bond as families and friends, to lend stability and shape to the cycles of life, and to come to terms with life transitions. Believers receive a useful (but not a complete) set of rituals for grief and transitions. American consumer culture presses many more on us in order to make us better consumers. But ritual is easy to create. Once we are aware of the role that ritual plays in our lives, we can inventory the rituals we have adopted without thinking, and can add new rituals that meet our needs.

6. Pursuing Bliss

Historically, the mystical experience has motivated the founding of religions, and mystics have sought it within the context of religions. However, practical people tend to dismiss it as hallucination, and psychologists have tended to categorize it as illness.

Research over the past half-century has shown that the mystic experience is real and probably benign — not a form of illness or delusion. These conclusions have strong implications for philosophy, psychology, and neurology, and we will look at some of them. But they also suggest that mystic experience could be sought in a secular context. The main question we want to answer is: would that be a worthwhile quest?

Describing bliss

The object of the mystic's quest has many names. Zen Buddhists call it *kensho*, Theravada Buddhists, a taste of *nibbana*; and both pursue it across multiple lifetimes. Richard Bucke called it Cosmic Consciousness, and thought he could detect it in the words of Christ, Dante, and Whitman[1]. Margahnita Laski called it Ecstasy, and performed one of the first properly-documented surveys of its frequency[2]. Abraham Maslow included it in the category he dubbed peak experiences, the defining moments of a self-actualizing life[3]. For this chapter I will call it Bliss, the term Nona Coxhead uses in her comprehensive survey[4].

One thing Bliss can be called is: surprisingly common. It is so common that if you haven't had it, you probably have met someone who has — although they may not have told you, because those who experience it are often reluctant to talk. Their reticence has three causes. There's the fear of being seen as some kind of nut. Second, the experience is very difficult to describe adequately in words. Finally, some who have had it feel that to force it into ordinary words would cheapen it.

Just the same, given the right encouragement, people will tell of it, and you can read first-person accounts in many books[5]. I have extracted brief snippets from a handful of these stories and pasted them into the following collage in order to give the flavor of the experience. Has something like this happened to you?

A bliss collage

It is an ordinary day. Possibly you are fretting about illness, money, or a relationship, but equally likely, you have no special cares at the moment. You are probably alone and outdoors. The first thing you might notice is a peculiar change in the light.

> ...the next thing I noted was that the whole locality was illumined by an extraordinary, bright light. It was a cloudy and dull day and this extremely intense illumination did not appear to originate in any fixed centre, but was diffused equally throughout the entire terrain.

> ...All at once, without warning of any kind, I found myself wrapped in a flame-colored cloud.

At the same time you perceive a scintillating aliveness in everything you see.

> ...I became intensely aware of many of the objects which were in the area. The rocks, the trees, the birds, the stream, the clouds, the flowers, became extremely meaningful to me.

> ...Every little pine needle expanded and swelled with sympathy and befriended me.

> ...The brush in my hand, my dustpan, the stairs, seemed to come alive with love.

> ...Every human being moving across that porch, every sparrow that flew, every branch tossing in the wind, was caught in and was a part of the whole mad ecstasy of loveliness, of joy, of importance.

Instantly you grasp, with a stamp of authenticity that utterly excludes doubt, that you and all things are facets of a single, universal process. You can *see* it, and you *know* that it is proceeding exactly as it should, and that you, as part of it, have nothing to fear.

...I realised the rocks, trees, etc. were I; I they; all brothers. And I was exceedingly joyful in realising this kinship.

...Everything seemed to be connected with everything else. Although all separate forms, and all vibrating with their own intensity of life, yet they all seemed to be connected by their vibrations into one whole thing, as the different coloured parts of a picture are yet the same picture.

...Nothing changed in my outward perception. ...Yet everything became part of a single Unity, a glorious symphonic resonance in which every part of the universe was a part and illuminated every other part, and I knew that in some way it all worked together and was very good.

Your own identity evaporates into this knowledge.

...One felt at one with it all and yet retained one's individuality. (This is one of those times when language fails, for it is a paradox when expressed in words, but while being experienced no difficulty exists.)

...When I say "the I had ceased to exist" I refer to a concrete experience that is verbally as incommunicable as the feeling aroused by a piano concerto, yet just as real — only much more real. In fact its primary mark is the sensation that this state is more real than any other one has experienced before.

Possibly you are flooded with a sense of great discovery, a feeling that you can grasp immense knowledge that is beyond telling.

...One day, being in orison, it was granted me to perceive in one instant how all things are seen and contained in God. I did not perceive them in their proper form, and nevertheless the view I had of them was of a sovereign clearness, and has remained vividly impressed upon my soul.

...It began with an overwhelming awareness that ... the Universe wasn't complex at all, but beautifully, exquisitely, simple ... No doubt you know the jubilantly satisfying click one experiences when one finds the solution to, for instance, a complicated mathematical problem. Well, the experience I had was of a similar kind but carried to the ultimate. A king-size, super-hyper-Click!!

You are saturated with positive emotion: joy, immense security, exultation at the perfection you see. Later you cannot say how long the experience lasted; it could have been from one second to several minutes. An afterglow of joy and buoyant energy remains; and the memory stays with you the rest of your life.

> ...The effects of the experience remained with me, in enhanced awareness of every form of life and experience, for at least three months, during which time I possessed boundless energy and vitality.

> ...The memory of my vision of the 'Garden' has never left me. Now in my eighty-fourth year I find life peaceful and pleasant and... I constantly give thanks for the wonder and joy of life.

Implications of spontaneous bliss

The different first-person stories that went into the preceding passage, and many others, tell of the spontaneous experience — Bliss that simply erupts, unheralded, into an unprepared mind. These spontaneous visitations happen to ordinary people, often nonreligious people, people with no history of mental illness. They are among the most vivid, compelling, memorable experiences these people ever have, and they make a permanent change in people's attitudes. But how common are they?

Frequency of spontaneous bliss

Starting in the 1970s, a few people began to investigate the occurrence of "spiritual" experience in a scientific way[6]. The following question, or a similar one, has been used in various opinion surveys in the US and in Britain:

> Have you ever been aware of or influenced by a presence or power, whether you call it God or not, which is different from your everyday self?

Consistently, one-third of the people polled answered 'yes' in both nations[7]. But when Hay went out to conduct detailed face-to-face interviews, he found more:

> By the time we had made 172 visits we had collected 124 positive responses... We decided that seventeen of these 'yeses' had come from people who either didn't seem to have understood the question properly or who couldn't actually describe the experience they claimed... That left us with 107 people, 62 per cent, who claimed to have had an experience of this type, more than double what we had predicted on the basis of the national survey.[8]

It is important to note that these surveys cast a net with a rather fine mesh: a positive response to the survey question often reflects any memorable, unnatural experience, such as a premonition that came true, a feeling that a deceased loved one is very close, even a moment of deep awe or reverence in a natural setting or in church.

What fraction of this one-third (or two-thirds, if Hay's interview experiences can be generalized) are reporting a genuine Bliss experience of the sort sketched above, with its key feature of egoless unity with all things? I have found only a few numerical clues. The most detailed sample is found in the summary report of the first eight years and 4,000 accounts collected by the Religious Experience Research Centre[9]. Hardy and his co-workers used a system of 92 features when tabulating thousands of first-person stories. The following list shows the features from their scheme that should be associated with an account of Bliss:

- 1(b) Illuminations (perceptions of a change in ambient lighting, as opposed to seeing specific lights) (45)
- 1(d) Feeling of unity with surroundings and/or with other people (60)
- 7(f) Sense of certainty, clarity, enlightenment (195)
- 7(i) Sense of harmony, order, unity (67)
- 7(n) Sense of integration, wholeness, fulfillment (13)

The number in parenthesis is the number of times they assigned that feature code per 1,000 accounts. For example, 60 stories in 1000 were marked by feature 1(d), feelings of unity.

These feature codes are not mutually exclusive. A complete Bliss story should be tagged with most of them. Unfortunately, Hardy doesn't give numbers that would let us judge, for example, how many reports were tagged with (7(i) *and* (1(d) *or* 7(n))). Based on the bare counts-per-thousand, it would be risky to hope that as many as 50 reports per 1,000 tell a full Bliss experience. The true count could be much less[10].

The TASTE website is a repository for scientists' accounts of "transcendent" experiences[11]. The editor defines "transcendent" rather broadly, so the site, like the opinion survey question, collects a wide range of experience. However, four of the forty-four accounts in its archive seem to me to be definitely Bliss experiences. This ratio of 9% is encouraging but not definitive because of the small sample size.

Thomas and Cooper asked 305 people a similar question and got the typical 34% positive response[12]; however, they analyzed the responses and concluded that only two of the positive responses represented a mystical experience. Two in 300 is less than 1%, but again the sample is small.

An unsupported guess, but one that is not contradicted by these numbers, is that one percent of all reports of spiritual experience tell of Bliss. Extending that to the 33% of the general population that freely admits to some kind of experience suggests that at least one person in 300 in the United States and Britain has experienced Bliss. If a sympathetic face-to-face interviewer can turn up 62% experiencers, the guesstimate rises to one in 150. This is the basis for my assertion that you probably have met someone who has known spontaneous Bliss.

Distribution of spontaneous bliss

Nobody has yet identified a consistent set of preconditions or "triggers" for the spontaneous experience[13]. Are there common factors among the people who have them? Hay and Morisey and Gallup reported some demographic features. In summary, people who report an experience are:

- More likely to be in the middle or upper social class than lower-class.

- More likely to be better-educated.

- "Significantly more likely to report a high level of psychological well-being than those who do not."[14]

In the U.S., positive responses are somewhat more frequent among churchgoers, parents, Protestants, Afro-Americans, southerners, and westerners; but they are by no means exclusive to these groups[15].

Some psychologists like to label "spiritual" experience as a type of psychological regression or escape mechanism. However, these trends — a tendency to be well-off both psychologically and economically, and to be integrated into a community (parents and church-goers) — argue against that idea. The people you might expect would need regressions or escapes — the poor and those reporting low psychological well-being — are not the ones most likely to answer 'yes' to the question.

Both reports underscore the point that experiences are reported in significant numbers by nonreligious people:

> A last point of interest is that in the "agnostic," "atheist," and "don't know" groups, not far short of a quarter of the respondents, claim they have had an "awareness of a presence or power" ... such a large proportion of responses from them raises interesting questions.[16]

> One of the most interesting aspects of these experiences is that they happen to the unchurched and nonreligious... For example, in the 1988 survey, 25 percent of unchurched Americans reported having had a religious experience. The survey defined the unchurched as those who had not attended church or synagogue within the past six months except for occasions like weddings and funerals.[17]

Bliss at random

Hay and Morisey found the frequency of reports going up with increasing age, from 29% for ages 16-24 rising to 47% at age 65 and up (Gallup did not note this effect). It is possible to think of more than one explanation; for example, older people are more likely to be "religious" by other measures. However, the simplest hypothesis is that these experiences simply happen *at random*, so that the longer one lives, the more likely one is to have one.

In fact, there's no data to contradict the guess that spontaneous Bliss visits one person in every two or three hundred, sometime in their lives, and that it visits people pretty much at random. While this can only be a working hypothesis, there's no evidence of any more systematic distribution.

In fact, a sparse, random rain of "spiritual" experiences of all types goes some way toward explaining the permanence of religions and their continual renewal. As Hay and Morisey put it,

> Could it be that a significant proportion of the population in Western industrial society remain "unsecular," not because of a residual loyalty to an ancient institution, but because of the vividness, reality, and unexpectedness with which some of their perceptual experiences challenge the taken-for-granted quality of secular reality?

There's also no reason to suppose that this is confined to the English-speaking peoples, or to the current century. It is reasonable to assume, as a working hypothesis, that these experiences have happened throughout history, and that they continue to happen today, throughout the population of the world, like a sparse rain of invisible meteorites. Most of the time, the person struck is just quietly grateful. His or her life may be deflected in a major way, but other people are not much affected.

Once in a long while, a spontaneous experience must visit a mind that is prepared, equipped, and disposed to become a prophet[18]. If this is the case, one implication is that the human race will never lack for new prophets.

Inducing bliss

Besides the spontaneous experience, there is *induced* Bliss; that is, Bliss that is laboriously sought using the ancient methods, including meditation in any of a hundred traditions; starvation, as in the Native American vision quest; rhythmic movement, as in Sufi dancing; or chanting; or flagellation; or, of course, mind-altering drugs.

There is endless debate as to whether an induced experience is the same as the spontaneous one, or fundamentally different, and whether one method induces a more true or more healthy experience than another.

But it seems clear to me that the reason that people pursue any induction method is simply because the spontaneous experience does happen. Over historic time, some of the people who had a spontaneous experience went in search of a repetition. Others, who had only heard about the spontaneous experience, sought to have one of their own. They all used whatever means was available to them in their culture that seemed likely to work.

Now, here's the tricky part: *all* methods will "work" if pursued long enough. If the spontaneous experience does occur more or less at random, it will sooner or later occur to someone who is pursuing it by method X. This is reported as a success for method X, which encourages more people to use it.

The Buddha received his first experience while sitting in meditation. Accordingly, his followers sit in meditation, hoping for the same. If a thousand people sit in meditation every day for a year, it's a statistical near-certainty that one or two of them will have a spontaneous experience in that time. And the same can be said of any other tradition of Bliss-seeking.

This is *not* to say that meditation is ineffective at inducing Bliss. It may be very effective. So might Sufi dancing, or peyote, or any of the other methods employed by mystics down through the ages. The point is, an anecdote of success can be perfectly true, yet still not be proof of efficacy.

Bliss and philosophy

Historically, the pursuit of Bliss has always been conducted in the context of a religion. In the past century, science and secular philosophy have gradually begun to take notice. (If you do not enjoy thinking about philosophy, you will lose nothing by skipping ahead to the next major topic — although a stop at "Unity as intellectual insight" on page 89 might repay you.)

Religious traditions

There are long, rich traditions of mysticism in Hinduism, Buddhism, Judaism (Kabbalism), Christianity, and Islam (Sufism)[19]. Until the Twentieth Century, the mystics who wrote down their experiences wrote within their religions, using religious vocabularies and imagery. And why not? They believed in the tenets of the religion, and its images and vocabulary were deeply familiar to them. In addition, in Christianity at least, a mystic's book would not be published if he or she wrote something that conflicted with doctrine. Mystical experience does tend to make mystics say things that don't align with doctrine. (For example, it is not easy to reconcile the doctrine of the Holy Trinity with a vivid perception that the universe is a unity.) However, one characteristic part of the Bliss experience is its feeling of absolute, unshakable authenticity — a feeling that makes the mystic stubborn about receiving spiritual direction. More than one Christian mystic was suspected of heresy, and one of the best-known, Meister Eckhart, was put on trial, but died before its conclusion.[20]

Early secular discussions

When secular scholars of the twentieth century began to survey mystical writings, they noticed that despite the differences in language and imagery, there was a striking similarity of feeling and even of meaning.

The first secular writer to tackle the issue was Dr. Richard Bucke. Bucke was a fabulous character. Born on the Canadian prairie, an intelligent and adventurous youth, he set off to see the world. He worked a wagon train to California, participated in the Gold Rush, lost a foot to frostbite in the Sierra Nevada. Using a small inheritance, he put himself through college and medical school in London, and led a long career as a respected psychologist, a pioneer of medical treatment of mental illness in Canada.

While in medical school, Bucke had a powerful, spontaneous Bliss experience, one that included all the elements: strange light (he's the one who said "All at once, without warning of any kind, I found myself wrapped in a flame-colored cloud"), perception of unity of all things, a sense of grasping cosmic knowledge, a lasting sense of utter security. He called this Cosmic Consciousness, and made a hobby of collecting other writers who, it seemed to him, were talking about the same experience. His book[21] was the first to lay out ecstatic writings from many sources and point to their parallels.

Bucke's contemporary, William James, included accounts of several Bliss experiences, including Bucke's, in his classic work *The Varieties of Religious Experience*[22], and he, too, pointed to their common features.

Thesis: Perennialism

In the first half of the century, others went further. Writers such as Aldous Huxley tried to show that the common features of mystical writings pointed to a universal, verifiable basis for all religion. This notion was based on three assumptions: first, that Bliss experiences were the original inspiration of all religions; second, that all mystics had basically the same experience; and third, that the experience was "real" in the sense that it reported a truth about the external world.

There were flaws in this Perennialist view[23]. In their enthusiasm to display a solid, anthropological basis for an ecumenical religion, the writers tended to edit, retranslate, select, and over-interpret the texts they collected to make them fit the thesis. Second, they tended to dismiss or flatten the differences between religious doctrines. It is true that religions are broadly similar, if only because they address similar concerns. However, doctrines do have serious differences that are not merely academic, but advocate different behavior. Also, each religion is a highly complex product of its culture and its history. To minimize the differences is to neglect the nuances of these great edifices of human thought.

Most important, Perennialists simply ignored a belief which was, by mid-century, nearly universal among scholars of the humanities: the belief that all conscious experience is conditioned by language and culture.

Antithesis: Constructivism

In the 1970s and 1980s, a backlash to Perennialism developed within the confines of academic philosophy. Modern philosophy asserts that it is not possible to have an experience that is not mediated by the brain; in fact, "to experience" *means* "to experience via the brain." More strongly, it asserts that all experience is filtered through the contents of brain, that is, through our culture and language — and even further, that this filtering is so thorough that we literally cannot see a thing unless it is translatable in our cultural vocabulary. We are said to "construct" what we call our experience by assembling our raw sense data on scaffolds provided by culture and language.

Under this Constructivist view, it is simply not meaningful to claim that mystics of all times and religions had "the same" experience. Even if the experience itself is based in brain physiology, each person has to modulate it with a different culture, language, and memories. So there can't be a single mystic experience, nor a single *ur*-religion. They are multiple, unique experiences and multiple, unique religions, and none of them are directly comparable.

Constructivists basically conclude that all reports of mystical experience are exclusively based in and shaped by religious tradition. As a result, whether they report anything useful, about either external reality or the architecture of the mind, is simply unknowable.

Synthesis: Awareness preceding construction

To a non-academic, there are fairly obvious problems with the Constructivist view. One is that it does not account well for the spontaneous experience. When nonreligious people, of different occupations, backgrounds, classes, genders, and centuries, voluntarily "construct" the same claim — that for one unexpected moment they felt literally part of everything — it is hard to avoid supposing that these experiences are, in some quite strong sense, "the same."

Within the past decade, some scholars have begun to create a synthesis. Some of these writers begin with the physical anatomy of the brain and central nervous system, and we will review them in the next section.

Among philosophers, Robert Forman argues[24] that mystic experience precedes language. Based partly on his own experiences of deep meditative absorptions, and partly on writings from different mystical traditions, he argues that advanced meditators in all traditions routinely enjoy *awareness without an object*, awareness that has no subject except itself. This is a paradoxical state: if one is alert, aware, yet not aware of anything but awareness — how is it possible to remember the time spent in this state? Forman, as well as mystical writers in several traditions, attest that it is possible. You look back on a period during meditation and realize "I was not asleep, yet there was no subject in my awareness. I could not say how long it was, but I was aware and alert." Such a state should not be possible under the modern philosopher's assumption that awareness is literally inconceivable without "intentionality" toward an object.

Forman also points to teachings from several traditions to show that all seek to induce mystical experience by abandoning or deconstructing words and concepts. In other words, mystics intentionally try to rid themselves of the very material of Constructivism! The mystic is trying to get to a state that precedes all the stuff that Constructivists say is essential for experience to happen. For example, a central element of Zen training is the "creation of great doubt" — Zen monks spend years, several hours a day, sitting and asking simply "What is this?"[25] When the experience comes, it is then wordless. It precedes concepts.

Forman suggests that a small adjustment to philosophy can accommodate this. William James introduced the division of knowledge into two categories: knowledge by acquaintance (knowledge based in sense data: how I know *my* toothache) and knowledge-about (knowledge based in language or rational inference: how I know *your* toothache). Both are necessarily "intentional," having a subject and an object. Forman proposes a third class, knowledge by identity, which arises internally but has only a subject, no object. He points to a similar division in Buddhist epistemology[26]. We'll find this same idea arising in a different context next chapter ("Pirsig's metaphysics of quality" on page 109).

Of course, as soon as the person tries to remember, integrate, and talk about the experience, the whole process of construction through language and culture must come into play. In other words, everything the person might ever do with the experience, other than simply to remember it in a nonverbal form, is false to the experience. Of course, this is exactly what people say about their experiences: they can't be conveyed in words![27]

Unity as intellectual insight

The Bliss experience delivers two things: a flood of positive emotions, and a convincing experiential insight showing, loosely speaking, that everything is one unitary process. As Alan Watts saw it in a spontaneous experience:

> ...the present seemed to become a kind of moving stillness, an eternal stream from which neither I nor anything could

deviate. I saw that everything, just as it is now, is IT — is the whole point of there being life and a universe.[28]

There is a vast gap between experiencing unity directly, as Watts describes, and understanding it as a concept. Just the same, the second-hand, intellectual concept is credible and useful.

Indeed, everything *is* related. This can be worked out intellectually[29]. Start by accounting for a simple wooden table, as if you had to explain it to an alien from another galaxy. Whenever you use a noun or verb, the alien says "What's that mean?" and forces you into another level of explanation. In order to tell the *whole* story of the table you have to tell about all the human economic and transport systems that brought the finished table to the room where it is now. By the time you have explained only this much — how the table was bought, paid for, and delivered — you have had to explain all human economic activity, which requires you to tell of the economic history of the human race. Well, consider that done; now tell about the shaping of the table, about lathes and saws and varnish. You will end up explaining all of metallurgy, and industry, and science. And you have yet to account for the wood itself, which means explaining forests, vegetation, sunlight, soil, and seasons; and explaining those means describing the earth and the solar system, which leads on to cosmology.

The point is, no matter what object you start with, you will end up explaining *everything* to your inquisitive alien. Reality is like an fishnet, with each knot an object. Lift up whichever knot you choose; you end up lifting the entire net. Ultimately, any phenomenon is contingent on all other phenomena. To render a complete account of *anything* requires telling the story of *everything*.

Moreover, this understanding operates forward in time as well as backward. If each present phenomenon was caused, in some measure, by every phenomenon that went before, then it follows that every *future* phenomenon will depend, in some measure, on each phenomenon that exists *now*.[30]

Think about that, and consider: actions are "phenomena," too. In principle, *every action you perform now has some effect on everything that will ever come to be hereafter*. You are indeed an integral part of a universal process, connected to everything, everything connected to you — and not in metaphor, but in plain, literal fact.[31]

That's philosophy. As a practical issue, we can't cope with this view of things in mundane life. There isn't *time* to consider how the table depends on everything else when you are laying the silverware for supper. However, it is intuitively clear that if you could keep a thread of this insight alive in the back of the mind, it would make you a wiser person, more sensitive to the implications of every act.

Bliss and psychology

Richard Bucke and William James both considered themselves psychologists, and tried to describe mystical experience as a feature of human psychology. These pioneers of psychology granted respect to the experience because they assumed that it revealed something transcendent about the real world.

After their day, and through the middle of the century, mainstream psychology followed the hard sciences in dismissing any idea of non-material transcendence. Given that belief, the mystical experience must arise from an internal state of the mind, and it can only tell us about the subjective mind; it doesn't tell anything about the world. (This moved psychologists out of the Perennialist camp; Perennialists generally assumed that mystical experience was saying something important about the external world.)

Psychologists also assumed that every aspect of the mind must somehow serve the needs of the ego[32]. Freud established the basic interpretation of mysticism; he said the unitive experience was a regression to an infantile solipsism. The mystic who felt one with all things was said to revert to early infancy, when (psychologists supposed) the entire world *was* an extension of one's self.

Today, psychological thinking rejects the idea of regression for several reasons. One is that research in child development has shown that infants recognize a difference between "self" and "other" right from birth; there is no natural condition of infantile unity[33]. Another is that a state of perfect, unitive solipsism is never seen, even in adult pathology. There's no remembered state to be "regressed" to.

As late as 1976, the Group for the Advancement of Psychiatry published a report titled "Mysticism: Spiritual Quest or Psychic Disorder?" The report waffled on the stark question in its title, but treated mystical experience as being an adaptation to pain, one that might be either pathological or creative.

Jung, the other great psychological trend-setter of the century, approved of mystical experience, seeing it as a natural, creative force arising from the collective unconscious. More recently, other psychologists have attempted to come to terms with the elusive mystical experience as something that might be healthy or useful. In the 1960s, Abraham Maslow, feeling that psychology was too preoccupied with illness and pathology, began to study the psychology of healthy, high-achieving people. He discovered that these people tended to report particularly vivid, compelling moments which he dubbed peak experiences. He included mystical experience in the category of peak experience:

> ...the B-love experience [selfless, adult love], the parental experience, *the mystic, or oceanic, or nature experience*, the aesthetic perception, the creative moment, the therapeutic or intellectual insight, the orgasmic experience, certain forms of athletic fulfillment, etc. These and other moments of highest happiness and fulfillment I call the peak-experiences.[34]

Maslow compiled a list of features that a peak experience displays[35], and it reads like a check-list for the perceptions commonly reported in the spontaneous Bliss experience: reality, rightness, connectedness, aliveness, perfection, and finality. Maslow also suggested that these features of peak-experiences could also define the proper values and goals of all life-experience.

Bliss in the brain

Whatever else it is, the Bliss experience arises in the brain. Recently scientists have tried to use what we know of Bliss as a probe to explore the function of the brain. (Again, if you are not interested in studies and speculations on brain structure and function, you will lose nothing by skipping to the next topic, "Addressing the obvious question" on page 96.)

Austin and the neuroanatomy of bliss

Richard Bucke was a doctor who had a Bliss experience and spent years following up on its implications. A century later James H. Austin, a neurologist by profession and a part time student of Zen, experienced a few deep meditative absorptions and then a full *kensho*, or Bliss moment. As a neurologist, he felt compelled to ask how such a powerful, unusual experience could arise from the brain as he knew it. As his attempt to answer that question, Austin put together a magnificent book, *Zen and the Brain*[36]. The theme of the book is:

> ...where does the experience of this Great Self come from? The premise of this book is that it must come from the brain, because the brain is the organ of the mind. The same perspective holds whether mystical or peak experiences arise spontaneously, are cultivated, or are drug-induced. Our thesis is that prior meditative training and daily life practice help release basic, preexisting neurophysiological functions. This thesis will lead to the following proposition: mystical experiences arise when normal functions reassemble in novel conjunctions.[37]

Austin agrees in essence with Forman that mystical experiences occur prior to words: "Their raw data anticipate all words, doctrines, and sacred texts, all theological, philosophical, and neurological interpretations."

Quite a few modern writers on mysticism are aware of brain anatomy and the high-level functions of organs like the hypothalamus, hippocampus, and amygdala, and everyone now seems to know that the left and right hemispheres contain different functions. But Austin reminds us to be very careful about making easy assumptions about the location of any mental function:

> ...there is no "simple" way to account for even our elementary perceptions and memories, or our most routine behaviors. They are the result of many smaller functions drawn together into very large constellations. They cannot be localized to any one lobe. Nor to any single part of the cortex, nor to any other particular spot in the brain. Instead, each represents a dynamic emergent function, expressing the integration of these many widely distributed columnar systems.[38]

It is impossible to summarize *Zen and the Brain*; it contains detailed surveys of dozens of separate topics, each bearing in some way on how the brain might produce meditative and ecstatic experiences. Some of the questions it addresses: How does the brain map sensations? How is it possible to shut off sensation within a meditative absorption while maintaining conscious awareness? Where are emotions generated and modulated? What might produce the flood of positive emotion in Bliss? How does the brain produce attention at all? How is it possible for meditators to train their attention, and what part of the brain are they modifying when they do so?

Austin writes at length on sleep. The sleep-wake cycle is an exceedingly complex mechanism. Austin goes through it carefully, looking for clues to how some part of the machinery that regulates sleep might operate out of its normal phase to produce elements of mystic experience.

Anecdotal accounts of drug experiences have some features in common with the Bliss experience. Austin reviews the literature of psychoactive drug experience sympathetically, starting with the oldest drug, nitrous oxide. William James was one of the first to describe how it often produces a sense that one has grasped great metaphysical insights. Alas, the insights disappear as soon as the gas stops. By contrast, the insights that come as part of Bliss remain to influence the person's life for years.

Austin reviews the voluminous literature on human and animal experiments with LSD. In common with many Bliss reports, some LSD takers have an impression of brilliant, hyperacute vision. Well, LSD dilates the pupils of the eye, and tends to reduce its normal, constant, jerky motions (saccadic motion). Could that cause the visual sensations?

The effects of LSD are unpredictable and highly variable, both from one subject to another and for the same subject at different times. Reviewing one study, Austin notes that of 206 "guided" LSD users, only 5% reported a "positive, integrative transformation" and only 3% reached a unitive experience in which time and the ego dissolved. Reviewing Grof's long career of giving multiple LSD sessions to over 1700 subjects, Austin notes that a few of Grof's subjects had unitive experiences with resemblances to *kensho* — although vastly more of them had a wide variety of other experiences, some very frightening. Austin also reviews the records on psilocybin and mescaline; then examines what is known about how all psychedelic drugs affect the brain's use of neurotransmitter chemicals. In general, he concludes, the effects of psychoactive drugs tell us a lot about how the brain works. However, drug experiences are unpredictable; and when they do produce valid insight, it is usually accompanied with hallucination and negative emotions. No drug delivers only the clear unitive insight of Bliss.

In all of these interlocking essays, Austin limits himself to what is definitely known about brain anatomy and function. However, other writers use neuroanatomy as a springboard to a higher level of theorizing.

d'Aquili and the neurotheology of bliss

Andrew Newberg and the late Eugene d'Aquili described a general model of brain architecture that, they feel, could account for the universal human drive to create religious accounts of the world[39]. Besides their rather grand goal of a *metatheology*, a descriptive system "that can explain the essential features of any theology arising out of any specific religious tradition," they also want to explain the mechanisms behind meditation absorption, near-death experience, and Bliss (which they called Absolute Unity of Being, or AUB).

These authors step back from the brain and view its structure at a much higher (and much more speculative) level than Austin permits himself. In their high-level description of brain systems, d'Aquili and Newberg are not afraid to make fairly sweeping claims. For one small example, they postulate that the brain contains both a "reduction operator," a unit with the function of analyzing any experience into component parts, and a complementary "holistic operator," a unit whose constant duty is to try to assemble the scattered flow of sensory input into coherent wholes. Although they base some of their speculations on MRI scans of brains in action, it seems likely that some of their more specific predictions may turn out not to be well-founded (recall Austin's caution against trying to locate brain functions in particular places). However, anatomical placement is not crucial. The model that d'Aquili and Newberg present is built on a small number of parts, each of which seems likely to exist as a functional unit somewhere in the brain. Out of the interactions of these parts come credible explanations for religious attitudes and experience. Even if the model does not map perfectly onto anatomy, it works as a metaphor.

A key concept of the model is "deafferentation," the effect of cutting off the inputs to some unit of the brain. (They could as well have said "disconnection" or "isolation.") The brain contains a number of gatekeeper structures that control the flow of inputs to other structures. Austin discusses some of these: the thalamus cuts off sensory input from higher brain levels during sleep; the reticular nucleus can selectively block input to the thalamus; and so on.

d'Aquili and Newberg stress what sometimes happens within a functional unit that has been cut off from its normal inputs: it resonates, processing its own fed-back outputs. This effect is the basis for their explanation of mystical and meditative experience. Suppose there is a distinct brain unit whose job is to maintain your perception of your physical self in space. Suppose this unit is simultaneously cut off from sensory input and strongly stimulated? The result could be a perception that the self extends to all of space. This is a sketchy summary of one element of their model of the Bliss experience.

Addressing the obvious question

Now let us set aside all the speculation about physiology, psychology, and philosophy. It remains likely that the Bliss experience is "real" in the sense that it is a rare, involuntary, intense state of the mind — not a form of dream or hallucination, nor an inflated account of a normal mood of awe or reverence. But the practical issue remains: what is the cost of pursuing it?

Let's assume that you have not received a Bliss experience. Nor have I. How much time, risk, and expense can we justify spending in pursuit of it? The answer lies somewhere between "zero" and "our lives, our fortunes, and our sacred honors." What does the pursuit entail?

Science no help

Alas, science can't help us here. Because Bliss cannot be repeated under any sort of controlled condition (remember, many people have devoted their lives to trying to do just that) it can't be studied except by examining people's verbal accounts. This creates many difficulties. People who are willing to describe their experiences, and who have the verbal skills to describe them clearly, are a minority and may not be typical. Anyway, the first thing they all say is that the experience cannot be conveyed in words; and when they try, each description is constructed out of the person's cultural and linguistic set. The farther we go from our contemporaries in time or culture, the harder it is to make sense of their accounts. And so on.

Common induction methods

Methods of Bliss induction, as practiced in various mystical traditions[40], have two consistent elements. Evelyn Underhill, a turn-of-the-century scholar of (primarily Christian) mysticism, put it so:

> There are two great phases in the education of every contemplative: and they are called in the language of the mystics the purification of the senses and the purification of the will.[41]

Based on what I have read, I would rename these two phases using postmodern terminology. I would call purification of the senses "deconstruction of cognition"; and purification of the will I would call "deconstruction of the self." "Deconstruction" is the precise word for the process a serious mystic applies to cognition and to ego. Each is analyzed into smaller and smaller parts until they cease to have any importance at all.

Deconstruction of cognition

In deconstruction of cognition, the mystic tries to give up the automatic association of experience with words and categories. The mystic tries to remain at all times in the physical present without interpretation or judgment, treating every sensory input as unique — not an abstraction, not a type, not a member of a class, but as itself only.

The Zen schools use several techniques to train the seeker in this way of thinking (or not-thinking). One is the *koan*, an unanswerable question. Koans aren't riddles; they don't have clever answers that one could discover by thinking hard[42]. The Zen master tries to convince the student of two things: that the koan is significant and interesting; and that it is futile to attempt to solve it using any intellectual method such as analogy, abstraction, or symbolism. The student willingly enters this bind of needing an answer when no rational answer is possible, and may, when the training works, arrive at a deep, nonverbal, insight.

The Theravada Buddhist approach is not so regimented, but it is no less determined to deconstruct cognition. The theravadan practice of vipassana meditation — we introduced the basic form of it earlier under "Sitting meditation" on page 50 — involves persistent, cool examination of each thought and emotion that floats into the mind. The student labels each mental event, "thinking," "hearing," "itching," or whatever, and observes it: especially observes how the event arises and fades away. Gradually the student achieves an internal margin on which to stand and observe thoughts as they come and go. Gradually it sinks in: *every* thought and sensation is ephemeral; nothing in the mind is permanent, and not one is even fractionally as compelling or significant as it presents itself[43]. With this, it supposedly becomes easier to maintain "mindfulness" at all times:

> While washing the dishes one should only be washing the dishes, which means that while washing the dishes one should be completely aware of the fact that one is washing the dishes. At first glance, that might seem a little silly: why put so much stress on a simple thing? But that's precisely the point. The fact that I am standing there and washing these bowls is a wondrous reality.[44]

Teachers like the Vietnamese Buddhist monk Thich Nhat Hanh present this state of mindful perception of reality as a better way to live. Nhat Hanh, like teachers in many traditions, claims it is somehow better or saner to be fully present to the physical reality of dishwater.

I find myself dubious about this teaching. Through a modest meditative practice I have become able to reside in the moment, unreflective and without mental chatter, for a few seconds at a time; but I find no great satisfaction in this. Perhaps it would be a release for a person whose mind is full of obsessive or frightened thoughts; probably it would be a refuge for person in the throes of bereavement. But when your stream of consciousness is connected, constructive, and enjoyable it is much more entertaining to reside with your thoughts than with the physical dishes[45].

Nevertheless, this advice is consistent in mystical traditions. A typical sentence from Underhill:

> Ambitions and affections, tastes and prejudices, are fighting for your attention. Your poor, worried consciousness flies to and fro amongst them.[41]

The consensus seems to be that silencing the internal dialogue is a necessary step on the road to Bliss. Remember the common-sense statement from a few paragraphs back: "There isn't *time* to consider how the table depends on everything else when you are laying the silverware on it for supper." The seeker in pursuit of Bliss cannot agree. Seeing the table and silverware as unique elements of reality is a primary aim of the seeker's practice.

Deconstruction of self

The other consistent teaching is the deconstruction of the self. I choose the word carefully: "deconstruction" is not "destruction"; it is analysis and realistic appreciation. The mystical seeker is taught to pick apart the components of the sense of self, to examine them, to appreciate them in a realistic way and, inevitably, to be tolerantly amused by them.

The abnegation of self is well-known in Christian teachings, from "not my will, but thine, be done" (Luke 22:42) to "whoever exalts himself will be humbled, and whoever humbles himself will be exalted" (Mat 23:12).

In the Christian contemplative orders, life is formed around the triad of poverty, chastity, and obedience. In the practice of poverty, the seeker gives up all thought of owning anything at all. This undermines the ego by removing all the psychological masks and props that our possessions give us. At the same time, it removes all need to defend and maintain an economic status. The practice of chastity deletes all the psychological complexities of man-woman and parent-child interactions. The practice of obedience is designed to silence the will. James quotes St. Ignatius of Loyola on obedience:

> In the hands of my Superior, I must be a soft wax, a thing, from which he is to require whatever pleases him... I must consider myself as a corpse which has neither intelligence nor will; be like a mass of matter which without resistance lets itself be placed wherever it may please any one...[46]

This goes beyond the military concept of discipline; the seeker is asked to deconstruct the elements of personal volition and discard them individually and collectively.

Buddhism preceded the Christian orders in establishing principles of poverty and chastity for contemplatives. The Buddhist approach to the further deconstruction of self proceeds at a deeper level.

The doctrine of not-self (*anatta*) is central to Buddhism. It is one of the three characteristics of existence: no phenomenon, in Buddhist philosophy, has a permanent self; all phenomena are "conditioned," that is, arising by cause then passing away, transient. The doctrine is applied directly and personally in Buddhist practice. The Pali

Canon contains several versions of the Buddha's teaching of non-self. In most of them, he deconstructs the perception of the self, piece by piece, and denies each piece:

> Form, monks, is not self. If form were the self, this form would not lend itself to dis-ease. It would be possible [to say] with regard to form, 'Let this form be thus. Let this form not be thus.'
>
> – Samyutta Nikaya XXII.59

Form, that is, the physical body, cannot be a (permanent, trustworthy) self because it is a mutable and failure-prone. The body is seen as a collection of conditioned phenomena, all in the process of passing away at different rates. If you identify "self" with the body, you set yourself up for an identity crisis when the body falls ill, or needs an amputation, or merely ages.

In the sentences following that quote, the same argument is applied first to emotions — if you identify "self" with emotions, are you a different person when you pass from anger to sadness to joy? — and then to your senses, and to your thoughts, and finally to consciousness itself. All possible components of a sense of self — the body, the emotions, the senses, thoughts and memories, and consciousness — are examined in turn and shown to be inadequate as a foundation for a sense of self.

In my youth I had strong negative reactions to Christian teachings like "not my will, but thine, be done." This is understandable in hindsight. First, I was an adolescent, nervously preoccupied with proving some value in my self. And second, it seemed as if such passages were always quoted to support manipulation from above — not aimed at my benefit, but for the benefit of a system. At a greater age, and with plenty of experience of the unreliability of the body, emotions, and memory, the Buddhist doctrine of *anatta* seems much easier to swallow. However, I can well imagine how many people could find either of these practices of self-abnegation threatening or offensive. Just the same, this kind of dismantling of the self is a standard part of every tradition of Bliss seeking.

Secular search for Bliss

There is nothing uniquely religious about either of these disciplines. Anyone who wants badly to pursue Bliss can find secular ways to practice deconstruction of cognition and deconstruction of the self.

The practices are demanding; serious seekers devote full time to them. And the deconstruction of cognition demands that you give up the habit of mental reverie. There is a very high cost in time and comforts. On the other hand, neither practice is likely to cause any psychological damage. To judge by their writings, mystics are rather happy people.

Summary

The Bliss experience, conventionally sought in a religious context, is a real experience that seems to be available to anyone, at least in the form of rare, and possibly random, spontaneous experiences. The active search for the experience also is available, to the extent that the two basic practices, deconstruction of normal cognition and deconstruction of the ego, can be practiced in a secular context. This search is likely to be long and demanding, and there is simply no data on how effective it might be.

7. Inspiring Self-Transcendence

Religions regularly expose people to models of magnificent achievement: Moses, Jesus, the Prophet, the Buddha, and all the ancient and modern saints of every religion. Over and over the believer is reminded "You *can* do better, you *can* display your Buddha-nature; you *can* attempt the Imitation of Christ." And sometimes these injunctions click with the believer, and motivate him or her to be stronger, wiser, more honest, more compassionate.

Where can we find inspirations like these outside religion? It has become fashionable punditry to say that rising secularism has cut us all off from mythic models. In this chapter we will first consider whether that's so (my answer is "no").

Then we have to ask, how do we recognize a saint or a hero, or any kind of excellence, when we see it? The answer is not at all simple; but it has deep implications for how we should go about finding role models for ourselves and our children.

Why do we need heros at all? Because we need them as standards in order to define ourselves; but what does "self-definition" mean? After we know that, we can finally plan a program for collecting heros.

No more mythic ideals?

For many years, writers have regularly noted that the rise of secularism, and the supposed eviction of religion from the center of life, has left people without models. Here are two genuinely wise men who fretted about it a third of a century ago:

> Every age but ours has had its model, its ideal. All of these have been given up by our culture; the saint, the hero, the gentleman, the knight, the mystic. About all we have left is the well-adjusted man without problems, a very pale and doubtful substitute.
>
> – Abraham Maslow[1]

> ...the democratic ideal of the self-determining individual, the invention of the power-driven machine, and the development of the scientific method of research, have so transformed human life that the long-inherited, timeless universe of symbols has collapsed. In the fateful, epoch-announcing words of Nietzsche's Zarathustra: "Dead are all the gods."
>
> – Joseph Campbell[2]

But Joseph Campbell probably knew that Thomas Carlyle had said something quite similar in 1840:

> I am well aware that in these days Hero-worship, the thing I call Hero-worship, professes to have gone out, and finally ceased. This... is an age that as it were denies the existence of great men; denies the desirableness of great men.[3]

One hundred fifty-nine years after Carlyle, the message from children's book critic Marjorie Allen was the same, with added details:

> Once upon a time, role models were public figures who exhibited virtues that parents hoped their children might emulate... Today, public figures have been dissected into oblivion by the media. Sports heroes gamble and take drugs. Presidents don't always tell the truth. Entertainers have feet of clay. The pedestals have toppled, and young people are hard pressed to find anyone to meet their expectations.[4]

Do we truly suffer a dearth of Heros? Even as I revved up my best rhetoric to echo these pundits, I had to stop and wonder. For one thing, when was this golden time when everyone had untainted heroes? Carlyle's testimony pushes it back at least into the eighteenth century. Perhaps, I began to suspect, it was only the most sophisticated thinkers who had been failed by their heroes. Was the absence real for everyone?

All heroes tainted?

Certainly anyone who keeps up with the news will be tempted to agree Marjorie Allen. But step back a bit and think about her examples. "Sports heroes gamble"? Well, it was a tragedy that Pete Rose, for many years a model of dedication and high achievement, was caught being greedy. But is that late news? The greatest gambling scandal in baseball history, beside which Rose's alleged sins are peccadillos, occurred in 1919!

True, every few months a sports figure is exposed as taking drugs. But really, what's new is not the drugs; what's new is the public exposure. We are aware of it because of regular testing and greater awareness among officials, the media, and the public. And keep in mind, there are two kinds of sports drug scandals. There are players who take banned substances for competitive advantage, like the Bulgarian weight-lifters in the 2000 Olympics. In essence, this is cheating at the game, looking for an illegitimate edge. Just the accusation is enough to humiliate a player and damage the player's career.

Less often, entertainment figures or players are outed for using illegal, recreational drugs like cocaine (in the week I write, the unhappy Darryl Strawberry has failed yet another urine test). They are punished legally as well as being humiliated and kept from their game.

All these exposures serve a public purpose. They are presented to us as morality plays. The solemn press conferences and well-publicized court appearances are the modern equivalent of the Puritans' stocks and ducking stool. It's our way of displaying social offenders to the community as bad examples to be avoided. We need those negative examples; they keep our rules credible. Fallen heroes are just as useful, in their way, as saints.

Entertainers with feet of clay? I can't think of any modern entertainers who party as hard or sleep around as widely as those in Hollywood of the 20s, 30s, and 40s. We permit entertainers to be outrageous, and admire them for doing it well (think: Madonna); but when they step even slightly out of line, we come down on them hard (think: Hugh Grant). We didn't do that even as recently as the 60s; President Kennedy's amours were ignored, as was Eisenhower's wartime relationship with an aide that, today, would bring deadly serious treatment as sexual harassment. We are holding public figures to higher standards than ever before, and when they betray even a little clay on their toenails we give them a good public spanking. The ones that are left are a pretty clean bunch.

As for presidents who lie: I'm sure Allen, writing in 1999, had Bill Clinton in mind, but I can remember how Richard Nixon made a whole career of lying; can even remember the now-sainted Eisenhower who, through Dulles and other aides, lied quite blatantly about U.S. interference in Latin America. The most visibly moral President of recent times, Jimmy Carter, was one of our least successful leaders.

I'm not saying it's OK for a president (or anyone) to lie. I am saying that anyone who looks to a president or other political leader for a model of moral behavior is bound to be disappointed. People with sense will look to political leaders for models of effectiveness and vision, and look elsewhere for models of morality or kindness.

Dearth of models?

Then I asked myself, is it true there are no positive, public role models? And realized that, not only is there no dearth of them, but that we have a wide and ever-shifting pantheon of modern cultural heroes who are regularly held up to display some kind of beauty or skill or courage. I had not noticed because, curmudgeon that I am, I usually dismiss them.

Think of the continued, reverent display of historical icons like Martin Luther King, Abe Lincoln, George Washington. School kids are subjected to their stories every year as their holidays roll around. Gettysburg address, yeah, yeah; "I have a dream," sure, sure; crossing the Delaware, ho-hum. Those old chestnuts don't resonate with me; they're for kids. Oh! Er, wait a minute... Just because *I* am a jaded old poop who finds the annual eulogizing of Reverend King overblown and irritating does not mean that he can't inspire other, younger people.

So I asked an experienced primary-school teacher what kinds of role models she was offering children these days. "Oh, lots; there's a whole new pantheon," she replied. She mentioned Ruby Bridges Hall, the 6-year-old girl who was the first African-American to integrate a segregated school, and the video on Rev. King, *Our Friend Martin*. In a school where the student body is about one-third

Asian and one-third African-American, the Disney movie *Mulan*
was "a huge hit." But when she polled her classes on who were their
heroes, almost half named their parents first, ahead of any
culturally-supplied icon. Another large fraction named an older
sibling, aunt, uncle, or teacher[5]. At least for young children, the
figures who define excellence are most often the people they live
with — which suggests that the search should start at home.

The offerings of pop culture

Not only had I been blind to elementary-school role models, I'd
been ignoring the crowds of faces that American popular culture
thrusts at us. Think of the popularity of sports figures like Barry
Bonds and Tiger Woods. I'm not interested in golf, and did not think
that Tiger's winning the U.S. Open by 15 strokes justified ranking
him with the greatest sports heroes of all time; but that doesn't
mean that he isn't a hero to many. And reasonably so: his skills are
superb, his personality affable, his public behavior exemplary.

And so on: just because *I* have no interest in Ellen DeGeneris's
sexuality and wish she'd get back to being funny... just because *I*
think Oprah Winfrey is a calculating panderer to the worst in
human nature... just because *I* think Britney Spears, Eminem, and
Christina Aguilera — to name three who have top-10 hits in the
week I write — make vapid, boring music... In short, just because
current media icons leave *me* bored and uninspired, does not mean
that each one does not excite and inspire some group of people.

In fact, when I actually *look* without prejudging or condescending, I
see that my culture presents a veritable smorgasbord of models in
sports, entertainment, politics and the news. Every one of them is
given a place under the spotlight because he or she displays some
quality that grips the imagination of some number of people.

There is a problem of emphasis. My culture offers its greatest
rewards to models of health, beauty, fashion sense, witty chat,
physical skill, and physical courage. It gives small reward to
exemplars of quieter virtues like charity, forgiveness, or patience.

Yet this culture, so often called shallow, regularly displays and
celebrates models of intelligence, for example Bill Moyers, Stephen
Hawking, the late Carl Sagan. This culture, so often called grasping
and materialistic, takes pains to celebrate public service. You don't
think so? What, then, is the subtext of shows like *NYPD Blue*, *ER*,

and *The West Wing*, if not the display of mythic icons of self-sacrificing public service — people who, when the chips are down, put the good of the public ahead of their personal concerns?

Indeed, my culture is so rich, and has so many specialist nooks and minority crannies, that there must be an idol to match anyone's interests. There are probably heroes of Persian cat breeding, Olympian figures of garden railway design.

And when the culture fails to thrust idols at us, we can fall back on the grade-school method, and find some real people to admire.

There are role models everywhere for everyone. The real issue is how we recognize them.

Perceiving excellence

How do we recognize something as good, as worth adoring or emulating? Let me tell two personal anecdotes; then we can get theoretical.

Vaaahh-rooooom

The time: a summer afternoon in 1956 or 1957, my 13th or 14th year. The place: a flat, straight, quiet stretch of two-lane asphalt highway south of Tacoma, Washington. The sky is overcast, the air cool and damp, the empty road lined on both sides by dark, shaggy Douglas firs. I am riding my bicycle slowly homeward, with several miles to go and a long hill yet to climb.

From around a bend half a mile behind comes a sports car. I am almost certain, now, that it was an MG-A coupe; a check of the history of the marque shows that the closed coupe was first produced in 1956. It's a stretch to suppose that one of the little British coupes reached the Puget Sound country in its first year, but it could have happened.

So: riding casually along, listening to the scrunch of the gravel shoulder under the balloon tires, I hear behind me the boom of an engine at high RPM. Stop, put a foot down, turn, and see this tiny, white, streamlined coupe, its roof barely higher than my belt-buckle, come past at high speed, *vaaahhh-roooooom!* and disappear around the bend half a mile ahead.

In only a few seconds exposure, the sight and sound of that little car defined and clarified so many things to my adolescent brain. That image became, for years, my personal icon of freedom, of speed, of self-sufficiency, of elegance. I had no particular choice in this; it simply occurred: perception and comprehension, unverbalized and instant.

Now batting... Rod Carew

Fast-forward 25 years or so, to a different state, a different life, different concerns. Sometime around 1983, I became aware of Rod Carew for the first time. I had only been paying serious attention to baseball for a couple of years, mostly to the local San Francisco Giants. For some reason, I tuned into an American League game on television, and when a slight, wiry man took his stance at the plate, I was transfixed.

Carew at that time was near the end of his career[6]. His batting stance was unusual. He somehow coiled his body like a spring, in a way that suggested a rattlesnake preparing to strike. All his weight was on his back foot; his arms holding the bat framed his head; the toe of his leading shoe probed delicately for balance. He awaited each pitch in that coiled stance, rocking gently, conveying an impression of absolute concentration, of perfect readiness. When he swung, his whole body uncoiled like a whip and his bat simply flashed through the flight of the ball. Quite often, the ball rocketed precisely between or over the defenders for a base hit.

I only watched Carew bat a few times, and never in person, always on television. But his batting style gripped my imagination for months. I had never seen anything that so mingled delicacy, precision, and power. For quite a while (and occasionally still) I used a mental image of Rod Carew at the plate as a kind of visual metaphor for the right approach to any physical task: delicately balanced, perfectly focussed, moving only at the exact moment and with the exact force needed.

Pirsig's metaphysics of quality

The point of these two anecdotes is that in each case, a *single momentary exposure* was enough to create a heroic or mythic image in my mind. And I think this is typical: when we recognize quality, we do so instantly, without cogitation, usually without any comment beyond "wow!" The process is not intentional. We do not *create* heroes and we are definitely not *taught* heroes; we *recognize* heroes, instantly. This has important implications.

The phrase "recognize quality" in the previous paragraph may have reminded you of something you've read. "How we recognize quality" is a summary of the theme of Robert Pirsig's *Zen and the Art of Motorcycle Maintenance*[7], a best-seller in the 1970s and still popular. Pirsig has continued to develop his Metaphysics of Quality into a detailed philosophy of human perception[8], a philosophy that resonates strongly with many people[9].

Here's how Pirsig stated his theme in *Zen and the Art of Motorcycle Maintenance*:

> Quality — you know what it is, yet you don't know what it is. But that's self-contradictory. .. Obviously some things are better than others — but what's the "betterness"?

You know from watching and from introspection that, generally speaking, people instantly agree on measures of quality: who or what is more beautiful, more elegant, more graceful, more amazing, more affecting. There are differences between cultures and between individuals within a culture; yet if you show a group of people from one culture a choice between two faces, or two natural scenes, or two poems, you'll get a clear majority preferring one over the other. And it doesn't take any significant time, any debate or analysis, to make these choices. What are people detecting so readily?

I remember pondering this while hiking in Yosemite valley. Walking on North Dome, looking through a mile of air at the faces of Cloud's Rest and Half Dome, I wondered, in what is the magnificence?

There's no magnificent-o-meter we can apply to the material scene. No physical measurement could describe anything but granite, trees, air. Yet nine of ten people shown this scene would agree that it is magnificent — of high quality, in Pirsig's sense. (And the tenth would probably be thinking about philosophy.)

Pirsig dives into this problem. If Quality can't be measured in an objective way, it is automatically assigned to the other side of a cruel dichotomy: things that aren't objective must be subjective, and subjective things have a doubly bad reputation. First, the tradition of scientific materialism discards the subjective:

> The whole purpose of scientific method is to ... eliminate the subjective, unreal, imaginary elements from one's work ... When he said Quality was subjective, to them he was just saying Quality is imaginary and could therefore be disregarded in any serious consideration of reality.

Also the academic tradition of classic formalism "insists that what isn't understood intellectually isn't understood at all," a doctrine that labels any instant, unthinking judgment as worthless. Yet the perception of Quality is clearly instant and unthinking, yet real and worthwhile. How can that be resolved with scientific and academic thought?

Pirsig's resolution is to short out the subjective/objective dichotomy by moving earlier in the process of perception. He declares that Quality is the instantaneous event at which the subject becomes aware of the object:

> ...at the cutting edge of time, before an object can be distinguished, there must be a kind of nonintellectual awareness, which he called awareness of Quality. You can't be aware that you've seen a tree until after you've seen the tree, and between the instant of vision and instant of awareness there must be a time lag. ... Reality is always the moment of vision before the intellectualization takes place. There is no other reality. This preintellectual reality is what Phædrus felt he had properly identified as Quality.

In the terms I used in Chapter 6 ("Synthesis: Awareness preceding construction" on page 88), Pirsig bases his Metaphysics of Quality on the assertion that awareness precedes construction — coincidentally, just the conclusion needed to account for the Bliss experience and other meditative phenomena.[10]

If Pirsig is correct, we recognize Quality in the timeless instant of seeing, before thinking happens. The perception of Yosemite valley as magnificent occurs in much less time than it takes to dredge up the word "magnificent." In the same way, I registered that MG-A coupe, or Rod Carew in his batting stance, as something unusually good, and did so in a thoughtless instant. How might the mind be organized so that instant recognitions like this can happen?

The intersection of quality with growth

Recognition of a remarkable thing is instant and precedes cogitation and analysis. Of course, the thinking does follow. We become aware that the incredibly beautiful person of the opposite sex is wearing a ring. Time reveals that the singer had only the one decent song. And so on. But we don't spend *any* time thinking about things that don't capture our imagination in the first place. We don't check for wedding rings on the hands of boring people; we don't listen for more music by a performer when we didn't like the first number we heard. So the first hurdle a hero or saint must cross in entering our mind is to make a powerful first impression.

But powerful first impressions are unpredictable and rare. When will we suddenly realize that a certain person is amazingly skillful, or intelligent, or brave, or is heroically honest, or persevering, or self-sacrificing? Each such impression is a happy accident that occurs when the moment that we apprehend the person intersects with our changing ability to value those qualities. A month earlier in our own growth, or even a day, and we wouldn't be ready to appreciate that person. And if we encounter them in the wrong context — Rod Carew had to be seen batting, Rod Carew muffing a ground ball on defense would make no impression — then we don't even see them.

Since the process is basically random, the basic strategy for finding Heros is to seek widely, in order to increase the chances of a hit. Now we can appreciate the wisdom of the Catholic Church in developing a vast range of saints, each with distinct qualities, which makes an approved hero available to any parishioner at any stage of development. But what about the rest of us? We'll come back to that after considering what we are trying to accomplish.

Celebrating contingency

In Chapter 2 I urged you to accept and to celebrate having a contingent nature; that is, being an incomputably improbable accident. Being contingent means that each of us is the only representative of our personal genome that will *ever* exist. It's a position of incredible freedom because you are positioned to know and exploit every possibility of that inheritance. It's a position of responsibility because *only* you can realize the possibilities of your inheritance.

Fortunately, realizing our own best possibilities is, quite literally, the natural thing for us to do:

> Man demonstrates in his own nature a pressure toward more and more perfect actualization of his humanness in exactly the same naturalistic, scientific sense that an acorn may be said to be "pressing toward" being an oak tree, or a horse toward being equine ... And creativeness, spontaneity, self-hood, authenticity, caring for others, being able to love, yearning for truth are embryonic potentialities belonging to his species-membership just as much as are his arms and legs and brain and eyes.[11]

Self-definition

The process of filling out the envelope of our humanness is often called "self-definition." The positive message of the Existentialists was that self-definition is both possible and necessary as a direct consequence of our contingency: we are able to define ourselves precisely, and only, because nothing predefined us.

Alas, this notion that you must define yourself is usually stated in a frightening way — as if there were some Self-Definition Examining Board you must face, or an annual Self-Definer license you must have in order to avoid arrest by the Existence Police. People who have no problem with the idea that they are contingent can still frighten themselves with this idea.

But if we are contingent, then not only is there no external authority that defined our natures, there is also no external authority to judge what we do with them! There can't be; if there were a supernatural Examining Board to judge our self-definition against some standard, that would simply re-introduce the divine plan and determined nature in an ex-post-facto version that would be even less fair.

Once you accept the Existentialist's motto "existence precedes essence," you have claimed not only the absolute freedom to define yourself, but also the absolute right to establish the standards by which that definition, and your achievement of it, will be judged. In other words, not only are we allowed to write our own entries in the great Dictionary of Human DNA, but we get to invent the language in which we write them!

One small caveat

The Existentialists emphasized the freedom and responsibility of self-definition. Maslow, the late savant of self-definition from whom I am drawing frequent quotes, cautioned that this freedom is not open-ended. Unqualified, the Existentialist message can be misread as a "denial of specieshood and of a biological human nature:"

> Yes, man is in a way his own project and he does make himself. But also there are limits upon what he can make himself into. The 'project' is predetermined biologically for all men; it is to become a man. He cannot adopt as his project

for himself to become a chimpanzee. Or even a female. Or
even a baby.[12]

This reminder from Maslow is comforting; it trims an ill-defined
project of self-definition back to a much clearer, achievable job. You
need not choose a goal from an infinite array of possibilities. Your
goal is only to demonstrate the strength and beauty that is implicit
in your very particular genome, in the context of your very
particular culture and historical moment.

Be a *mensch*.
– traditional Yiddish invitation to self-actualization.

Standards of self-definition

Of course, we still need standards of comparison, and there is no
source of them except the ones we receive from other people. We
rely completely on other people's opinions to tell us how successful
we are at being ourselves. Think it through: what is your "self,"
anyway?

It is not that physical carcass you inhabit, however handsome it may
be just now. This truth can be argued in several ways. The Buddha
focussed on the impermanence of the body, how it changes, ages,
succumbs to disease. If you base your definition of yourself on the
form of your body, you build on a foundation of sand. Again, you
can give up almost any part of your body that the surgeon may
demand: limbs, lungs, "liver and lights"; hack 'em off in the name of
survival; swap in a transplant; "you" remain.

But your self can't be the present contents of your mind, either,
because they also change constantly. Just as your body contains
hardly a single molecule it had when you were a child, your mind
also contains hardly a single opinion that is the same as when you
were young.

What constitutes a "self" is memory: the internal recollection of a
history, of a personal, continuous trajectory through time. It is only
that trajectory — the curve of the wake you leave on the surface of
time — that is at least slightly under your control, and at least semi-
permanent in your memory and other peoples' memories.

We evaluate our historic selves by contrasting them to the stories we
receive about other people, both real and fictional. This is natural
and appropriate: we are social beings. But for best results, we need

to use good, challenging, standards for comparison. And that points up the importance of our selection of heroes.

Publishing a self-definition

One tragedy of life is that nobody else will ever comprehend your personal history as you understand it. There's no way to download your memories in full to somebody else (although, pathetically, we often try). Words are inadequate; and anyway, there's no audience with the patience to sit through the whole story.

Yet we have strong practical reasons for letting other people know how we currently understand ourselves. It is also useful to quickly learn other peoples' self-definitions. And this is why we dress our bodies and furnish our lives with material symbols: in order to summarize ourselves to others. In gesture and accent, in choice of possessions and style of facial hair, in a thousand subtle ways we advertise what we think to be our own present co-ordinates and direction in life-space. This is a communal effort using a common language: we continually read other peoples' advertisements and adjust our own to match theirs, or to compete with them.

In adolescence, the whole thing seemed impossibly difficult. Like many, I adopted a public attitude of scorn toward the "pretension" of dress, of "fitting a niche." And, of course, I dressed and wore my hair in a way that advertised how I saw myself in relation to the communal language of dress and hair, like someone chanting "English is trivial," in English. The only way to really step out of the game of self-advertisement is to step completely out of society.

But the idea of a human life lived in complete isolation, without reference to a society even for contrast, is almost as hard to conceive as the sound of one hand clapping. We have no choice but to define ourselves using the symbology that is understood in our community; and have no choice but to interact with other people on the basis of their self-descriptions given in the same language.

In short, *why* we have to define ourselves is to establish and justify our place in a community; and *how* we do it is by using the cultural symbols that are understood in that community; and *why we bother* is because other people are of critical importance to our own health and happiness (as discussed in Chapter 3).

Professional help for the project of self

The project of self-definition is automatically a project of self-improvement, because inevitably the images we form of how we ought to be are always at least slightly larger than we are at the moment. And self-improvement can be grandly called self-transcendence: we try to get beyond our present limitations, try to begin to prove there is a butterfly in this cocoon.

One way toward self-transcendence is to choose a few good models and strive to be more like them (the ostensible subject of this chapter, toward which we are slowly returning). But another is to work directly on your own psychology, trying to understand and remove its weaknesses and build up its strengths. For this, you might consider getting professional advice. There isn't a lot of it around, however.

One school of Psychology is directed toward the study and improvement of the healthy mind. This is the school of Humanistic Psychology, founded in the 1950s by the late Abraham Maslow, Carl Rogers, and others. Humanistic psychology "emphasizes the independent dignity and worth of human beings and their conscious capacity to develop personal competence and self respect," and it aims "to enhance such distinctly human qualities as choice, creativity, the interaction of the body, mind and spirit, and the capacity to become more aware, free, responsible, life-affirming and trustworthy."[13] The flavor of writings in Humanistic Psychology tends to be practical and people-oriented.

Transpersonal Psychology, although it was founded in the same effervescent years of the 50s and 60s, is a rather different school. Transpersonal psychologists are the only ones to give serious attention to the mystical experience (Chapter 6), and the literature of this school speaks often of self-transcendence. Unfortunately, a great deal of its literature also accepts and promotes "mysticism, occultism, supernaturalism, and religiosity."[14] A cautious person should be careful when looking for help from a Transpersonal (or indeed, any) therapist.

In Europe there is a small but growing trend toward "philosophical counseling"; that is, persons schooled in philosophy who offer personal counseling on life issues[15]. This idea has a certain appeal. After all, classical philosophy contains as many sound answers to questions of "How should we live?" as any other body of thought.

A sensitive person who listens well and who is well-versed in philosophy ought to be able to give good advice. However, there are no professional standards for "philosophical counselors." It would be as easy to set up shop as a philosophical counselor as it is to go into business as, say, a Feng Shui advisor, although perhaps not as lucrative.

Modesty and impermanence

There is a mistake in the notion of "defining yourself." It lies in two unstated implications: that the definition is supposed, somehow, to be permanent; and that its function is to benefit the future. When these ideas are examined (not often) they are quickly seen as false. The only use of your self-definition is to serve you, in the moment and in your present context.

Permanence is impossible because you can never finish the project. A human life isn't a word that can be stated, it's a continuous process. You are not an obelisk, you are a fountain; not a fine granite spire engraved with a statement, but a spray of particles outlining a form that sways in the wind of circumstance. Everyone who survives to old age will have had several different careers and will have played several different life roles. There's never a point when you can dust off your hands and say, "There, that's me, finished." Even on your deathbed, there's still the challenge of demonstrating how well you can die.

And then, after you've died, the life that you sculpted so carefully will be ruthlessly condensed in the memory of your descendants. What survives of it will be reinterpreted according to the standards of days you can't imagine. Do you suppose your great-grandfather would be flattered if he could know how you think of him? Your great-grandchild's concept of you will be just as detailed and just as fair as that.

Finally, modesty is important. Consider for a moment what it means to be one of six billion people (the UN noted the six-billionth birth the week I wrote this). In order to bring this number home, you need 1,000 of something, or at least 124 small coins, like U.S. pennies.

On your living-room carpet, lay out a square array of 32 by 32 coins. If that isn't convenient, lay out just the perimeter of such a grid, 124 coins defining a 32x32 array. Now you have an image of a thousand coins, near enough. (Actually 32x32 is 1024, a computer "K.") The U.S. penny is 3/4-inch in diameter (19mm), so a thousand-penny array is 24 inches square (0.6m).

Now, visualize 1000 such grids. In your mind's eye, imagine that each one of the coins in your grid swells and divides into a new square of 1000 coins. There you have a solid sheet of 1024x1024 coins — if pennies, it is 64 feet on a side (19.5m). Pace off this distance in your front yard. Can you visualize that sheet of shiny coins? This is a million coins. It is a visual model of the population of a medium city, and coincidentally about the number by which the human population increases each week.

Now imagine 1000 such sheets of pennies. Picture an array of sheets, 32 on a side. As pennies, they would carpet a field 2,000 feet on a side (622m). Picture the largest parking lot you have ever seen at a business office or shopping mall, with every square inch carpeted with coins. That's just *one* billion coins.

Got that image clear? Now recall that there are *six* billion people alive today. And they are all busily defining themselves.

The good news: if you can do it only average well, there are still three billion who aren't doing it as well as you. And, among the three billion people doing it better, you ought to be able to find some heroes.

Finding heroes

We are surrounded by people being heroic in some way — heroically brave, heroically tolerant, heroically clever, heroically compassionate — but they are hard to notice because they look like just ordinary people. Our media parade others before us; and we have thousands of books, fiction and nonfiction, describing more. The problem is to notice them and appreciate them.

Finding your own heroes

In fiction you can find complete heroes: people who are wholly admirable, or whose failings are limited and chosen to highlight their virtues. Actual people are more mixed, but also far more numerous and accessible. In looking for real-life heroes you have to be content to look at facets of lives. You have to be willing to admire one skill or virtue contained in a very ordinary life.

This is especially true of sports, entertainment and political figures. You know very little about these people; you have no idea what they are like when they go home at night. All you know is what you see on the field or stage. And that's all right. You are able to watch them do their best, to see exactly those facets of their lives that are worth admiring. It would be silly to assume they are anything but ordinary when they are out of the spotlight, but that in no way invalidates the power or brilliance of their performance when they are in it.

And you can extrapolate in some remarkable ways. Sports really can supply metaphors for the rest of life. I don't think I was silly when I tried to drive a car the way Rod Carew batted; it worked, for me, for a while. Anyone could take the laser-like intensity of a Tiger Woods or a Mia Hamm and use it as an icon for the right way to approach *any* task.

Give up jadedness

You are unlikely to see quality if you don't concede that quality exists. You won't notice value in public figures, especially ones in popular culture, if you are jaded.

A condescending air, as any adolescent quickly learns, is a protection. It permits you to dismiss things that might otherwise upset you or make you look small or inadequate. Adolescents need protection like this to avoid being overwhelmed by life. Alas, an unconsidered habit of condescension, carried into adulthood, blocks our ability to see quality in great chunks of our culture.

This is why I am suspicious of people who mention smugly how little TV they watch. I don't watch a lot of TV either, but that is only because I don't know of shows that are more interesting than other things I want to do. Two considerations keep me from feeling smug about this. First, I know that there are thousands of talented people working in the TV industry. They can't all be failing all the time. Somewhere on the 70-odd channels on my cable system, sometime during every day, something is shown that would interest me, perhaps even dazzle me, if I watched it. Further, every minute of air time on those channels contains content that interests somebody, that is, some human being who is not so very different from me. I don't have the time to look, but I have no basis for assuming it's all uninteresting.

I and my wife have a private expression for this: "the Niagara Effect." Planning a trip through the Northeast, we debated whether to stop at Niagara Falls. We had a world-weary impression that it was just some tourist thing, a place for honeymooners who had no imagination. But finally we did include a stop at Niagara Falls and, guess what? The falls are spectacular! We looked at them from every vantage point; we took the boat ride; we even had to confess that we were impressed when they were lit up at night with colored searchlights. We decided it was a pretty good rule of thumb that, if a whole lot of people go to a place over a long period of time, it is not because the people are sheep. It's because there is something genuinely worth seeing there.

Apply the Niagara Rule to celebrities of the culture. There are almost no wholly manufactured celebrities[16]. It's a pretty sure bet that every celebrity has some genuinely admirable facet. Perhaps that isn't a facet that excites you; that's fine, just be willing to concede that it excites some people. And keep looking; there are thousands of celebrities and new ones every minute.

Give up cynicism

Jadedness is the feeling that you've seen everything good and everything to come is just repetition. Condescension is the feeling that there's nothing happening that rises to your standards, your level of sophistication. Cynicism is worse yet; it's the feeling that there simply is nothing good, everyone is venal and everything they make is intentional trash.

Clearly, a habit of cynicism is a highly effective filter against recognizing any sort of hero. Try to give up such a habit. Persuade yourself that there might really be admirable people around you. Be prepared to encounter examples of goodness, virtue, genuine Quality. One of the commonest virtues is courage, the simple guts it takes to go on living and not collapse in despair. You meet people who display that courage every day, if you will deign to notice them.

Because people are such mixtures, it is necessary to notice and admire tiny facets. You never know when a person you meet will display one momentary instance of courage, of grace, of gallantry, of forbearance, of wit, and in that instant become a lasting icon in your private collection of mythic images.

Inventing a hero

Your icons of excellence do not have to be drawn from the real world. After all, icons are flashes, striking moments, powerful impressions in your mind — which means that they have only a tenuous link to the reality of the people that inspired them. There is nothing wrong with finding such an image in a book. There is no telling when a powerful idea from a page will intersect with your own development to spark an explosion in your mind.

Finding heroes for children

Children aren't troubled by cynicism or ennui; they are wide open to perceiving Quality and storing it. But they also make radical adjustments in the contents of their minds every hour, so you can never guess what will impress them. And because they spend the greatest amount of time among their peers, the greatest number of things that catch their imaginations will be drawn from the behavior and attitudes of their friends. (Wasn't that how it was with you?)

You probably can't hope to be more influential than your children's peer group, but you could try to come in second by adopting a strategy like that of the Catholic Church: make sure there are lots of potential heroes and saints around at all times. The most convenient way to do that is through books.

There are a number of books specifically designed to present historical figures as heroes. These days, girls are better served than boys, with many books on admirable females. Marjorie Allen discusses more than 100 books that contain characters, male and female, who are admirable in some way[17].

Beyond that, be alert to the process of hero-acquisition as it happens. What makes your child gasp "wow!"? What rivets his usually wandering attention? Who does she suddenly begin to imitate? You can't control a process as instantaneous as the perception of Quality, but you can pick up clues as to what other icons might work at this momentary stage of growth.

Summary

We don't intentionally select our heroes, our mythic icons of goodness; we discover them, in a rare and near-instantaneous process of recognizing Quality. We use these heroes and icons to guide us in a necessary and never-ending process of self-definition. We can always use more examples of Quality. Fortunately, and contrary to conventional wisdom, we are surrounded by potential heroes,and if we shed our habits of condescension and cynicism we can recognize them anywhere.

8. Articulating Your Ethics

You have been living an ethical life, have you not? I doubt that a really wicked person would pick up a book like this, or at any rate, would never stick with it this far, so I shall assume that your daily life is reasonably free of violence, lies, theft, intoxication, and sexual misconduct — the big tickets in all ethical systems.

If you are like me, you remain moral because the temptation to any really unethical action trips one or more of the following alarm wires in your mind:

- A list of don't-do items deeply internalized during your childhood.

- Your natural empathy with other humans: if you do this thing, it will cause pain, and that distresses you.

- Self-image: people would think poorly of you if it were known you did this thing (or, in nobler terms, this act would be unworthy of you).

- An adult's foresight: experience tells you that actions like this one have bad outcomes, ugly repercussions, or hidden costs.

- Your philosophy of life: you feel that nobody ought to do things like this, so you can't do it without being a hypocrite.

- Last and least: there are legal penalties for being caught doing this.

Uses of an ethical code

These native guardians of behavior serve us pretty well most of the time. But there are two times when we need to refer to a systematic, clearly-articulated, code of ethics.

One is when we are suddenly presented with a quick choice to act or not to act, maybe under social pressure, maybe in the heat of strong emotion. Given quiet time to think, you could form a good decision based on your experience and beliefs. But it is hard to be courageous in a hurry, or when angry, or when dizzy with drink or hormones. If you haven't thought out some kind of system, a personal code, in advance, it is all too easy to do what is easiest, or whatever will call the least attention to you.

The second use for a systematic code is when you want to pass on your own ethics to a child. Children unerringly detect waffling, indecision, and pretence, and give them exactly as much respect as they deserve. If you don't have a clear, systematic, easily-recited code of ethics at hand, you find yourself falling back too often on "Because I said so."

An ethical code must have two features to be useful to you and to your child:

- Clarity: it must be short and worded simply and clearly, so that you can easily recall it under pressure.

- Coverage: within the limit of clarity, the code must apply to as many of the big issues of life as possible.

What a code is not

We are not looking for a complete ethical system. That would be a philosopher's life work, a task that few people want to tackle or read about. And we are not interested in legalisms, complex formal arguments, deep philosophy, or clever debating points. We are talking about an *ethical touchstone*: a simple set of rules that we can recall at short notice, to guide snap judgments.

Because of its brevity, such a code must be approximate. It isn't an algorithm into which you can plug any situation and read out an absolute right/wrong label. The best it can do is warn, "stop, this doesn't smell right, better think again."

In this chapter we will look at existing touchstones, some of which have both the broad generality and the conciseness we want. In the end I will urge you to compose your own from the essential features of others. First we need to establish an ethical basis.

Your Ethical Basis

The *basis* for an ethical code is an absolute, unquestioned belief against which you can test the rightness of any proposed action. In the traditional Jewish, Christian, or Islamic ethical systems, that absolute standard is the believer's understanding of God's pleasure. The believer, wondering whether or not to do something, can ask "Would this thing please God or not?" If the believer's gut feel, based on his or her training, is "it could displease God," then the action is ethically suspect, and needs to be considered further.

You will sometimes hear believers say things like "Without belief in God there is no morality." What they really mean is that they cannot imagine a standard they could use as a test of good or bad actions, in place of this internal image of God's pleasure. But in fact, there are at least three purely secular absolutes that have equal breadth and certainty.

The basis in unity of being

The broadest, most general basis arises out of the understanding that everything is connected. In discussing the Bliss experience ("Unity as intellectual insight" on page 89) we saw how, through a perfectly logical sequence of ideas, we end with the conclusion that, at least in principle, every action you perform now has some effect on everything that will ever come to be hereafter.

As long as this idea remains only an intellectual insight, it isn't much use as an ethical basis. However, if a person could internalize it, come to really believe in it and enshrine it as a part of daily life, it could act as the foundation for ethical living. Before acting, you would ask yourself "As the effects of this action echo down through time, are they likely to be negative and destructive?" And if so, that action is ethically suspect and should be reconsidered.

Buddhist doctrine attempts to codify and systematize exactly this ethical basis under the name *karma*.

The basis in sociality

The basis in unity can be focussed and applied specifically to our connections in society. We all need human contacts to stay healthy (we reviewed this at length in Chapter 3), but our dependency goes far beyond this. Think about it: you quite literally depend on the good will of other people for your survival — not just sometimes, but every day and every minute.

In this modern world our lives depend on all the economic and social structures that keep our cities running. Where I live, the water in my tap comes from a mountain range 150 miles away. If tomorrow morning I turned the tap and no water came out, what could I do, other than go thirsty? Do you know where your water comes from, and how many people are involved in keeping it flowing, and clean, and free of bacteria?

The fruit at my market comes from places as distant as Peru and New Zealand. If I went to the store and found no fruit or vegetables, no canned tuna, no milk, no bread, what could I do to feed myself?

If any of the intricate social organizations that bring us our food, electricity, medicine, clothing, or gasoline were disrupted, we would quickly be in mortal danger. Never mind the huge investments in "infrastructure"; the crucial element in every one of those systems is the good will of people who do their work consistently and correctly. We ride trains and airplanes, and drive on freeways where a single person's single failure to observe the rules can kill us in a split second.

Given these webs of absolutely vital dependencies, is it not clear that any act that tends to destroy or undermine social groups, also undermines the survival and health of you and of others? Any action (by me, you, or anyone) that creates anger, alienation, and distrust in society weakens society, and that puts us all in danger. Granted, our industrial society has great inertia, and our systems have great redundancy. But you only have to look around the world at places like the former Yugoslavia, or Lebanon, or any of half a dozen African nations, to see graphic examples of what happens to every person's safety when society is degraded by anger, hatred, greed, stupidity, shortsightedness, and violence. You being nasty or self-destructive will not turn your country into a Kosovo, but there is a connection between our behavior as individuals and the health of our society.

I cannot think of an act that is forbidden by a religious ethical system that does not in some way undermine trust, or create anger, pain or alienation in other people, thereby harming the morale of a group. Even acts with no direct victim, like vandalism or aggressive driving, have the effect of creating hostility and distrust among strangers, who will carry those emotions into their groups.

Therefore, when considering whether or not to do something, you can ask "Would this act undermine the morale of a group — increasing distrust, anger, alienation at any level of society?" If so, that act is ethically suspect and needs to be considered further.

The basis in empathy

A third secular basis is argued eloquently by His Holiness the Dalai Lama. It arises from the observation that every person seeks to avoid suffering and to reach happiness.

> The desire or inclination to be happy and to avoid suffering knows no boundaries. It is in our nature. As such, it needs no justification and is validated by the simple fact that we naturally and correctly want this.[1]

We would like to claim this drive to avoid suffering and seek happiness as a right. Wouldn't you say that you have a right to avoid suffering and seek happiness? We even have it in our Declaration of Independence as an "inalienable right."

Now, when we use the words "as a right" we mean it as a shorthand way to say "it is ethical for me to do this, and it is unethical for others to interfere with me."

However, the only logical basis on which I can claim the pursuit of happiness as a right is if I simultaneously grant the same right to all other people[2]. In other words, before I can say that it is unethical for anyone to cause me suffering, I have to concede that it is equally unethical for me to cause suffering for anyone else. Before I can assert that it is unethical for anyone else to thwart my drive toward happiness, I have to admit that it is unethical for me to deny happiness to anyone else.

Once you grant this principle, it provides a comprehensive basis for ethics. Before any action, you can ask yourself "Will this cause suffering for any other person, or prevent another person from gaining happiness?" If so, that action is ethically suspect and needs to be considered further.

When you have committed to any of these ethical bases, you have established a foundation for all ethical decisions, including the tough ones. However, it can take long, careful thought to connect a specific situation to your ethical basis. The purpose of an ethical touchstone is to make the basis more specific and easier to apply. Let's look at some possible touchstones.

Candidate codes

We start with two of the least familiar, and then one of the most familiar. We dive into philosophy and hastily climb out again. Then we have to look at the Ten Commandments in some detail because of their influence in American political and social debate. As a counterbalance, we spend almost as much space examining the less familiar Five Precepts of Buddhism.

Solon's dicta

Solon of Athens was an eminent politician, philosopher, and poet of his age. In 594 B.C.E. he established the first democratic constitution of the Athenian state, which was also the world's first written constitution. As recorded by Diogenes Laertius[3], Solon recommended the following list of rules to live by:

1. Put more trust in nobility of character than in an oath.
2. Never tell a lie.
3. Pursue worthy aims.
4. Do not be rash to make friends and, when once they are made, do not drop them.
5. Learn to obey before you command.
6. When giving advice, seek to help, not to please.
7. Be led by reason.
8. Shun evil company.
9. Honor the gods.
10. Reverence parents.

Solon's dicta are simple and practical, the kind of advice one would like to hear from a wise parent. However, as a touchstone they do not cover the ethical ground very thoroughly. For example, Solon says nothing about violence, not even "thou shalt not murder"; nor does he allude to sexual misbehavior or intoxication.

The Rotarian's 4-Way Test

Rotary International is an organization for business and professional people who want to infuse their daily work with morality and public service. In the 1930s, a businessman named Herbert J. Taylor, later a president of Rotary, was casting about for what, today, we would call a corporate mission statement: a capsule expression of the way he wanted his company to do business. Eventually he distilled his statement of business ethics to just twenty-four words:

> Of the things we think, say or do:
> 1. Is it the truth?
> 2. Is it fair to all concerned?
> 3. Will it build goodwill and better friendships?
> 4. Will it be beneficial to all concerned?

Taylor insisted that his company adhere to this ethical code even when it was apparently not to his financial advantage. Eventually the 4-Way Test was adopted as an ethical code for its members by Rotary International[4].

The 4-Way Test is both simple and has broad coverage. Can you think of an act that you would call unethical that is not also un-true, or un-fair, or destructive of good will or friendship, or at least un-beneficial to someone?

As a guide to business and professional activities, or as part of a corporate mission statement, the 4-Way Test is exemplary. And yet, when I consider it as a personal guide to the private choices of daily life, it seems to me to somehow miss the point. When I am tempted to do something self-indulgent, self-destructive, or sneaky, "Is it the truth? Is it fair?" are not the first things I need to ask. "Is it *right*?" is the immediate test, and a code needs to be more specific to answer that quickly.

The Golden Rule

The Golden Rule can be written this way: *Behave toward others as you want them to behave toward you.* It is a straightforward rule that harnesses and strengthens the natural empathy that all healthy people feel; and its clever, self-referential hook makes it memorable. Most Americans know the Golden Rule as a teaching of Jesus. There are two New Testament versions:

> Therefore all things whatsoever ye would that men should do to you, do ye even so to them: for this is the law and the prophets.
>
> – Matthew 7:12

> And as ye would that men should do to you, do ye also to them likewise.
>
> – Luke 6:31

In both of these, Jesus is portrayed as drawing out the meaning of the Hebrew Law. There does not seem to be a Golden Rule statement in this form in the Old Testament. Leviticus 19:18 says in part "Thou shalt love thy neighbor as thyself," which is a related (and broader) precept.

Isaac Asimov points to a previous version in the Book of Tobit[5]:

> And what you hate, do not do to any one.

I have seen an internet citation to Rabbi Hillel, *the Babylonian Talmud*,

> What is hateful to you, do not do to your neighbor.

Confucius put it this way,

> What you do not want done to yourself, do not do to others.

and the Buddha, thus:

> For what is unpleasant to me must be unpleasant to another, and how could I burden someone with that?

and it also appears in the great Indian epic, the *Mahabharata*, as

> Let no man do to another that which would be repugnant to himself.

In Great Britain, the Golden Rule is given this marvelously succinct form:

> Do as you'd be done by.

Clever as it is, the Golden Rule has a limited scope: it covers only direct interactions between people. It has nothing to say about actions you take that have no direct impact on another person, for example wasteful use of resources, cruelty to animals, or private self-destruction. It doesn't cover actions directed against the world at large, like vandalism, nor actions that have no defined victim, like a terrorist bomb or angry driving on the freeway.

Nor does it seem to apply when you are interacting with a corporation; for example when you are considering whether or not to cheat an insurance company, or whether to steal stationery from your employer. A corporation does not "do unto" you in the same sense you "do unto" it. Nor does the Golden Rule cover interactions with mobs, gangs, or groups. It makes no sense to say you should "do unto" a group the way you want the group to reciprocate; the kinds of actions an individual directs toward a group (e.g. being loyal, paying dues, cooperating) are of a different order than the actions the group could direct back to the individual.

While the Golden Rule is a good code for person-to-person interaction, it leaves a lot of ethical ground unfenced. It's a good teaching tool that speaks to a lot of playground issues, but not the general touchstone we seek.

Three imperatives

An imperative is a rule that commands agreement from our reason. Kant, who more or less created the modern job of academic philosopher, attempted to define an ethics based solely on reason. His idea was to base his ethics on a single imperative:

> There is therefore but one categorical imperative, namely, this: Act only on that maxim whereby thou canst at the same time will that it should become a universal law.[6]

In this system, a moral choice becomes a four-step algorithm:

1. Choose a course of action.

2. Before you act, deduce the maxim (general rule) that guided your choice.

3. Ask yourself, could this maxim be a universal law, incumbent on everyone, without logical contradiction?

4.   If not, return to step 1; otherwise, go ahead with the chosen action.

Here's an example. You are preparing your income taxes. Your dead-beat brother-in-law has been living in your garage and occasionally paying you rent in cash. Should you report this as income?

1.   You decide that you will not.

2.   Your maxim was: Money the government can't trace, I needn't claim.

3.   Reformulate it as a universal law: Cash the government doesn't know about, needn't be claimed as income by anyone. Can you agree with this as a universal law?

4.   You decide that it effectively is a universal law already, but in any case there is no *logical* reason it shouldn't be one.

Kant uses similar examples and claims that immoral maxims do not make logically consistent universal laws. I find the arguments unconvincing, but no matter; Kant's imperative is of little use as an ethical touchstone. Who's got time or inclination to ask themselves questions about maxims and universal laws when they are under peer pressure, or caught up in a rage?

Jean-Paul Sartre wrote little on ethics. However, in one essay he outlines an imperative that is a close relative of Kant's:

> In fact, in creating the man that we want to be, there is not a single one of our acts which does not at the same time create an image of man as we think he ought to be. To choose to be this or that is to affirm at the same time the value of what we choose... at every moment I'm obliged to perform exemplary acts. For every man, everything happens as if all mankind had its eyes fixed on him and were guiding itself by what he does.[7]

Sartre's idea can be phrased as a rule this way:

> When choosing a course of action, assume that all humankind will take you as a model.

Now, at this point any reader who has had a mother, or who is a mother, is doubting the practical value of all philosophy. Here are two monster intellects who flew to the glittering sky of cogitation and returned with — what? Nothing more nor less than the voice of mommy giving you a shake and saying "What if *everybody* acted that way? Wouldn't *that* be nice!"

After dismissing the imperatives of Sartre and Kant, I decided to try my own hand at composing a one-rule ethical imperative. I call it the *Mortal* Imperative:

> Always choose the action that maximizes the number of people who will be sorry to learn of your death.

In my humble opinion, this Mortal Imperative is at least as good a guide to right behavior as Sartre's or Kant's. It does not depend on abstract reasoning, but rather invokes our instinctive knowledge of how other people feel about what we do. That makes it much easier to apply under pressure. It is proactive: not only does it tell you not to do things that other people would call bad, it urges you to get up and go do things other people would call good, in order to make more people regret your passing.

In short, while no one-line rule makes a very good ethical touchstone, the Mortal Imperative is better than most. I think Solon of Athens would have liked it.

The Ten Commandments

The Ten Commandments have been dragged into American political dialog. People who feel deeply that our public morals need a boost have tried to get the Commandments posted in courtrooms and schools. Their attempts have been rejected by the courts in verdicts that caused controversy.

Let us actually look at this set of verses about which some people feel so strongly. Keep in mind that our main objective is to ask if they provide material for a good ethical touchstone, a terse, comprehensive, memorable list of guidelines. We can also ask if it is a good idea to post these particular rules in public places as semi-official reminders to the public at large. However, that political question is apart from our main goal.

The Ten Commandments can be found in Exodus 20:1-17 and again, in not quite identical words, in Deuteronomy 5:6-21[8].

According to the story in Exodus, the Israelites, having fled out of Egypt, wandered and starved in the desert until God put in a personal appearance.

> And the Lord said unto Moses, Lo, I come unto thee in a thick cloud, that the people may hear when I speak to thee, and believe thee for ever.

First, the people had to purify themselves. Then, according to Exodus chapter 19,

> Moses brought for the people out of the camp to meet with God; and they stood at the nether part of the Mount. And mount Sinai was altogether on a smoke, because the Lord descended upon it in fire; and the smoke thereof ascended as the smoke of a furnace, and the whole mount quaked greatly. And when the voice of the trumpet sounded long, and waxed louder and louder, Moses spake, and God answered him by a voice. ... And God spake all these words, saying,...

And the Ten Commandments follow. These particular verses, out of all the hundreds of rules that comprise the Law, have emotional significance because they are the first ten rules of the Law, and because they are the only words said to be spoken directly by God to the ears of his people, without the intermediation of Moses or another prophet. It is no exaggeration to call this a climactic moment in the Bible, for Jews, Christians, and Moslems too.

Here are the Commandments, with their conventional numbers for reference. If you are not already familiar with them (many people are not), read them carefully and think about how they apply to the issues of your life.

1. I am the Lord thy God, which have brought thee out of the land of Egypt, out of the house of bondage. Thou shalt have no other gods before me.

2. Thou shalt not make unto thee any graven image, or any likeness of any thing that is in heaven above, or that is in the earth beneath, or that is in the water under the earth: Thou shalt not bow down thyself to them, nor serve them: for I the Lord thy God am a jealous God, visiting the iniquity of the fathers upon the children unto the third and fourth generation of them that hate me; and shewing mercy unto thousands of them that love me, and keep my commandments.

3. Thou shalt not take the name of the Lord thy God in vain; for the Lord will not hold him guiltless that taketh his name in vain.

4. Remember the sabbath day, to keep it holy. Six days shalt thou labour, and do all thy work: But the seventh day is the sabbath of the Lord thy God: in it thou shalt not do any work, thou, nor thy son, nor thy daughter, thy manservant, nor thy maidservant, nor thy cattle, nor the stranger that is within thy gates. For in six days the Lord made heaven and earth, the sea, and all that in them is, and rested the seventh day: wherefore the Lord blessed the sabbath day, and hallowed it.

5. Honour they father and thy mother: that thy days may be long upon the land which the Lord thy God giveth thee.

6. Thou shalt not murder.

7. Thou shalt not commit adultery.

8. Thou shalt not steal.

9. Thou shalt not bear false witness against thy neighbor.

10. Thou shalt not covet thy neighbor's house, thou shalt not covet thy neighbor's wife, nor his manservant, nor his maidservant, nor his ox, nor his ass, nor any thing that is thy neighbor's.

These verses are the opening of the Law, but (if you continue to read Exodus and the following three books) they are neither the essence nor the whole of it. The giving of the Law continues for many more chapters and books of the Bible or Torah. But how do these ten work as a touchstone?

The first four commandments are liturgical in nature, telling the people of Israel how to behave toward their partner in the great compact between God and their nation. As such, these verses have no contribution to make to our touchstone. (As for posting them in public places: it can't be good policy to post rules that are irrelevant to the daily life of the typical person who would read them. Doing so only invites people to ignore the rest of the rules you post. Take for example the fourth commandment. If taken literally, it is broken weekly by all Christians other than Seventh Day Adventists. If interpreted freely as calling for weekly worship, it is still broken by a majority of Americans[9]. Hence a majority of the people who see an officially-sanctioned Ten Commandments on a wall at school or in a courtroom can only feel alienated by rule 4.)

If we look only at commandments 5-10, we find a concise ethical touchstone that has a rather patchy coverage of ethical issues. How many common sins are not proscribed by those verses? Suicide, battery, gluttony, intoxication with alcohol or drugs, treachery, torture, rape, arson, unmarried promiscuity, sexual or physical child abuse, oath-breaking, vandalism, laziness, deceit of every sort other than "false witness"[10] — it is a stretch to make these and other evil acts fit the actual words of the commandments.

However, these gaps in coverage are easily repaired by restoring just one missing element — an element that is actually present, further on in both the Old and New Testaments.

The commandments in the New Testament

There is scriptural evidence that most Jews did use a shorter list of important laws as an ethical touchstone. For example, Matthew 19:17-21 describes a scene in which Jesus summarizes the Law:

> And, behold, one came and said unto him, Good Master, what good thing shall I do, that I may have eternal life? And he [Jesus] said unto him, ... if thou wilt enter into life, keep the commandments. He saith unto him, Which? Jesus said, Thou shalt do no murder, Thou shalt not commit adultery, Thou shalt not steal, Thou shalt not bear false witness, Honour thy father and mother: and, Thou shalt love thy neighbor as thyself.

Jesus is portrayed as saying that the essential commandments of the Law are numbers 6, 7, 8, 9, and 5. He omits number 10, covetousness. However — and this is the crucial point — he includes that additional command from Leviticus 19:18, to love thy neighbor as thyself. At this point in the Bible, Jesus, a Jew, is depicted as addressing a Jewish crowd, who could be expected to know their own Law. The text doesn't suggest that Jesus is presenting any radical new doctrine; rather, the point seems to be that he is demonstrating his familiarity with, and drawing meaning from, the Law that his audience was familiar with.

Saint Paul summarized the Law to the congregation in Rome (Romans 13:9) this way:

> ...Thou shalt not commit adultery, Thou shalt not kill, Thou shalt not steal, Thou shalt not bear false witness, Thou shalt not covet; and if [there be] any other commandment, it is

briefly comprehended in this saying, namely, Thou shalt love thy neighbor as thyself.

Saint Paul wrote that the essential commandments were numbers 7, 6, 8, 9, 10 (adding back covetousness but omitting honor to parents); and he strongly underscores the importance of "love thy neighbor" from Leviticus.

How does this New-Testament summary of the Hebrew Law look as an ethical Touchstone? Merging the versions of Jesus and St. Paul gives a list of seven commandments:

1. Thou shalt not murder.

2. Thou shalt not commit adultery.

3. Thou shalt not steal.

4. Thou shalt not bear false witness.

5. Thou shalt not covet.

6. Thou shalt honor thy father and mother.

7. Thou shalt love thy neighbor as thyself.

It is wonderful to see how the addition of a commandment to be empathetic — to love other people as much as you love your own sweet self — plugs the holes in the Ten Commandments of Exodus. It does so in two ways. First, most of the wrong, or ugly, or cruel, or self-destructive thing you might be tempted to do will usually arise out of anger, fear or malice — emotions that are the antithesis of love. In order to remain true to the command to love others, you must constantly do battle with these elements in your own nature.

Second, it blocks hairsplitting and legalistic debate — for example, legalisms like the ones that I indulged in a few paragraphs back, when I pointed out all the sins that were not specifically ruled out by the Ten Commandments. There is no commandment against torture, true; but could you torture someone and still love them as yourself?

With some rewording (for instance, changing "thy neighbor" to the more general "other people"), and some editing (for instance, number 6 becomes redundant when number 7 is changed to "other people"), these Seven Commandments of the New Testament begin to look like a useful ethical touchstone. We'll return to it after looking at another great tradition.

The Five Precepts of Buddhism

The ritual by which a person formally becomes a Buddhist is called "Taking Refuge." The applicant publicly takes refuge in — that is, seeks the protection and help of — the Buddha, his teachings, and the community of Buddhists. As part of this ritual, the applicant recites a promise to adhere to the Five Precepts that the Buddha established as the minimal behavior standards for a lay practitioner. Often recited in sonorous Pali (the cousin to Sanskrit in which the teachings were first recorded in writing), and chanted in chorus by the whole group, the taking of the Precepts becomes a powerful ritual:

1. *Panatipata veramani sikkhapadam samadiyami*

    I undertake the precept to refrain from destroying living creatures.

2. *Adinnadana veramani sikkhapadam samadiyami*

    I undertake the precept to refrain from taking that which is not given.

3. *Kamesu micchacara veramani sikkhapadam samadiyami*

    I undertake the precept to refrain from sexual misconduct.

4. *Musavada veramani sikkhapadam samadiyami*

    I undertake the precept to refrain from incorrect speech.

5. *Suramerayamajja pamadatthana veramani sikkhapadam samadiyami*

    I undertake the precept to refrain from intoxicating drinks and drugs which lead to carelessness.

These five rules govern the behavior of Buddhists in about the same way as the Ten Commandments govern the behavior of Christians. That is, these are the basic "don'ts" Buddhists apply to daily life. Because they are not as familiar, and because they have some unusual features compared to the other codes we have looked at, we should consider the five individually.

Do not destroy living things

The first precept, not to destroy living creatures, is rather broader than "do not do murder." People who take it literally feel it means, among other things, being a vegetarian. And indeed, Buddhist monastics are vegetarian, and do not even swat flies or mosquitoes. On the other hand, Peter Singer observes that

> when I visited Japan some years ago to study Japanese attitudes to animals, I found that very few Japanese Buddhists were vegetarians ... Buddhist priests even bless the Japanese whaling fleet before it sails off to bring death to Antarctic whales.[11]

But worries like these are beside the point. In order to live according to the first precept, a person has to cultivate respect for the value of life, and learn to control or eliminate the fear and anger that can lead to striking out at living things, especially people.

Take only what is given

The second precept, to take only what is given to you, is also quite a bit broader than its parallel in the Ten Commandments, "do not steal." "Take only what is given to you" also extends to not picking up things that just happen to be lying around unattended, as well as to active theft. It would apply to taking unearned credit for another's work; or to taking unofficial work compensations that aren't part of one's employment contract, like unauthorized copying or internet use.

There is nothing in this second precept to forbid commerce in the sense of free exchanges of value. It would clearly be taking what was not given to cheat someone by giving short measure or by deceiving the buyer about the value of the goods. But when a buyer and seller, or an employer and an employee, agree with full knowledge to exchange value for money, each is taking what the other willingly gives.

"Take only what is given to you" is also a useful maxim to drum into the heads of children before visiting someone else's house.

Refrain from sexual misconduct

In the West, the third precept is often translated as "refrain from sex outside of a committed relationship." The Buddha specifically taught against adultery and against sex with minors, with dependents, and with those committed to others. At any rate, this precept is wider in application than the Biblical "do not commit adultery."

Speak what is true and helpful

The fourth precept seems puzzling when stated as "refrain from incorrect speech." The meaning of correct speech is clarified in a different part of Buddhist doctrine, the Eightfold Path, a set of positive guidelines that extend the negatives of the precepts. "Correct" speech is speech that meets a two-fold test: it is both true *and* helpful. The precept goes beyond a simple "don't tell lies"; it proscribes also speech that might be literally true, but is hurtful, or divisive, or misleading, or just distracting. A good way to phrase the fourth precept is "speak only what is both true and helpful."

Do not intoxicate yourself

It is no surprise that Buddhism, which places the highest value on clear-headed insight and mental focus, would prominently feature a precept against intoxication. In hindsight, it is a surprise that no other ethical code proscribes it. When you get drunk on any substance (even, or perhaps especially, your own hormones) it becomes much harder to make good ethical decisions. Intoxication releases and amplifies all the emotions that motivate you to violate other precepts: anger and fear that lead to harming, greed that leads to stealing, lust that leads to sexual misconduct. And of course, intoxication is notorious for motivating thoughtless speech.

The Precepts in practice

Buddhist teachers say that the Precepts are so designed that they reinforce each other, both positively and negatively. For example, if you get intoxicated you are liable to sexual misconduct or theft, which can motivate you to tell lies, which can lead to anger and violence, and so on into an ugly, descending spiral, with the result that you become entangled in a clinging web of stress, anger, and self-deception.

On the other hand, when you follow the precepts, you create a zone of calm and safety around yourself. People can trust you to not harm them, not take their things, not seduce their partners, not lie to them. That makes them feel safe, and makes it easier for them to follow the precepts too. Although the precepts are phrased as "shalt nots," to follow them is seen as a positive act of creating an atmosphere of trust, within the bounds of which other people also can find it easy to give the gift of safety and trust to each other and to you[12].

Your own touchstone

One thing ought to stand out from this brisk survey of ethical codes:
The fundamental issues are not strange, abstruse, inaccessible.
Ethics is a matter of how we behave from moment to moment, and
especially what we do in moments of crisis or emotional heat. To
memorize a simple code will not armor you against all temptations,
but it can help you to act in accord with your best self in a crisis.
And having a short list of memorable rules at the tip of your tongue
should definitely help you rear a child.

In the following table, the New Testament commandments and the
Buddhist Precepts are restated for easy comparison. The items that
are applicable in adult life, but not in the lives of small children, are
put last in the list.

Commandment	Precept
Love others as you love yourself.	Do not harm living things.
Do not murder.	
Do not steal.	Take only what is freely given.
Do not bear false witness.	Speak only what is both true and helpful.
Do not covet.	
Do not commit adultery.	Do not have sex outside a committed relationship.
	Do not intoxicate yourself.

These are the essential gems of the ethical codes of two great
philosophical traditions. From them anyone can craft a simple code
to guide them through life.

The choice and wording of your code needs to be your own, because
the words will only be real and meaningful if you compose them
and commit to them. If you have a family, you want to compose
rules jointly with your partner. When you have a short, numbered
list of terse rules, it could become a private family code, so that, for
instance, discreetly waving two fingers becomes a private reminder

of Rule 2, meaning "take only what is given," or, in context, "put that back!"

Summary

Ethics is about how you behave when you don't have time to ask advice. The general shape of your ethics is the product of your deepest personality and the shaping of your childhood. But having an ethical touchstone at the tip of your tongue can help you to act, under pressure, like the person you would prefer to be, rather than the person you might sometimes have been. Having a shared family code means you can guide your children with fewer resorts to "Because I said so!"

9. Dancing With Mister D.

Let death and exile and all other things which appear terrible
be daily before your eyes, but chiefly death, and you will
never entertain any abject thought, nor too eagerly covet
anything.

– Epictetus

Death is all about us. Religions remind people of this and urge them
to prepare. We who don't practice a religion find it all too easy to
overlook or ignore death throughout our youth and middle age,
until finally death steps into life and demands to be acknowledged.
Yet we can gain a lot from a clear-eyed understanding of death's
omnipresence.

In this chapter we first consider the omnipresence of death, and the
reasons not to fear our personal death. Although our own deaths
are, in the words of Epicurus, "nothing to us," the deaths of others
cause grief. We look at what is known about grieving, how to help
grieving friends, and how to survive our own bereavements.

At some point some of us will need to comfort or care for a dying
person, or deal with a death in the family, so we look at the help
available for these duties. Finally, we look at the very practical steps
everyone can take to prepare a legacy — a legacy of common sense
and wisdom that tells our survivors how much we cared about
them.

Ten billion to die

Earlier I described a way for you to visualize the six billion people alive today ("Modesty and impermanence" on page 118). Picture the largest parking lot you have ever seen, closely carpeted with coins; that's about *one* billion coins. There are *six* billion people alive today. Now think:

100 years from today, *all those six billion people will be dead.*

Dead along with them will be a few billion more people who were born in the interim. *Ten Billion to Die!* It's a great headline, but one that no paper will ever run. Although it's true and amazing, it is not news, only life.

Among those myriad corpses will be a few truly important people: Me. You. Everyone you or I have loved. All our friends, and everyone our friends loved. Every person we envied or desired; every person we feared or despised; every artist or performer we applauded; every fool we mocked; every hero we admired; every candidate we voted for — all dead and buried.

The logistics alone are staggering. Every year, there are roughly one hundred million funerals to arrange and burials or cremations to carry out. If each dead person was important to only three other people, that's three hundred million bereaved persons — more than the current population of the United States bereaved each year.

What makes this mighty river of death even more remarkable is that in our American culture we can avoid almost all contact with it. The historical and sociological reasons for this are beyond my unravelling[1]. But it is true of me, of you, of everyone: we *will* be required to respond to deaths: to the deaths of people our friends love; to the deaths of people we love; and to our own deaths. Unless we take thought now, we will be less prepared for these deaths than we should be.

It can be liberating to discover the omnipresence of death at a personal level, as in this account:

> Not until past thirty did I really become aware that people were dying around me all the time; that I was dying all the time, parts of me, old cells, old ideas, old ways of being. Death was hidden out of sight in hospitals, in statistics, in a compartment of my being I didn't look at. I saw a friend lonely and isolated because fear kept friends from talking

with her about the most important thing happening in her
life — her dying. ... Most of us are cheated out of the fullness
of life by fear and embarrassment. We experience the pain
and joy of birth and life and then many of us deny ourselves
our death, the closure of a circle. Denial comes from fear —
our fear, doctors' fear, loved ones' fear, our whole culture's
fear.[2]

An unfearful awareness of death can be used to motivate profound
changes in life. But first the fear has to be mastered.

Removing fear

Deborah Duda echoes many observers in saying "Denial comes
from fear." But I would add the reverse: the fear arises from the
denial. Many people are well into adulthood before they come as
close to death as the sanitized ritual of a funeral. People avoid
talking about death, and use all sorts of circumlocutions to avoid the
word itself. Hospitals and nursing homes take pains to make sure
that nonprofessionals don't see corpses. What is a child or a young
person to think? What could be the reason for this silence, which is
even deeper than the silence around sex? Surely there must be some
awful secret, something deadly, shocking, or contagious; *something*
against which people are protecting themselves?

In fact, no. Death and dead people are only quiet and sad. Death
itself is not contagious. Corpses, even fresh ones, aren't awful; they
are only pitiful.

Once we face this, none of the old magical threats has any power:
Talking about death won't kill you; thinking that a sick person
might die doesn't make them any less likely to get well; putting
your own affairs in order will not hasten your death.[3]

Some fears are appropriate. It is reasonable to fear *bereavement*, the
loss of a precious person. Bereavement robs you of companionship,
steals your certainties, and pitches you into a new, hostile, future.

It is also reasonable to dread serious illness. Illness and its treatment
are painful, humiliating, and expensive. Illness plows up your life
and your family's. Hospitals are dismal places to spend any amount
of time if you are conscious.

Finally, it is reasonable to fear, or at least to regret, the effect your
own death will have on the people who care about you — to fear

what grief it might cause them, and what loose ends it will leave them to wrap up.

All of these are productive fears: we can use them to motivate action. The rest of this chapter is about ideas for useful actions.

But as for death itself: what is there to fear? I don't know about you, but I expect to find myself in the same state I was in before I was born. That is a state of unknowing and nonexisting, but it is also a state that contains, by definition, no pain and no regret.[4] Before death I worry about unfinished projects; I regret that I will not see how the great human saga plays out; I worry about the effect of my death on others. After death, all such concerns cease. This attitude has ancient roots:

> Accustom yourself to believe that death is nothing to us, for good and evil imply awareness, and death is the privation of all awareness... Foolish, therefore, is the person who says that he fears death, not because it will pain when it comes, but because it pains in the prospect. ... Death, therefore, the most awful of evils, is nothing to us, seeing that, when we are, death is not come, and, when death is come, we are not.[5]

Even the transition from life into death is, apparently, calm. This is the one sure lesson we can draw from the voluminous literature on near-death experiences (NDEs). There is controversy about the cause and meaning of NDEs. Set those issues aside; the fact remains that these are reports on how people felt during severe physical trauma and approaching death. The consistent report is that people found themselves serene, emotionally detached from their bodies, and without pain or fear[6].

When the fear is gone, or at least mastered, you can begin to use your understanding of death to make life richer for yourself and others.

Using death to motivate virtue

When you accept the presence of death in life, and accept death as the expected conclusion to your own life, it changes your outlook on yourself and other people. At least, my outlook has changed since I began work on this chapter.

Everywhere, all around us but mostly invisible, people are receiving terminal diagnoses, enduring miscarriages, burying dead children, caring with great kindness for their dying parents, dying spouses, dying lovers, dying strangers. Quietly and with awesome courage, people like you and me are coping with death every minute. When you begin to understand the universality of death, you begin to understand how lucky you are that you are not, at least just now, involved. And your respect for the courage of your fellow humans goes up.

On a trivial level, I find that increased awareness of death gives me a way of dealing patiently with irritating people. When I find myself getting angry at some stranger who has done something arrogant or stupid, I remind myself, "Let it go; he's dying."

In general, remaining aware that I and everyone else is dying is a way of keeping perspective on all kinds of concerns. It adds power to the old saying, "Will it matter in a hundred years?" That old saw coyly hints, but avoids saying outright, that very few current concerns will matter in a hundred years *because* everyone now alive will be dead, and most of their ideas and prejudices will die along with them.

Indeed, you can use this insight as a way of finding genuinely valuable issues in life. If you can find an issue whose outcome *will* matter in a hundred years (or even fifty), you have found a battle worth joining.

Awareness of death can motivate us to repair personal relationships. It is a common regret of survivors that they can never repair their relationship with the dead person — never apologize for some slight, never make up a quarrel, never thank the person for a favor, never tell the person how much they love or value them.

When we don't think let ourselves think about death in general, we can't think about the very real possibility that a friend or relative could die tonight. Or that we could! Either way, important words will be left unsaid. Turn this around: become aware of the ubiquitous, hovering presence of death so that you have a reason to see every friend and relative as a fragile, transient presence that could disappear at any moment. Being aware of death gives you this motive to reach out and repair relationships, so that you will never, at a funeral, have to think "Oh, if only..."

Grieving

Because death is inevitable, grief is inevitable. When someone you care about dies, you will grieve. When someone you care about is grieving, you would like to help. No matter whether it is you who grieves or a friend who is grieving, it helps to know something about grief.

Bereavements

Any loss is a bereavement, but some bereavements are worse than others. You can be bereaved by smaller injuries than death. If your car is stolen, or you are mugged, or your home is destroyed in a fire or flood, you lose more than property. The main loss in these cases, as in rape, is your sense of security, your feeling of being at home in the world.

If you are dumped by a lover, you lose the secure feeling of being a worthy, lovable person. If you are diagnosed with a life-threatening illness, you lose the security of a healthy body, and you are forced into a new life as a dependent and, sometimes, an object.

The death of your spouse or child or sibling is a triple loss: you lose companionship; you lose all the planned future that you founded on that person's existence; and you lose the social roles you founded on being that person's spouse or parent or brother or sister. With these losses, you literally no longer know who you were.

A surprisingly common type of bereavement, and one that is rarely discussed, is the loss of an unborn child to miscarriage or stillbirth. Approximately 20% of all pregnancies end in miscarriage[7]. What is lost is every imagined future plan for the child, as well as the waste of all your preparation for parenthood. Cruelly, there are no mementos you can use to remember the child that will not be.

Grief and grieving

Grief is the name for the emotional condition that follows bereavement. Grief is a general term for a painful psychological readjustment[8]. It is the pain that comes from a forced, unwanted, revision of your beliefs about the world and your place in it. Each of us carries a model of the world in our heads, a well-organized and highly-detailed set of beliefs about where we are, who we are, and what we can and should do. A bereavement falsifies crucial parts of this world-model. Colin Parkes, a psychologist who has written extensively on grief, classifies bereavements and similar upheavals as psychosocial transitions (PSTs). He illustrates the effects as follows:

> The death of a spouse invalidates assumptions that penetrate many aspects of life, from the moment of rising to going to sleep in an empty bed. Habits of action (setting the table for two) and thought ("I must ask my husband about that") must be revised if the survivor is to live... These examples begin to explain why PSTs are so painful and take so much time and energy. For a long time it is necessary to take care in everything we think, say, or do; nothing can be taken for granted any more. The familiar world suddenly seems to be unfamiliar, habits of thought and behavior let us down, and we lose confidence in our own internal world.[9]

It takes time to tear up and remodel our fundamental beliefs about life as well as our expectations for the future. The grief following the death of spouse or child typically needs more than a year to work itself out to the point we feel at least sometimes at home in life once more. According to one study, more than a year after their husband's death, a majority of widows still cannot look toward either past or future with pleasure, and 13% still show signs of clinical depression[10].

There are common features to this lengthy process. Some simple-minded bosh has been written about "stages" of grief. It seems obvious to me that each grief is a unique intersection of events with a stressed human personality. Given the complexity and fluidity of human emotions, it should be no surprise that grief is

> such an individualized process — one that varies from person to person and moment to moment and encompasses simultaneously so many facets of the bereaved's being — that attempts to limit its scope or demarcate its boundaries by arbitrarily defining normal grief are bound to fail.[10]

That said, it is common for the bereaved to be emotionally numb and uncomprehending in the first few hours or days. When a TV reporter pushes a microphone into the face of someone who has just survived a disaster and they look blank and say something like "I just can't believe it," you are hearing the voice of initial numbness.

As the reality of the loss is implacably hammered home — by the little shocks as feature after feature of the assumptive world is exposed as false — the bereaved person begins to feel intense emotional, and sometimes physical, discomfort. As time passes and the person's internal map of the world is redrawn with new borders, the discomfort becomes less intense and less frequent, and the person begins to reengage with the world.

However, it is true that loss is forever. Eventually you might have another house, another child, another spouse, another friend, but you can never have *that* house, child, spouse, or friend again. So although grief ceases to dominate life after a year or eighteen months, the sadness at the loss is a part of you forever:

> I can recall that Ann cried out in the night years later, remembering even after two decades: "Today would have been his birthday. He would have been twenty-one."[11]

Even though remembering can cause pain, it is important to realize that grieving is not about forgetting, not about discarding or avoiding the memory of the lost one. It is about becoming familiar with a world in which the lost person is only present as a memory. As that new world grows more familiar, the memories can be valuable and comforting.

First-person grieving

The following is what I would like said to me when I am bereaved. I have kept it simple because a really grief-struck person is just too distracted to pay attention to anything complicated. If you are bereaved, I hope it helps.

OK, this is going to hurt. You have sustained a major loss.

Don't let them tell you it doesn't hurt; it does. What it cannot do is kill you. It is not possible for feelings to kill, no matter how bad they are. Like it or not, you are living through this.

There's no way to finesse this, dance around it, sleep through it, or numb it. The only way *out* is *through*.

Waves of grief hit when you least expect them. When a wave hits, stop what you are doing and pay attention to it. If it's strong, express it. Cry. Stamp your feet. Beat on pillows. If that bothers people, it's their problem, not yours.

Remember your mindfulness. Observe the pain: where does it affect the body? Note the key fact: this pain, like everything, arises and passes away. Observe yet again how all things are transient, even the worst ones.

You have won a pathetic booby-prize: the status of a victim. People will make allowances for you, and offer to help you. Be generous; accept their help. It makes them feel better. If you insist on being a stoic, you short-change the helpers along with yourself.

Important: your beliefs about yourself are impaired. Your opinions and attitudes will be different a year from now. Don't commit to anything permanent, or buy anything expensive, for a while.

You still have your competence and skills. Using them is better than doing nothing. The hours are going to pass anyway; you can sit and watch them, or you can occupy them.

Hang onto this: It hurts; it won't kill you; it *will* end.

Helping a grieving person

One of life's tougher challenges comes up when someone you care about is grieving. You want to help, but what can you say? Obviously, nothing you can do will repair their loss. Conversation seems impossible. The fact of their loss sits beside you like a hippopotamus that everyone is too polite to mention. Grieving people don't take well to helpful suggestions like "you're doing fine" or "you'll soon find another interest." And they are not a lot of fun to be around. Your suggestions about going out ("to take your mind off ...um... things") are met with a brave little "You go ahead, I'll be all right."

Worst of all, the grieving person is all too likely to break out in displays that embarrass you, involving heaving shoulders and wads of damp tissue. Stronger people than you have reacted by running away. But if you are willing to try, it is possible to really help this person.

Grieving is a process of reweaving the tattered ends of one's life, and this can only be done by living, one hour at a time, until every tiny circumstance of this new loss-world has become familiar and comprehensible. It is a process of rediscovering the details of a new world, one in which the lost person is not a presence but a valued memory. Like any exploration, it is easier with companions. There is nothing you can do for the grieving person that will relieve them of their loss or of the necessity to rebuild their experience of life, but you can assist them to do it by just being there, being willing to help and to listen.

Ann Kaiser Stearns, author of one of the classics of self-help literature, says you can play either or both of two roles[12]. You can be the Empathic Friend who, among other things:

- Is not easily shocked, and accepts the grieving person's feelings as natural.
- Is not embarrassed by tears.
- Is warm and affectionate.
- Is not afraid to ask the grieving person directly about their feelings of loss.
- Says so honestly when emotions or attitudes make them uncomfortable.

Or you can be the Basic Care Provider who, among other things,

- Helps the grieving person work out practical problems.
- Makes the grieving person welcome in the provider's house.
- Includes the grieving person in social occasions.
- Does small acts of kindness to make life smoother.

Either kind of helper will, of course,

- Not insist on giving unwanted advice.
- Treat the grieving person like an adult who is able to make decisions.
- Anticipate anniversary dates that will be difficult and be especially understanding at those times.
- Keep confidences confidential.

Using these guidelines and a great deal of patience, you can contribute to shortening and softening the grieving period. That's a considerable gift that is in your power to give.

Living with the dying

Someone you know and care about is seriously ill and may be dying. Perhaps they've been given a diagnosis of one of those cancers that make people shake their heads and change the subject. Or they have AIDS and are moving into a yet another serious crisis. Or they are just very old and show increasing symptoms of congestive circulatory failure. Do you have any idea how to help the dying person?

Of course, everything depends on your relationship, whether you are this person's child or parent or sibling, lover or spouse, or merely a friend or second cousin. But there are some general guidelines that are useful for all these cases.

Supporting the dying

The first guideline is that every dying person (like every person) has unique attitudes and a unique personality and history. Now, if ever, they may claim the right to exercise their uniqueness. Therefore, your first rule must be to take your cues from the person and support them as they wish to be supported. If you insist on imposing your own preferences, styles, or prejudices on them, you will at best do no good, and at worst create added distress.

When Ted Menten first began to work with dying children, an experienced nurse told him about "Rule One" which is, "They get it their way":

> They know what's happening, don't think for a minute they don't. Even the very little ones. So the best and kindest thing we can do is let them set the rules. They wanna talk — you listen up. They wanna be alone — you scoot. They wanna laugh, or cry, or swing from the trees — you let 'em.[13]

Rule One should apply to all dying people. Almost never will they need your unsolicited advice or your unsolicited help, or anything else you might give unsolicited, except, perhaps, a hug.

A second guideline is to be sensitive to the way in which the fact of death forces everyone out of their normal social roles[14]. Begin with the doctors and other hospital personnel. Their social role is to make people well. That is the function that endows them with status and authority and gives structure to their days. When they can no longer do that, they face being, at best, useless, and possibly failures. For this reason, hospital personnel are often reluctant to admit that death is possible, let alone likely.

But social displacement affects others as well. Parents of a dying child are profoundly affected by the fact that they cannot perform the essential roles of parenting: to nurture and protect the child.

And the dying person: whatever claims of status and position in society he or she once had are now in question. Simply to enter a hospital is to take on a new social role as a patient. Like any social role, it has both rights and responsibilities: the right to be exempt from work and to receive special care; the responsibility to be cooperative and grateful for the care, and to get well. When a person begins to realize they are dying, they can't maintain their end of that unspoken bargain. They receive the special care and can be grateful, but they can no longer hope to "justify" all the effort by getting well.

To admit to be dying is effectively to resign from the future, to abdicate the role of father or mother or spouse or child, even the role of patient, and to become a person with no role except to consume people's labor and sympathy. The person won't articulate it this way, but the unspoken question is: if I'm dying, then what good am I? For this reason, well-meant words like "Now, you don't have to do a thing, you just lie there and get well" are not really reassuring — they only emphasize the patient's increasing distance from life.

Myra Bluebond-Langner, who documented social relationships in a ward for dying children, noted that the only way people could continue to function was to engage in a mutual dance of pretence. Parents and caregivers continued to treat each other as if a cure would be somehow possible. Even the children, who knew their own conditions quite well, pretended not to know in order to protect the feelings of their parents and caregivers.[15]

Do you talk about death to the patient? The answer is in Rule One: you talk about what they want to talk about. If they say to you (as my mother said to me), "You may as well face it, I'm dying," you do *not* deny it, shrug it off, pretend not to hear, insist on raising hopes. You respect their wish to be open about the most important fact in their life at this time: their dying. You don't have to find anything meaningful to say. You certainly don't have to cast about for something cute or (please!) funny. You don't have to say words at all; a squeeze of the hand or a hug is a good response. You merely have to be a human being who hears, respects, and understands.

> Being with someone who is dying does not mean that we must become comfortable, but that we learn to accept our discomfort. We learn that we cannot expect to have all the answers.[16]

Choosing where to die

Less than a century ago, the majority of people who died of old age or illness, died at home. Sometime after the Second World War, that changed. More and more people died in an institutional setting: a hospital or a nursing home. As a result,

> In the United States, death at home in the care of family has been widely superseded by a technological, professional, and institutional process of treatment for the dying.[17]

It is depressing to think about dying in a typical hospital ward, with its lack of privacy, its fluorescent glare and round-the-clock noise, and its constant rotation of strange staff faces, each apparently having the right to invade your personal space without warning or permission. Possibly the worst thing about being a patient in a hospital is that your family can't care for you. Family members are denied the opportunity to do more than hold the patient's hand, and that impoverishes them as much as it does the patient.

When a person dies quickly from accident or acute illness, the setting hardly matters. But if the dying process is to be extended for days, weeks or longer — as it so often is with AIDS or cancer — an alternative should be sought[18].

A skilled nursing facility is slightly better than a hospital. A nursing room affords a little space for personal belongings, more quiet, and more opportunity for interaction with the family. (Most nursing facilities are understaffed and are happy to let family members perform any services they want to, apart from giving medications.) In the USA it is almost automatic for an elderly patient to transfer to a skilled nursing facility from hospital because of a rule that Medicare will pay for several weeks of skilled nursing after a hospital stay.

The next alternative is home. For the dying person, home is — well, *home*, with all that may imply of familiarity and serenity. And there

are a few practical benefits: at least people who want to visit don't
have to find a sitter, travel across town, and endure hospital parking
and lobbies. But there are problems. First, few homes are well laid
out to be sick wards. Having a very ill person in residence causes a
major disruption of the home arrangements. Second, few family
members are qualified to do even routine nursing tasks like taking
vital signs and assisting a feeble person at the toilet or bath. The
stress on family members of full-time nursing care is extreme.
(Hiring a paid caregiver at least one shift a day can make a huge
difference.) Finally, it is essential to have not merely the doctor's
agreement but the doctor's active participation in preparing a
palliative care plan that can be implemented without frequent trips
back to the hospital. (See note[18] for help with these and many other
practical issues.)

A third alternative is a hospice: an institution designed for the
sympathetic care of terminally-ill people. The number of hospices in
the United States has mushroomed in the last decade, at least in part
as a response to the AIDS epidemic with its army of slowly-dying
young people. A hospice attempts to provide a home-like
atmosphere combined with professional nursing care.

To a disinterested third party, going to a hospice to die may seem
like a highly practical solution, but it is not an obvious or easy
conclusion for the patient to reach, nor the patient's doctor or
family. After all, everyone knows what the hospice is for. As long as
you stay in a hospital you can at least pretend you are still hoping
for a cure; and if you go home, well, you might yet move back to the
hospital. Moving to the hospice means you concede that death is
inevitable and coming soon. Although the patient's doctor and
family may find this difficult to admit, some patients — exhausted
by medical treatment and by the need to keep up a front — may find
it a relief.

Final arrangements

When someone close to you dies, it may fall to you to make the
arrangements for the handling of the body. This is a daunting
experience, as full of choices and trade-offs as buying a new car,
which it can rival in cost. If you have not prepared for this ordeal,

and especially if you are dazed with fatigue and grief, you will almost certainly end up spending far more money than you need to.

> Just knowing what to ask, what to say, and who to call can save your family 50% or more on funeral services, burial plots, or monuments, and as much as 75% on the cost of a casket.[19]

Pressure to make decisions starts almost immediately: the hospital or nursing facility wants you to arrange to move the body off their premises quickly. (A hospital staff person may offer to call a funeral home for you. Sometimes this is because the person wants to be helpful; sometimes because they will be paid a finder's fee by the funeral home.)

Once you commit to a funeral home and the body is on their premises, you are subjected to heavy salesmanship aimed at getting you to purchase a wide array of expensive goods and services. The sales people are personable, solicitous, patient, respectful — and relentless. You will be helpless before them unless you are prepared with a clear idea of, first, what the dead person wanted; second, what the other relatives expect; and third, what is essential versus what is optional and needless.

The dying person's wishes come first. Finding out their wishes for how they want their bodies to be memorialized and disposed of can be a wonderful excuse for some real, substantive talk during their last days. (If they prefer to retain some hope of a reprieve, you can always couch it in hypothetical terms.) My mother specified everything; not only how to treat her body, where to bury her ashes, and what to write on her marker, but the complete order of the memorial service she wanted: who was to speak, what scriptures to use as a text, what hymns to sing. It gave her a lot of pleasure to work all this out at a time when her pleasures were few; and it was a relief and a pleasure for me and her other mourners to carry her wishes out.

The other relatives come next. If you don't have directions from the dead person, you have to create a family consensus on what is to be done. Consensus is essential; you can precipitate major family feuds by proceeding high-handedly without the consent of others who think they deserve a say. It can take hours on the phone to get consensus among a far-flung family. Obviously it would be good to do this in advance of the death, not in the hectic hours after it.

Finally, you need to be armed with consumer advice on purchasing funeral services, from a book[20] or from online resources[21]. Only then can you face a sales person at the funeral home with a hope of not being fleeced. Read some of these resources now, while all your loved ones are in good health, so you know what the issues are[22]. Knowing these things in advance will help you maintain your poise in difficult times, and greatly improve your reputation as a rock of reliability in your family circle.

Arranging your own affairs

The final benefit that you can gain from an honest understanding of death is the motivation to put your own financial and legal affairs in order. There are only a few important steps and, unless your finances or family situation are unusually complicated, you can handle them without a lawyer. First let's remember why this is worth doing.

Expecting the unlikely end

Suppose that the next time you fly, your airplane falls out of the sky. It could happen. Think about the people on that airliner that crashed just a few weeks ago. (I'm sure there was a recent crash no matter when you read this. When I drafted these words, it was an Air France Concorde that crashed on takeoff, ending the lives of 100 well-to-do vacationers.) Or suppose that the next time you drive, your life ends in one of the tens of thousands of fatal auto wrecks that happen each year. Stay at home: you can catch a fast-moving infection and go from the peak of health and success into death over a weekend, just like the late Jim Henson.

> The man immersed in
> gathering blossoms,
> his heart distracted:
> death sweeps him away —
>   as a great flood,
>   a village asleep.
>
> – *Dhammapada* IV, 46[23]

Your life has unexpectedly ended. How will the people who depend on you cope? In the days after your death, would your shocked survivors know where to find the bank and brokerage accounts, the title to the car, the insurance policy, the benefits you vested at a former employer, the combination to the safe, the key to the safety-deposit box? Would anyone have a clue as to what you wanted done with your body? And your estate: if, like many, you have a child from a former marriage, is there a will to show your desires as to how your money should be divided among your spouse, your children, and your exes?

> If you procrastinate until death, that will prove costly to your inheritors, and may well mean that your property will not be distributed as you wish. If you die without a will or other valid transfer device, your property will be divided between family members according to a formula established by state law. A judge will appoint someone of her choosing to supervise the distribution of your property. Your estate must pay this person's fee, which can become quite hefty.[24]

Suppose that, instead of simply dying, only your mind is damaged or destroyed. Every day, perfectly healthy people end up unconscious in a hospital from head injury, stroke, or infection. If you have not taken specific steps to make your desires known, or given legal authority to another person to represent you, the doctors are required by law and ethics to do everything they can to preserve your physical life — even if that means keeping your vegetable body alive on a ventilator and feeding tube forever.

Suppose you and your life-partner die together on that airplane or automobile trip. In the aftermath of this worst-case scenario, will the responsibility for raising your children rest with someone you know and trust, or will they go to a foster parent chosen by the state or county?

No matter when or how you die, your survivors will feel the grief of bereavement. You can't help that; in fact, the better the person you are, the more they'll miss you. But you do have the ability to prepare for them a generous legacy of reassurance and stability. The documents of your well-organized personal affairs will testify from beyond the grave that you loved and cared about your survivors. (And, not incidentally, that you were a smart, capable person.) If you want to be remembered with gratitude, you will take the steps outlined here.

Medical directives

Step one is to prepare a medical directive, sometimes called a "living will," that tells your desires about medical treatment. Its most common use is to refuse certain kinds of treatment that would be mandatory otherwise. What you can say, and how you must express it, differs from state to state. Here is some of the wording from a medical directive that is valid in the state of California:

> If I should have an incurable and irreversible condition that will result in my death within a relatively short time without life-sustaining treatment or that has produced a persistent vegetative state ... I direct my attending physician, pursuant to the Natural Death Act of California, to withhold or withdraw treatment that only prolongs the process of dying...

You can put in a variety of hedges, for instance you might specify how many physicians must agree that your condition is incurable. Or, you could use your medical directive to specify "I want it all, keep me going whatever it takes." That's the normal, default approach of the medical profession, but you could make it explicit if, for instance, you feared that someone in your family felt differently.

An important supplement to the medical directive is a Durable Power of Attorney for Health Care, a document that names a person who can speak for you to the doctors[25]. While you lie there, unconscious, with tubes running into your various orifices, there are many decisions to be made. Should they operate now, or wait? Should they get a second opinion? Should they transfer you to another hospital? Your medical directive can only set a general policy. You need a trusted agent who can demand treatment, or refuse it, in your name. If the person you would trust to do this is not your legal spouse or a close relative, his or her opinions will be ignored without a power of attorney.

These documents, using the form and language that is valid in your state of residence, must be signed in front of witnesses and (usually) notarized. Then you can give a copy to your doctor to put in your records, and give a copy to your trusted agent for use when needed.

Disposition of your body

There are many things that could be done with your body after you
are finished with it. If you don't specify your wishes in advance,
you make your survivors agonize over how to do the "right" thing.
Very possibly they will go to more trouble or expense than you
would have liked. Your second step should be to write a Letter of
Disposition to specify what you want done with your remains.

One possibility is that your body, or parts of it, could be useful to
other people. There are never enough healthy hearts, kidneys,
corneas, and other organs to help all the people who are waiting for
transplants. If you are willing to donate your organs for transplant,
you should say so both in this letter and in your medical directive.
(It needs to be in your medical directive because your disposition
letter might not be read until a day or so after your death, when
your body has already been sent off to a mortuary. Transplant
materials need to be "harvested" quickly.)

You can opt to have your body transferred to a medical school to be
used for training future doctors. However, you need to arrange this
with that medical school in advance of your death. If this idea
appeals to you, contact the medical school now; they will be happy
to help you with the paperwork. Typically, when the school is
finished with your body, they will cremate it. The ashes can be
buried, or can be returned to your survivors.

You may want to have your body cremated, with or without a
detour through a medical school. Cremation reduces a body to a few
pounds of clean, crumbly gray ash sealed in a small metal box or a
decorative urn[26]. Then the ashes can be scattered, either at sea or in
a place that has ritual meaning for you and your survivors. The
scattering can be done by your survivors, as part of your memorial
ritual; or you can contract to have it done by a professional
company[27].

Or, your ashes could be placed under a plaque or headstone as a
permanent memorial. If you want a permanent location for your
ashes or for your entire body, you have to buy it. Burial plots and
spaces in cemetery vaults are real-estate properties, and rather
expensive ones per square foot. If permanent burial is your choice,
you need to secure the purchase of a burial site while you are alive.
Otherwise, your wish to be buried might force your survivors into a
rushed, and likely a costly, purchase.

Make these decisions now and record them in a formal Letter of Disposition. The letter should specify how to dispose of your body, and list all the related documents, such as a deed to a burial plot, or the medical school donation forms. In addition, you can describe what kind of memorial service you would like. In this, you may be as detailed and lyrical as you like. Take your lead from Tim Leary:

> Instead of treating the last act of your life in terms of fear, weakness, and helplessness, think of it as a triumphant graduation. Friends and family members should treat the situation with openness, rather than avoidance. Celebrate. Discuss. Plan for that final moment.[28]

Do bear in mind that (we hope) this document will not be executed for many years. By that time your tastes may have changed.

This letter is not a legal document like a will or a power of attorney; it needs only a signature, not witnessing and notarizing.

Estate planning

Your estate is the value of everything you own when you die — money, stock, home equity, possessions. Estate planning entails four independent steps:

1. Making an estimate of the current and near-future value of your estate.

2. Forming a clear idea of how you want the value of the estate divided among your survivors after you have died.

3. If you are responsible for minor children, deciding who should be their guardian if both you and your life-partner should die.

4. Setting up legal documents to ensure that steps 2 and 3 will happen with minimum delay and cost.

The first two steps amount to a pleasant morning's work: a conference with your partner and some time drafting a one-page summary. Step 3 is a bit harder; at the very least you have to confer with the people you want to nominate as your children's guardians and make sure they are willing.

Step 4 has many details that can't be covered in this book, but which are clearly explained in books[29]. The simplest document that can do the job is a will. If you are reasonably young, so that there is only a very small chance of your will's being executed, a will is all you need. You can prepare a legal will in a few hours using inexpensive software[30].

Things are not as simple if your relationships are complicated by multiple marriages or by feuds and estrangements, or if your estate has a value approaching a million dollars or is entangled by complex debts or other problems. In these and other cases you will want to have more than a simple will.

There are two basic issues which are independent, although often confused. The first issue is avoiding federal and state estate taxes. For most people this is a non-issue, because the estate tax exemption is over $600,000 and scheduled to rise to $1,000,000 in 2007. (As I write, the federal estate tax itself is under political attack and might be removed entirely.) If you think your estate might be larger than a million, you should read a book or get advice to understand this issue and the answers.

The second issue applies to most estates. It is that probate, the legal process by which a will is executed, is slow and costly. If you leave your estate only through a will, your heirs will wait for months, possibly years, for probate to end, and might lose a significant fraction of the estate in fees. However, if you are young enough that your will is really only a hedge against an unlikely, worst-case event, there's no reason to spend the effort to avoid probate at this time. As you get older and your death in the forseeable future becomes more possible, you need to give more thought to avoiding probate. The legal methods of doing this are not difficult, although they can be time-consuming to carry out.

Letter of instruction

After you have completed these steps and have prepared your medical directive, your durable power of attorney for health care, your letter of disposition, and your will and other estate-management documents, you package them all neatly in a binder headed with a Letter of Instruction. This letter is for the use of your survivors in the days following your unexpected death. It tells them where to look for all the important papers and keys, and it details who they need to contact and gives telephone numbers.

Maintenance

Starting from scratch it might take you some weeks to get all these decisions made and all the necessary paperwork done[31]. When it is done, you can take well-earned satisfaction from closing the cover on your completed binder of documents.

However, the circumstances of life keep changing. Within a year or two, some of your documents will be out of date. You'll have a new child, or grandchild, or residence, or job; telephone numbers change and so do opinions. So you need to schedule an annual return visit to the state your affairs. (Perhaps you should make a ritual of it?)

Personal Memorials

Now that you've taken care of the business part, you can relax and have some fun. When people die, it's common for their survivors to wish there was more to remember them by. In Chapter 7 I mentioned in passing how rapidly people's memory of your life will become compressed and thinned, until they remember no more of you than you remember of your great-grandparents. You can address both problems by building a personal memory archive that you can pass on to your heirs. This doesn't have to be as elaborate as an autobiography. You can create quite a substantial inheritance just by organizing those drawers full of old snapshots into albums and documenting them. You can write letters of appreciation to people you love, and include them as an appendix of your binder of legal papers.

There are many other ways in which you can create a bundle of memorabilia to document and illuminate your life and times. It could even have real value. Have you watched the popular "Antiques Roadshow" on television? If so, you know that the most trifling stuff gains amazing value just from being old. The only thing needed to create this value is time. You don't expect to die for some decades yet, right? So each year, buy or collect a few small objects that reflect the times, and put them away in box. Add a note showing when each object was bought. Let us hope that, by the time your heirs open this trove, so many years will have passed that some of the things will be valuable antiques.

Summary

Incredible as it always seems, we're all dying and soon will be gone. By recognizing and accepting our own mortality and the mortality of everyone you meet, we become emotionally wiser and more tolerant. By taking a little thought now, we can prepare ourselves to be useful to others when they are bereaved. And we can take satisfaction in setting up our own affairs so that our survivors will have even more reasons to remember us with gratitude.

10. Being Happy

We spent a long time with death; now let's take a break and consider happiness. Choose an answer to this question:

Taking your life as a whole to this point, would you say that you are:
  a. Very happy.
  b. Somewhat happy.
  c. Not very happy.

Social psychologists have been asking questions like this of people for decades. Literally hundreds of thousands of people, randomly selected, in many nations, have answered this and more detailed questions. Their answers have been correlated with their answers to other questions of fact ("Are you married?" "How much money do you make?") and questions of attitude ("How well do you like your job?" "Do you feel in control of your life?").

When the psychologists analyze people's responses, the results sometimes confirm common wisdom (for example, money truly cannot buy happiness), but sometimes they contradict it (for example, the empty nest is often a happy nest). Out of all the analysis emerges a clear portrait of the happy person. Psychologists find they can reliably predict your answer to the question above based on the strength of four interrelated character traits. No external circumstances of life can predict the answer so well as these traits. Repeat, *no* external circumstance — not health, not age, not gender, not race, not physical beauty, not income, not country or place of residence, not job, not faith, not marital or parental status —

nothing predicts your answer to that question as reliably as the strength of four of your personal psychological traits.

There is good news and bad news in this. Good: it is possible to be happy no matter what circumstances you live in. Bad: changes in your circumstances, like more money or a better job, make little or no difference to your overall happiness. Bad: These personality traits that incline you toward or away from happiness are stable ones that normally persist over the decades, so if you are unhappy now, you are likely to stay that way. Good: Some schools of psychology emphatically claim that you can indeed change these traits, and teach how to do it.

In this chapter we will first survey the research on happiness. The research results clearly point to a number of practical strategies for being happier, and we examine many of them.

What's happiness?

There are at least four meanings to the word "happiness":

1. A pleasant, passing emotion that arises from immediate circumstances, for example being hugged by your lover, eating a chocolate, or finding money.

2. A pleasant feeling of anticipation: "Oh boy, tomorrow is Christmas."

3. A feeling of relief from stress and unpleasant feelings, as in "I'll be glad when this assignment is turned in," or "Good news, I don't have to go to the dentist today after all."

4. Retrospective satisfaction with a long-term situation: "We've had a pretty happy marriage," or "I'm happy in this job."

It is the fourth meaning that the psychologists try to study. It is called a "a pervasive sense of psychological well-being" in the literature[1]. This is a reasonable choice. The first three kinds of happiness are fleeting. The second and third are set up by some preceding stress, so to create them you have to first create the stress. All these feelings are welcome when they come, but it wouldn't be practical to say "I want a life of more hugs, Christmas mornings, and cancelled dental appointments." However, it *is* practical to say, "I want a life such that, when I look back over it, I evaluate it as very satisfying."

Oddly enough, people's reports of this fourth kind of happiness turn out to be ridiculously flexible, easily influenced by their recent experiences of the first three. In one of the sneaky experiments of which psychologists are so fond, subjects were asked to make a copy of a document before they sat down to an interview. Some of the subjects found a small coin, apparently forgotten on the copy machine; others did not. During the interview, people who had just found a coin were significantly more likely to express satisfaction with their lives than those who did not! Other studies have found that people express greater life satisfaction on sunny days than on rainy ones[2].

This very flexibility suggests one general truth about happiness. Shortly we will see that our sense of well-being reflects a running balance between good things and bad things. These experiments show that the most recent events weigh most heavily on these scales. So it is not at all silly to say that, if we want to feel happy in a general sense, we should cultivate an appreciation of frequent, small pleasures. Simply making a habit of being aware of the small, available pleasures of daily life — arising in good health, meeting a friend, feeling sunshine — helps to tip our running account of life toward the happy side.

Are people's reports of their own happiness reliable? Besides pivoting in the wind of their recent experiences, people being interviewed tend to over-report the good and downplay the bad. Just the same, if you poll enough people, selected randomly, over a range of locations and times, their responses show reasonably stable statistics. And when you retest them, people's responses tend to be consistent over time. Besides, people who say they are happy often show signs of being happy:

> They smile and laugh more during interviews. They have happier memories. They report more joy when their experience is sampled daily... their friends and family are more likely to see them as happy people.[3]

Very well, what makes happier people happy? And how do we get some?

Studying happiness

Here are some of the high points in the scientific study of happiness.

Happiness as a balance of feelings

One early milepost was that what people report as well-being or happiness is the net sum of two different sets of feelings, a set of positive feelings and a set of negative ones. An important second finding was that the sources of positive and negative "affect" (that is, feelings) are different, and are not related to each other:

> ...variations in negative affect are associated with difficulties in marriage and work adjustment, interpersonal tensions, and feelings of having a "nervous breakdown," as well as with some of the more standard indicators of anxiety and worry. None of these variables, however, is related to positive affect.

> ...positive affect appears to be related to ... the degree to which an individual is involved in the environment around him, social contact, and active interest in the world ... such things as the degree of social participation, which is reflected in organizational membership, number of friends ... companionship with one's spouse; and ... degree of variability in one's life experiences... [4]

One confusion in this summary is that it mixes up external issues ("difficulties in marriage," "number of friends") with internal ones ("anxiety and worry," "interest in the world"). The next milepost was to eliminate most of the influence of the external world. Costa and McCrea located the source of good and bad feelings in two clusters of personality traits:

> Under the heading of E [extraversion] come sociability, warmth, involvement with people, social participation, and activity. Under N [neuroticism] come such characteristics as ego strength, guilt proneness, anxiety, psychosomatic concerns, and worry. Extraverted traits contribute to one's positive enjoyment or satisfaction in life, although they do not generally appear to reduce the unpleasantness of adverse circumstances. Neurotic traits predispose one to suffer more acutely from one's misfortunes, but they do not necessarily diminish one's joy or pleasures. [5]

In this model, happiness is still the sum of good feelings and bad feelings, and the sources of the feelings are still separate, but now the feelings can be studied apart from the actual events that cause them. Each of us experiences a mix of good things and adversities.

Each of us reacts to these events with good feelings or bad ones. But people with strong extravertive traits extract more good feelings from good events. People with strong neurotic traits suffer more deeply from bad events. The strength of the traits determines the intensity of the good or bad reactions.

Consequences of happiness as a feeling balance

The revolutionary point in this is that both the overall intensity of our feelings and the balance point between good and bad feelings are more closely related to our personality traits than they are to the external circumstances of life. Happiness depends less on what happens than on how we feel about what happens.

If this is true, two things should follow. First, happiness should not change much when life circumstances change. That is just what was reported in a paper with the memorable title "Lottery winners and accident victims."[6] Surveying the happiness of 22 winners of a state lottery and that of 29 people who had become paraplegics in recent accidents, the researchers found that the lottery winners were not significantly more happy, and the unfortunate accident victims were not a great deal less happy, than a set of matched control subjects. And the lottery winners got less satisfaction from ordinary pleasures of life.

If happiness is determined by personality, a second outcome should be that, because personality is relatively stable over time, people should report consistent levels of happiness after a long interval, without any regard to any changes in their lives during that time. That is just the result from a number of longitudinal studies.

> We can predict future happiness far more accurately from measures of past happiness than from such significant life circumstances as marital status, sex, race, or age.[7]

In other words, there are happy people and unhappy people, and they tend to remain happy or unhappy throughout their lives, no matter what happens to them.

Personality traits of happiness

What are the personality traits that determine long-term happiness? The late Angus Campbell made a career of measuring the sense of well-being. He identified two key personality traits. One was a sense of efficacy, or personal control; the second was self-esteem:

> If we isolate that part of the population which expresses both a strong sense of personal control and a high level of satisfaction with self (about 15 percent of the total), we find that we have identified a group of people with extraordinarily positive feelings of well-being. Three out of five of these people describe themselves as "very happy," hardly any of them express themselves as dissatisfied with life in general, very few (4 percent) feel they have not received their reasonable share of happiness...[8]

Other studies isolated the balance of optimism versus pessimism as a key trait. David Myers, in his survey of happiness research[9], settles on a list of four general traits:

- Extraversion: the tendency to be sociable and outgoing. Costa and McCrea included "warmth" and "vigor" in this heading.

- Self-esteem: the tendency to approve of yourself, to answer Yes to survey questions like "I am a loyal friend" or "People tend to like me."

- Efficacy: a belief that you can control the circumstances of your life, so you answer Yes to questions like "I usually achieve what I set out to do," or "An individual can affect some government decisions."

- Optimism: the tendency to see good events as likely to continue and to view bad events as temporary setbacks.

Now, I (who, I have to admit, have no psychological credentials whatever) see a kind of circularity in this list. It seems to me that these traits interact with each other, and it is not simple to separate them.

For example: If you are optimistic, when walking into a group of strangers you will expect to meet kindly people, and so will be ready to greet them openly and ready to make friends, in other words, to act like an extravert. If you are an extravert, you tend to have more friends and to get more public approvals, and as a result you will automatically think better of yourself than if you were an introvert. But if you think well of yourself you will naturally think you are skilled and likely to succeed in what you attempt, so you would naturally have a stronger sense of personal control. But if you have a strong sense of personal control, you would of course tend to be optimistic about how things are going to work out.

In other words, it seems to me there might not be four distinct traits here; some of them might be the result of others. However many traits there are, it is clear that they interact in a positive way, sending the fortunate person who has them all into an upward spiral toward happiness. And the unlucky person who has the inverse traits of introversion, low self-esteem, helplessness, and pessimism is doomed to spiral into depression.

Optimism and pessimism

Martin Seligman made a specialty of the study of helplessness, depression, optimism and pessimism. He points to the fourth trait, optimism, as the one that is the key to happiness[10].

Seligman analyzes pessimism and optimism this way. When any event, good or bad, happens to us, we tend to characterize it along three axes:

- Whether its effect is permanent and lasting, or transient and temporary.

- Whether its effect is pervasive, affecting many parts of our life, or limited, affecting only a specific situation.

- Whether the event is caused by our personal acts, or whether it is due to external causes and not rooted in ourselves.

When an adverse event happens, the pessimist interprets it as *permanent*, *pervasive*, and *personal*. The optimist, in contrast, sees an adverse event as *transient*, *limited*, and *external*.

Here is an example. You are hosting a party. Hurrying to serve your guests, you scoop up a tray of snacks and start into the room, trip, stumble, and scatter juicy stuffed mushrooms across the carpet and your guests' laps. How do you react?

A pessimist says (or thinks) things like: "Well, that ruins the evening" (permanent), "Everything always goes wrong" (pervasive), and "I am such a clumsy oaf" (personal).

An optimist thinks things like: "It'll take several minutes to mop this up, who else could serve the wine?" (temporary), "At least I didn't drop the shrimp cocktails" (limited), and "I caught my foot on that stupid throw rug" (external).

Just the reverse happens following a happy event. The pessimist thinks the good thing was transient and unlikely to recur, limited in scope, and due to external causes. The optimist, however, sees it as evidence that good times are going to continue (permanent), that they will spill over to the rest of life (pervasive) and that they are probably due to the optimist's own skill and hard work (personal). Seligman's book contains a test you can administer to yourself to learn how you score on these scales[11].

It seems at least plausible that people who are strongly optimistic would naturally tend to be extraverted (because they always expect other people to be friendly and helpful), to have high self-esteem (because they always credit good events to their personal qualities and bad ones to external causes), and to have a sense of personal control (because they expect their plans to work out, and when the plans don't, they blame the failure on external causes).

On the other hand, it could be that the inborn traits are extraversion and self-confidence, and that they result in an optimistic outlook. Let's just leave it that all four traits interact to support each other. Which means that working on your optimism/pessimism balance would be as good a starting point as any.

The limits of external factors

One of the most striking results of the study of happiness is that the actual circumstances of life make little difference to our sense of well-being. Here are some of the things that have been conclusively shown to have at most a weak correlation to happiness:

- Income (with an exception to be mentioned shortly). Richer people are no happier than poor ones, and people in wealthy nations are not necessarily happier than people in poorer nations.

- Age. Adolescents are not significantly less happy than the average; nor are the elderly. Properly-conducted studies find no evidence whatever for either a male mid-life crisis or a female empty-nest crisis.

- Race or social class. It is not true that disadvantaged minorities have lower self-esteem or happiness than the average.

- Gender. Men and women react to *unhappiness* in different ways (women more often with depression, men more often with violence or alcohol), but they report similar levels of happiness.

- Physical good looks. Handsomeness does not correlate to happiness, except among young women.

- Faith and religion. Freedman looked for this correlation specifically, and found:

  Those who are religious are no happier than those who are not religious... Taken as a whole, there is no relationship between individual beliefs regarding the existence of God (and God's characteristics) and general happiness... we found no relationship between belief in an afterlife and general happiness.[12]

Money really doesn't matter

Money matters to happiness only in the following way: true poverty is hell, and almost always unhappy. By "true" poverty I mean an income so low that you cannot meet the basic needs of life: you cannot afford a secure place to sleep or to store your possessions, you cannot afford adequate food, adequate clothing, or needed medical care.

If you live in true poverty or on the edge of it, you are subject to constant, miserable stress. You aren't sure where you will sleep tonight, you need charity just to eat or clothe yourself, and so on. The stress of merely staying alive dominates your life. Everything conspires to hammer down your self-esteem. Everything works to prove you have no ability to control your life. If you are destitute, it is almost obscene to ask how "happy" you might be.

Raise your income to the level that meets the basic needs, so you have a secure place to live, enough to eat, adequate clothes and the ability to store them and launder them, and access to basic medical care. This is the condition of the great majority of American citizens. Beginning at this minimal level of income, and all the way up to the wealth of a professional ball-player, the amount of money you make does not correlate with the happiness you report. Furthermore, an increase in your income does not produce a matching increase in your happiness. A stark, obvious proof that increased affluence does not produce increased happiness is right in front of us. Here is how David Myers expresses it (with his italics):

> In 1957, the year John Galbraith was going to press with his famous book describing us as *The Affluent Society,* our per person income, expressed in today's dollars, was seventy-five hundred dollars. By 1990 it was over fifteen thousand, making us The Doubly Affluent Society... Compared to 1957, we now have twice as many cars per capita... and $12 billion a year worth of brand-name athletic shoes. ... *We're twice as rich — not just 20 percent richer — yet we're no happier.* ... In fact, between 1956 and 1988, the percentage of Americans who reported they were "pretty well satisfied with your present financial situation" *dropped* from 42 to 30 percent.[13]

Could anything be clearer? A real and measurable increase in affluence did not create happiness — a decrease if anything. This is absolutely undeniable, yet it contradicts almost everyone's casual assumption. Quickly: what would make you happier? Odds are that even now, your first thought is "more money." *Wrong!* And there are two good reasons.

Adaptation levels

The reason that a raise in pay won't make you permanently happier is that your wonderfully flexible brain is designed to adapt to any change of condition. When a condition changes, our brains quickly reset our expectations to make the current situation the norm. This is "adaptation level theory," the idea that we continually *adapt* to label the existing *level* of any stimulus as the norm.

We can see this in all types of perception. It explains how we find it useful to keep our headlights on when driving at noon, yet can distinguish a faint star in a dark sky; or why our attention is drawn equally to a whisper in a silent room, or to a shout while crossing a busy street. Each is an incremental change above a local norm[14].

It is built into us that what matters, what is worth focussing on, is a change from the current norm. It is also built into us that we are continually, and quite unconsciously, resetting the "norm-o-stat" to agree with current conditions. In any area, including income and social status, "what matters" is that things have changed. What is not changing is the norm, and the norm is not worth noticing. This is how luxuries gained become necessities. And it explains why,

> Even as we contemplate our satisfaction with a given accomplishment, the satisfaction fades, to be replaced finally by a new indifference and a new level of striving. This is, of course, a derivation from the fundamental postulate of adaptation level theory, namely, that the subjective experience of stimulus input is a function, not of the absolute level of that input but of the discrepancy between the input and past levels.[15]

Sliding standards

Various studies have shown that people's dissatisfaction with their income or status does not correlate with absolute income or social level. In other words, rich and poor are about equally likely to be satisfied or dissatisfied with what they have. Adaptation level theory explains some of this. The rest is explained by the fact that we do not judge our income or status on an absolute scale. We compare ourselves to three *relative* standards:

- People we take to be our peers.
- People a little above us on the ladder, who we hope to match.
- Our internal standard for how people our age ought to be doing.

The relativity of these standards explains how we could, as a society, become so much richer over the past 50 years and yet be no happier. We all got big-screen TVs, VCRs, and SUVs, and yet nothing changed, because we reset our standards of comparison to match. Everyone moved up together, so we still see the same relationship between ourselves and our peers and those better off than us.

If we are making less than our friends, or less than how much we think people of our age ought to be making, or if we aren't catching up with people who have a little more than we do, we get dissatisfied. That dissatisfaction can create bad feelings that feed into our overall balance of happiness. But getting a little more money will only ease that unhappiness temporarily; then it becomes a norm. And soon, our peers also move up, or we grow a little older and think we should be doing better, and we are dissatisfied once more.

This is why Brickman and Campbell dubbed adaptation to income as "the hedonic treadmill." With adaptation levels and sliding standards, the only way you could maintain permanent satisfaction with income is to do the impossible: to continually increase your income without limit.

This permanent condition might be very bad news, but later I will share some thoughts on how the treadmill can be jammed.

Some factors do matter

Here are some factors that do correlate to happiness, although never as strongly as personality factors:

- Location. Campbell found a weak correlation with population density (the higher the density, the lower the happiness). There is little difference in happiness among the industrialized nations, although people in third-world countries are definitely less happy. Myers says that people in countries with a long history of democratic government average out slightly happier than people in countries with a history of instability[16].

- Education level. The better-educated tend to be slightly happier.

- Occupation. People who are happy in their jobs tend to be happier overall.

- Marital status. Married people in general are happier than single or divorced people, and people who are happy with their marriages tend to be happiest of all.

It is interesting to speculate how these factors could relate to the happiness personality traits (but I have no sources for these speculations). Consider education level: Meeting the day-to-day challenges of classwork can only help your sense of personal control; and having a degree can only improve your self-esteem. Then, consider occupation: A satisfying job has many opportunities for socializing and for building self-esteem; and meeting the daily challenges of work contributes to a feeling of personal control.

As for marriage, we have already talked about how important your intimate family is to your health ("Intimate family" on page 35). Here we highlight your family's importance to happiness.

Marriage, family, and friends are among the major contributors to the satisfaction of people's need for relating, and we find that satisfaction in these domains of life is affected very little by considerations of income, education, or other aspects of status.[17]

...a conclusion drawn from several large studies: Social support — feeling liked, affirmed, and encouraged by intimate friends and family — promotes both health and happiness.[18]

Myers is eloquent on the benefits of marriage, pointing out how in a good marriage you find a confidant, friend, supporter, and lover. In addition, marriage eases you into mastery of new social roles as spouse and parent. Success in taking on these roles helps build your sense of self-esteem and efficacy.

Building toward happiness

Has this discussion of happiness made you unhappy? Perhaps you responded to the question at the head of the chapter with "b. Somewhat happy" or even "c. not very happy." If you did, everything that followed suggests that you are doomed by your personality to feel no happier, forever.

Wait! "Doomed?" "By your personality?" "Forever?" Why, that is precisely the pessimist's view of adversity as pervasive, personal and permanent! Away with pessimistic thinking; let's take the optimist's view that bad things are transient and fixable. There are three general approaches: boosting the happiness traits, changing the balance of good and bad feelings, and jamming the hedonic treadmill.

Put on a happiness face

To recap, the four traits that strongly correlate with self-reported well-being are extraversion, self-esteem, efficacy, and optimism ("Personality traits of happiness" on page 173). They are not clearly separable, and it seems (at least to this layman) that an improvement in any one of them cannot help but feed into the other three.

Apply your creative imagination: what practical changes can you imagine making in your life that would make you stronger in any of these traits? Here are some possibilities[19].

Exercise

Physical exercise nourishes all the happiness traits. If you set up and carry out an exercise plan, it gives you a sense of efficacy: You get daily proof that you can make plans and carry them out. The results of the exercise cannot help but improve how you feel about yourself. Learning in this intimate way that your body is capable of improvement boosts your optimism about the future. If you exercise with other people, you get chances to socialize and improve your extravertive abilities. At the least, you have a new subject of conversation.

Time management

Good time management supports efficacy and self-esteem. As with exercise, when you demonstrate your ability to set and meet deadlines on a daily and hourly basis, it improves your sense of efficacy and your self-esteem. One part of time management is breaking major goals down into small, doable sub-goals. This helps manage time, but it has the even more important result of giving you a constant flow of small successes to feed your sense of efficacy.

Another part of good time management is getting adequate sleep. Sleep deprivation is common in our culture, and it affects mood in negative ways.

Learning

Learning or improving any skill helps efficacy and self-esteem, and most learning situations put you in touch with new people, aiding extraversion. Learn photography; take up an instrument or join a chorus; take a course in astronomy or bird watching or web page design; join a hiking club; learn a new sport; take up any subject that remotely interests you. Or start a study, aiming toward becoming expert about anything: your town's history or your family's, local flora or fauna, civil war relics, dolls, Lhasa Apso dogs, stamps. Simply knowing a lot about anything raises your self-esteem, and the process of coming to know it feeds the sense of efficacy[20].

Volunteering

Involvement with other people makes extravertive behavior easier for a shy person, and volunteer activity is an easy way to get that involvement, as we already saw ("Volunteering" on page 40). Successful interactions with others improves your self-esteem.

Giving of yourself through volunteering makes you feel much better about yourself and your world, and contradicts feelings of helplessness.

Self-improvement

To conceive, plan, and carry out *any* intentional change in your life style is a powerful method of creating a sense of personal control and self-esteem. For example, at one point my wife and I, who were both then heavy smokers, decided as a couple to become nonsmokers. We got advice from a psychologist; we stocked up on nicotine gum (today it would be the nicotine patch), and on a selected day, we quit. Marian ritually smashed our biggest ashtray. And we haven't smoked since, except occasionally in dreams. It has been more than fifteen years, yet this still stands as a high point in our lives together and even now, recalling it gives satisfaction. Almost any positive change will do: you can make an intentional change in your diet, exercise, dwelling place, or occupation.

Shopping no recommended

There's one popular happiness technique that really can't be recommended. Some people, when something bad happens, try to compensate by buying things — "When the going gets tough, the tough go shopping." The relationship to the happiness traits is pretty plain: searching, comparing prices, choosing, and buying are all activities that make a person feel competent. Owning something new helps self-esteem. But compared to other techniques in this chapter, the cost is likely to be high for a small, temporary improvement. And getting (further) into debt is never a way to improve your happiness.

Psychological help

Recall how strongly the optimistic and pessimistic thinking patterns influence the other happiness traits. Do you tend to think like a pessimist, treating every aversive event as permanent, pervasive, and a personal failing? Or, have you have suffered from clinical depression? In either case, you might be able to benefit from a Cognitive Therapy approach to correcting negative patterns of thinking. Cognitive therapies focus on breaking habitual, negative, thought patterns and they aim at giving quick help without extended analysis[21].

Changing the balance

Recall the analysis of happiness as the balance between good feelings and bad feelings. It is true that the feelings are primary in the happiness balance, and true that our personalities control the strengths of good and bad feelings. Nevertheless, those external events do exist and are to some extent in our control. You can look beyond your personality at the external triggers of good and bad feelings, and consider what you can do to increase the frequency of actual pleasant events in your life.

Many of the practical actions listed in the preceding section are also direct producers of good feelings. Exercise, for example: never mind what it does for your sense of efficacy or self-esteem; it feels good in the doing. It's a pleasure to make a schedule or a task list and a pleasure to check off the items on it. Getting a good night's sleep is a pleasure. Every step of learning or collecting is a small satisfaction.

Recall that your evaluation of your overall happiness is influenced by your recent, momentary experiences of pleasure or pain. With this in mind, a very practical way to improve your sense of well-being is to make a habit of collecting and valuing the transient pleasures of daily life in a mindful and deliberate way. Or, as Thich Nhat Hanh puts it,

> When we have a toothache, we know that not having a toothache is happiness. But later, when we don't have a toothache, we don't treasure our non-toothache.[22]

Do you have one of those digital watches that can be set to chirp on the hour? Set it to do that. Then, every time it chirps, look around and find something to appreciate or enjoy — even if it is no more than the pattern of sunlight on the carpet, or the fact that you are healthy, warm, and safe.

Jamming the hedonic treadmill

Dissatisfaction with income or status is a potent source of bad feelings. If you can control or eliminate this dissatisfaction, you can give your balance of feelings a healthy shove toward happiness.

Dissatisfaction usually comes from comparing our circumstances to relative standards: to our peers; to our notion of where people our age should be; and to people just above us on the ladder. As we have seen, this is deadly because such dissatisfaction can never be cured. When we improve our standing a little, all those standards creep ahead to reopen the gap.

There can be only one answer: *change the standards*. But to attempt this is to enter a battle of epic scale. If you set out to change your standard of values, you will be like a character in a heroic fantasy, a lonely hero beset by powerful, amorphous forces. Yet, like a fantasy hero, you can call powerful allies to your side.

Beset by powerful forces

Consider: There are two huge industries that are totally dedicated to the single purpose of persuading us to accept standards that will leave us dissatisfied. The advertising industry comprises tens of thousands of bright, creative, industrious people who spend their working days figuring out ever more clever and subtle ways to make us *want stuff*. And the entertainment industry has battalions of energetic, talented people who know that what most entertains us: images of people living brighter, more exciting lives than we live.

The people in both of these industries would claim to be working for our benefit. But the inevitable outcome of their work is to school us in *how to evaluate our lives*. They supply us with colorful images of how people of our class or age ought to dress, act, eat, and drive, what kind of place we should live in, and how we should furnish it. Almost inevitably, that evaluation will leave us dissatisfied with our actual circumstances.

If we buy into these popular images — so convenient, so attractive — we automatically accept a dissatisfaction that, as we've seen, cannot be cured. We step onto the hedonic treadmill. But how can we detach from these standards, without also detaching from the comforts of our society, and from society itself? We admire the Amish their convictions; we don't envy their dowdy clothes, their hand tools, or their isolation.

Befriended by courageous allies

Popular culture is pervasive and powerful (oops, pessimistic words). Fortunately, like a fantasy hero going to war against vast evil, you can call on courageous allies. In this war, our allies are the people who, throughout history, have preached the value of simplicity in life. One of the most eloquent American voices was Thoreau's:

> Most of the luxuries, and many of the so-called comforts of life, are not only not indispensable, but positive hindrances to the elevation of mankind... None can be an impartial or wise observer of human life but from the vantage ground of what we should call voluntary poverty.

> ...the cost of a thing is the amount of what I will call life which is required to be exchanged for it, immediately or in the long run...[23]

But Thoreau has descendants in modern life. Today, the "voluntary simplicity" movement has many eager advocates.[24]

The findings of happiness research help us interpret the message from Thoreau and his modern counterparts. We get the same message from every advocate of simplicity: *We must replace our relative standards of comparison with absolute standards.*

They all tell us to compare our circumstances, not to an ever-sliding relative standard, but to an absolute standard of human comfort. For example, learn not to ask "Is our house as good as the neighbors'?" and ask instead, "Is our house as safe, comfortable, and welcoming *as we need it to be*?" And of course, the same for the car, the salary, the clothes.

When we begin to judge our possessions by absolute standards, we learn, in Katy Butler's words,

> ...to sever the link
> between consumption and happiness,
> between consumption and self-worth.[25]

And that puts sand in the gears of the hedonic treadmill.

There is freedom in this shift from relative to absolute standards! It brings freedom from having to purchase something only because other people have one and we don't want to be different or left out. It brings release from the pressure of striving for a standard of comfort invented by a script writer. It brings escape from the need to stay with a job because it has status. It brings relaxation from the pressure to own the things that properly express our personalities, in favor of owning the things that merely work.

There are more ways to seek happiness, but this is the first, the most radical, and the most difficult.

Summary

Happiness, defined as a pervasive sense of well-being, has been closely studied. It has been found to reflect a balance between the minute-to-minute flow of good and bad feelings, but these are strongly modulated by personality traits that are consistent over a person's life, the most important trait being optimism. There are lots of simple, practical strategies we can use to shift the balance of our emotions toward the side of well-being. The most revolutionary of these is to convert the unexamined, relative standards by which we judge our quality of life into deliberate, absolute standards; in short, to step off the treadmill of consumption.

11. Being Content

While reading the papers and books on happiness that went into the preceding chapter, I kept thinking that something important was being left out; some important consideration was being missed.

Finally I realized what it was. All the happiness researchers had no choice but to assume that life would permit happiness. They had to set aside any recognition that, in the pungent modern phrase, *shit happens*. Death happens; bereavement happens; accidents and fires and tornadoes and strokes and landslides and cancers and car wrecks and muggings and wars happen. The happiness personality traits affect how you recover from disaster over the long run, but they can't prevent disaster, and they can't make your immediate response any more resilient or efficacious.

One of the documented benefits of prayer and other "religious coping behaviors" is resilience in the face of disaster[1]. Are there secular techniques with the same effect? What habits of life make us more steadfast in the face of the inevitable disaster? What practices help us adjust quickly to loss and respond more constructively?

I can think of four answers. All four are ancient recipes, and it is not easy to write of them without sounding preachy or pompous. Still, I know from experience that they work.

Freedom from debt

Debt is mental slavery. Worry about debt is a wonderfully effective source of unhappy feelings. Owing money restricts your choices of occupation. When you owe, you can't freely change jobs or take a

sabbatical. Debt also restricts your choices of what to buy, where to
live, even how many children to have.

Sooner or later, you will experience an economic crisis. It might be a
general one like a national recession. Or it might be a personal one,
resulting from losing your job, or from a huge expense such as an
unexpected illness or a legal judgment. At some point, the financial
boom will be lowered. What makes such a catastrophe worse? Debt.

None of my readings on happiness mentioned this simple formula:
get out of debt. Yet the state of being debt-free is a steady source of
small pleasures, similar to the state of being healthy. Being debt-free
does wonders for your self-esteem. And, when you are debt-free
and want to remain so, you are much less likely to fall prey to
advertisements. "Oh, that looks lovely, but not lovely enough to go
into debt for."

It is possible for anyone to become debt-free. Consult a financial
advisor; work out a step-by-step plan; then carry it out. The
successful execution of each incremental step of your plan will leave
you feeling better; and the final result will be well worth the effort.

Having nothing to hide

A couple of years ago we spent several weeks touring Tuscany. The
Italian national police, the *carabinieri*, have a program of random
stops along the highway. You are driving along admiring the
beautiful countryside when you notice in the road ahead a police
car and a couple of *carabinieri* in trim uniforms. The underling has a
grim expression and an Uzi. The officer steps out in the road with a
little red wand and flags you down.

As I pulled over, I first felt a wave of nerves at being stopped by the
police, but it was followed by a wave of happiness when I realized
that I literally had nothing to fear. There was no contraband of any
kind in the car. All the papers were in order. No legal authorities
wanted me for anything. I had been driving at a legal speed. I
actually thought "My conscience is clear," and it felt good.

After the officer had filled out his paperwork (with much difficulty
because he had little English and we were not about to try out our
halting Italian) and we were again on our way, I thought about that
reaction. It feels very good, I realized, to have nothing to hide. And
it simplifies your response to both good things and disasters.

Part of a resilient, contented life, then, is owning a clear conscience. Of course this does not mean being without regret or guilt. Everyone can think of things in their past that they wish had never happened, and acts they wish they had never done. I am no different. Believe me, I can ruin an hour anytime, by recalling some of the stupid, cruel, or disgraceful things I've done.

No life is without error or regret, but an operational definition of a clear conscience addresses the three tenses of future, present, and past as follows. First, you have the intention of living ethically in the future. You have formed a clear ethical code, you are living by it, and you aren't planning to violate it. Second, there's nothing in your life right now that couldn't be posted on your web site to be read by the world and the FBI. And third, you have considered the major wrongs from your past and you have either done something to atone for them, or at least you have formed a clear understanding of why they were wrong and are determined not to repeat them.

Using detachment

One of my late father's characteristic expressions was "Well? What'r ya gonna do?" After discussing anything inevitable — politics, rain on the hay crop, the follies of his neighbors — he'd look at you, spread open his palms before him, and with a wry smile say, "Well? What'r ya gonna do?" Years after his death, I realized this was his expression of the principle of detachment.

My phrase to express detachment is "This is what is." It can be stressed in several ways, but I say it: *this* is what *is*. *This*, happening in front of me, is all that I can know; it *is* what actually exists, as opposed to what I might prefer to be.

The futility of judgment

As I understand detachment[2], it applies to all things you cannot personally influence. To judge such things on any subjective scale — good/bad, right/wrong, skillful/stupid, ugly/beautiful — is, first, futile, and second, harmful to yourself.

Judging is futile because, given that this is a thing you cannot personally influence — the weather, the outcome of an election, a stranger's behavior — your judgment does not and cannot alter the thing in any way. That you think it wrong, or stupid, or ugly does nothing to improve it or make it cease. Your thinking it right, moral, skillful, or beautiful cannot preserve it or multiply it. Your judgment is simply irrelevant to what is.

Judging is harmful because even to form a value-opinion creates an emotional pull or push you cannot resolve. Suppose the weather is not what you hoped it would be today. If you feel emotion about that (anger, distress, frustration) this emotion cannot be discharged. You have no choice but to eat your liver until the emotion subsides; or worse, until you vent your spleen on another person or thing.

Recognition, the Third Stance

The only productive attitude (and the only attitude supportable by logic) is the attitude of detachment: "this is what is." Now, this attitude of detachment is quite different from liking or disliking. It is not the absence of an attitude; it is a third attitude, a positive stance that is neither approval or disapproval.

The value of detachment has been known for millennia. Epictetus (50-125AD) put it this way:

> ... he who desires or avoids the things which are not in his power can neither be faithful nor free, but of necessity he must change with them and be tossed about with them as in a tempest, and of necessity must subject himself to others who have the power to procure or prevent what he desires or would avoid.[3]

Some might name the third attitude "acceptance," as in, "I must accept things as they are," but that word carries a sense of approval, or at least of acquiescence — as if you agreed to the event and would permit it to be, supposing you had any say in it at all. And that's not necessarily the case.

Recognition is the proper name for the attitude of "this is what is." You *recognize* what is; you see it, you comprehend it, and as far as possible you understand its causes and likely results. Recognition does not imply acceptance. Does the pathologist who looks at a biopsy and recognizes cancer approve of it?

Our society likes binary choices, and popular wisdom does not allow for a third attitude. People prefer slogans like, "If you aren't part of the solution, you're part of the problem," and "Silence is consent." If you only acknowledge that something exists, people may infer that you approve of it. "It looks as if it will rain on our school picnic tomorrow." "Well, you don't sound very unhappy about it! Aren't you sorry that the kids will be disappointed?"

One reason our culture prefers not to acknowledge the detached stance is that so many cliques and causes draw their power from your emotions. Advocates for any cause work to create strong value judgments in people's minds. When they have fomented a state of emotional distress, they promise to release that distress in group action. Political activists will never agree that it is possible to recognize an issue without also judging that issue. All their membership, contributions, and influence depend on getting people to make value judgments about issues that those people can't personally influence[4].

This third stance of recognition may also be called "denial." If we do not form an emotional judgment, especially of a wrong or a tragedy, we may be accused of denying that it has happened. In psychology, the mechanism of denial is seen as having a practical purpose, of sheltering the mind from overwhelming emotion. That also is the use of recognition! However, recognition does not deny; it investigates. It does not withhold vision — it is willing to see microscopically — it only withholds judgment and emotion because they are useless.

Recognition may also be mislabelled resignation, passivity, or apathy. If we do not react with conventional elation or dismay to some event we cannot influence, other people may say we are incapable of feeling or reacting. But feelings and reactions, when they cannot possibly lead to change, are pointless and damaging. It is much more helpful in the long run to seek a cool understanding of the situation, than to judge it.

It is definitely possible to recognize and comprehend events while not judging them on an emotional scale. You do it often. Look at your thumbnail; is this a virtuous thumbnail, or a pretty one? Think about the public transit system in your city. Is that a moral transit system, or an ugly one? Nobody asks these questions. You understand these ordinary things intimately; you could become expert on them if you needed to; but you don't judge them on any subjective scale of values.

The secret of detachment is to be able to have the same kind of clinical, intelligent, detailed knowledge about something that tugs at your emotions, that you have about your thumbnail. When you succeed in this, someone may accuse you of being "cold." Before you feel guilty for your coldness, ask yourself why the accusation was made. That person may want to influence you. Your quiet recognition calls into question the value of the person's own emotions. He or she needs you to join in the distress in order to validate it.

Benefits of Detachment

There are two reasons for developing detached recognition. The first is to reduce emotional distress and to achieve a measure of tranquility when catastrophe strikes. The second is to improve your own ability to understand and to influence events.[5]

If we say of an event in progress, "that's bad, that's evil, that's stupid, that's wrong" we harm ourselves by increased stress; but also, we tend to stop with these judgments, as if pronouncing judgment ended the matter. Worse, it could be that we judged hastily or superficially. But now we have to maintain our indignation, because we are emotionally invested in a belief that the event was bad. Our need to defend our indignation gives us a strong motive to select the details that will sustain and justify our emotions. In contrast, quiet recognition gives time to form a clear understanding, and leaves room for ideas to change as we learn[6].

Everything, when examined closely, turns out to be more complicated than we knew at first. If we can dispense with the pain of negative emotion and the distraction of futile judgment, we can look deeper into the why of a thing, and further forward in time at its consequences. We might very well discover that, if we are tranquil and prepared, there is an opportunity, after all, to influence this event or its sequels. And even if that does not turn out to be so, we will at least be wiser in how things like this come about, and be able to see them forming sooner in the future. Such penetrative wisdom is harder to come by if we are wrapped up in the stress of judging the quality of the thing or supporting a judgment.

Learning Forgiveness

There is one immense class of things that are definitely not in our control: the class of all the things that happened in the past! What's done's done. How you feel about what was done cannot possibly make the thing be undone, or differently done. In that case, isn't it obvious on the face of it, that to harbor strong feelings about errors and insults of the past is automatically pointless and probably harmful?

This is simply to extend the principle of detachment into the time dimension. If the best way to handle "what is" is with clinical examination, quiet understanding, and thoughtful appreciation, shouldn't that also be the best way to handle "what was"?

Epictetus noted two millenia ago that when you feel strongly about things not in your control, you have made yourself a slave of the person who does control those things. It should be clear that if you have an emotional investment in being hurt and angry about some past event, you make yourself a slave, not to a current person who might be influenced, but to the past, which is uncaring, implacable, and changeless.

The way to be released from this slavery to the past is to learn to forgive. Forgiveness is not easy to learn, but it is possible. Dr. Frederic Luskin at Stanford studies the process of forgiveness, trying to turn it from an art into a trainable skill. A large group of adults who undertook a six-week course in forgiveness showed significant reductions in stress and anger.[7]

Even the unforgivable can be forgiven. Dr. Luskin studied five women from Northern Ireland who had lost sons or close relatives to political violence. They underwent forgiveness training and showed significant improvements in feelings of hurt, depression, and optimism about the future.

Summary

Genuine disaster strikes every person's life sooner or later. Our resilience and strength to recover and cope can be improved by four ancient common-sense methods: being debt-free; having a clear conscience; learning to replace emotional reactions to events with detached recognition and clinical scrutiny; and practicing forgiveness to escape slavery to past damages.

12. A Partner in Infinity's Dance

> By nature, men are nearly alike; by practice, they get to be
> wide apart.
>
> > – Confucius

I began this book with the aim of solving a puzzle. I knew from observing the lives of my parents and others that a genuine religious practice — a practice that is pursued with enthusiasm and diligence, a practice integrated into everyday life — makes life better. Yet I was (and still am) sure there are no supernatural interventions in the world. If the benefits of religious practice didn't have supernatural causes, they must have a natural ones. What were they? Did they have secular sources?

Finding these answers that you have been reading was a very enjoyable process of discovery. I hope you agree with me that the benefits are there for the taking, and that it is possible to build a fulfilling life practice from secular elements.

Building a life of wholeness is neither quick nor simple. Alas, I have found no reason to think that a genuine secular practice is any less time-consuming than a genuine religious one. You need just as much enthusiasm and diligence, and your beliefs need to be integrated just as thoroughly into everyday life.

Here's one way to approach it. A religious person with a minimal practice must spend at least three hours per week attending services, praying, and doing congregational work. That seems to me the least one could do and still claim to be "practicing" a religion.

Very well, let's take three hours a week as the minimum time cost for a secular life practice, also. You can devote more time to it, but you couldn't devote much less without losing any feeling of having "a practice."

Block out a few sessions in your week's plan, each between 30 and 90 minutes, and make up your mind that you will devote those blocks of time to activities you have mindfully chosen as life-enhancing. (You might make a ritual of starting and ending each block!)

What sort of things will you do in these blocks of time? You could allocate 90 minutes a week to any of the areas we've looked at:

- In any of a dozen ways, knitting yourself more firmly into human society, connecting to more people and improving your relations with the people you already know.

- Starting or improving a meditation practice.

- With your intimate partner, making an inventory of the rituals in your life, deciding which to shed and which to retain or revivify.

- Inventing and carrying out new, constructive, meaningful rituals for yourself and your family.

- Seeking out new faces for your own, or your child's, gallery of heros (not overlooking ordinary people and unpopular types of excellence, like persistence or kindness).

- Thinking through your ethical stance and working out ways of integrating it in your life — or contemplatively reviewing the week to see where you fell short of your own ethical standards, and considering how to atone or improve.

- Arranging your affairs; and designing and preparing a memorial legacy.

- Improving your odds of feeling happy, in small ways (developing the habit of appreciating of small pleasures) and great ones (simplifying your life).

- Working at being debt-free; atoning for old crimes; practicing detachment; and forgiving old grudges.

And I am sure that your own creative imagination can run far ahead of mine using only the hints and pointers in the preceding pages. If it doesn't, read some of the books listed under "Recommended Books" on page 231.

Whichever of the many routes to a richer life practice you follow, you will choose it, not because you "ought to" in some abstract sense, but because you find it deeply satisfying to take deliberate, mindful control of your life — making yourself a skillful, jubilant partner in Infinity's great line-dance.

Whatever you choose to do, I hope that you will

Live long and prosper.

– Traditional Vulcan farewell

Notes

Citations to print sources begin with an author's name, like (Gardner 1997). They are keyed to the bibliography that starts on page 234. A citation beginning with "Web," like (Web Bible), refers to one of the Internet resources listed beginning on page 244.

Introduction

1. If this were an online document, the numbered notes would be hyperlinks. As with a web page, "link" to a note only if you want to know more about the topic.

1: Benefits of a Religious Practice

1. (Bergin and Richards 2000).

2. The phrase "peculiar people," used proudly by fundamentalists to distinguish themselves from "worldly" people, is found in three places in the Bible. Twice in Deuteronomy it is used in wording God's commitment to the Hebrew tribes:

> For thou [art] an holy people unto the LORD thy God, and the LORD hath chosen thee to be a peculiar people unto himself, above all the nations that [are] upon the earth.
> — Deuteronomy 14:2

> And the LORD hath avouched thee this day to be his peculiar people, as he hath promised thee, and that [thou] shouldest keep all his commandments...
> — Deuteronomy 26:18

These verses only justify the Jews as a "peculiar people." For Christians, the more significant use is found in the words of Peter in the New Testament:

> But ye [are] a chosen generation, a royal priesthood, an holy nation, a peculiar people; that ye should shew forth the praises of him who hath called you out of darkness into his marvellous light:...
> — I Peter 2:9

3. (Goodstein 1999). This news story continues,

> "I don't believe this is necessarily the end," she added,
> echoing several others who spoke of apocalyptic signs, "but
> it's definitely getting closer."

Apocalyptic ideas add spice to the great story. They are attractive
because they offer hope that the dramatic conclusion of the great
story might come in the believer's lifetime, rather than in some far
future.

4. Believers who say "Get thee behind me, Satan" as a way of
rejecting temptation are probably thinking of the story of Christ's
Temptation, told this way in the book of Luke:

> And the devil, taking him up into an high mountain, shewed
> unto him all the kingdoms of the world in a moment of time.
> And the devil said unto him, All this power will I give thee,
> and the glory of them... If thou therefore wilt worship me, all
> shall be thine. And Jesus answered and said unto him, Get
> thee behind me, Satan: for it is written, Thou shalt worship
> the Lord thy God, and him only shalt thou serve.
>
> – Luke 4:5-8

The phrase appears also in the two versions of Christ's rebuke of
Peter (Matthew 16:21-23 and Mark 8:31-33), when Peter wants to
reject a prophecy of the coming Passion. But this doesn't have the
drama of refusing "all the kingdoms of the world."

5. The phrase "two or three are gathered" is used by many
Christians to speak of the importance of meeting for worship. It
comes from the Gospel of Matthew, where Christ offers his disciples
this powerful promise:

> Verily I say unto you, Whatsoever ye shall bind on earth shall
> be bound in heaven: and whatsoever ye shall loose on earth
> shall be loosed in heaven. Again I say unto you, That if two of
> you shall agree on earth as touching any thing that they shall
> ask, it shall be done for them of my Father which is in
> heaven. For where two or three are gathered together in my
> name, there am I in the midst of them.
>
> – Matthew 18:18-20

In context, the passage appears to be about matters of discipline
within the community of believers, but pastors like to quote only

the final sentence as a way of reminding their congregations of the hope and solemnity of the service.

6. From (Web Quran),

> Ye are the best community that hath been raised up for mankind. Ye enjoin right conduct and forbid indecency; and ye believe in Allah.
>
> – Al-Imran 3:110.5

7. (Matthews et. al. 1998) is an authoritative survey article on the relationship of belief to health issues.

8. Our perception that others share our beliefs is even more important than that they share our ethnic group:

> We generally seem to prefer, to one degree or another, those with belief systems that are more congruent with our own. Our findings suggest that this organizing principle is far more important than other kinds of categorizations, such as race or ethnic grouping, in determining our relations with others. If race or ethnic categorizations are important it is primarily because they are convenient symbols that stand for complexes of beliefs which to one degree or another are seen to be similar to or different from our own. We find this organizing principle to hold for southerners as well as northerners, for those high in prejudice as well as low in prejudice, and for younger as well as older Jewish children. (Rokeach 1960)

9. For example, see Note 4 on page 209.

10. "Make show! Make show!" is what Allan Williams, their then-manager, urged the Beatles to do, when they were bombing in their first Hamburg gig.

> The German audience took up my shout and it soon became a late-night rallying call all over the Reeperbahn area: "Mak show!" (Williams and Marshall 1976)

11. (Berlin and Jahanbegloo 1992).

12. As quoted in (James 1902).

13. Dostoevsky is frequently quoted as having written "If God does not exist, everything is permitted." Often, only that sentence is quoted, leaving the impression that Dostoevsky himself had that

opinion, and implying that Dostoevsky felt morality was impossible without belief.

Two things are wrong with this. First, Dostoevsky did not write it in his own voice; he placed the opinion in the mouth of a character, Ivan Karamozov. Second, the sentence itself does not appear in *The Brothers Karamazov*! Anyone can verify this by searching the online text of the book. (For one of several online texts of this book, see (Web Dostoevsky)).

It is correct that the proposition "if God does not exist, everything is lawful" is a fair summary of an opinion that Ivan Fyodorovitch Karamazov advances, but Dostoevsky never has Ivan himself expound these beliefs. Other characters explain Ivan's beliefs to each other and to the reader, but they never use the often-quoted sentence. More important, there is nothing in *The Brothers Karamazov* to show how the author himself felt about this issue. To attribute the sentence to Dostoevsky himself is careless scholarship (carelessness of which Jean-Paul Sartre, among many others, seems to have been guilty).

But we can go further. The sentence "if God does not exist, everything is lawful" is a logical implication, "if A then B." In logic, an implication is true only if the antecedent, A, is true. When the antecedent is false, the statement is not negated; it is nullified, made meaningless: if *not-A* then *nothing* is asserted about B. So? Well, partway through *The Brothers Karamazov*, Ivan admits to Alyosha that in fact, he believes in God, and apparently has from the beginning. In other words, Ivan has known from the start that his proposition was null, and therefore no more than an intellectual toy. The great irony of the novel is that others act on Ivan's toy philosophy with tragic consequences. An irony of modern scholarship is that Dostoevsky's best-known phrase is a sham belief of a character who never states it as it is quoted.

14. (Shermer 1999).

15. Prager is of course not alone; I have seen opinions like his expressed in, for example, op-ed pieces by Boston's Jeff Jacoby and Detroit's Tony Snow. These sentiments can be given a charitable reading as a popularized version of the Existentialist concept of Nothingness: that without the anchor of a predetermined nature, humankind must make its own way through a void. However, the Existentialist understands that the consequence of Nothingness is

the freedom and responsibility to blaze an admirable trail into the void. The Nothingness of Existentialism is a challenge to self-transcendence. In contrast, the message that I get from writers like Prager and Jacoby is that there is *no* valid moral alternative to belief in God; and therefore, unbelievers *cannot* be moral; and therefore, unbelievers can only be *im*moral; and therefore — this is never stated but is clearly implied — unbelievers are dangerous people who ought to be isolated and controlled for the good of society.

16. (Hofstadter 1998).

17. When Josef Stalin died, I was in grade school. I still remember my mother saying with angry satisfaction, "I guess now he knows whether there's a God or not." It so impressed me that during "current events" period in school that day, I stuck up my pudgy little hand and said "My mother says,..." and quoted her. The teacher's reaction, as I remember, was to change the subject.

18. (Sagan 1996).

2: Finding Validity

1. (Camus 1955)

2. (Maslow 1964)

3. Remember, from Biology 101, every sperm and every egg contains a different, random selection of one-half of that parent's genes. You differ physically from your sibling because you got a different randomly selected half of your mother's genes, combined with a different randomly selected half of your father's. If it were not so, all siblings would be identical twins.

4. Whether we actually *do* have free will — and, if we do, how it emerges from the biochemical operations of our brains, which are essentially mechanical and hence, presumably, deterministic — are questions that have been debated by people with better minds than I have. For an introduction to the difficulties of this slippery problem, you might see (Gardner 1996).

5. (Malville 1981).

6. (Heinrich 1994)

7. Two books that do a good job of communicating this vision are (Malville 1981) and (Goodenough 1998).

8. The idea that Brahma creates the universe for sport is not only a poetic metaphor but a logical conclusion of Hindu doctrine. Hindu thinkers worked it out this way: If Brahma, the all, is truly infinite, it cannot have needs. Needs would imply a shortcoming, which is not possible of the infinite. And if Brahma is infinite, it cannot have a purpose, because all possible ends are accomplished and contained in the infinite. Yet Brahma clearly chooses to manifest as the physical universe. Why? Not because it needs to, and not to achieve a purpose. What does that leave, other than a desire to amuse itself? The concept is expressed in Sanskrit as *liilaa-vibhuuti*, playful manifestation. (Banerjee 1975)

9. For one example of this, read the Law, dictated by God to Moses in Exodus chapter 21, on slave-owning and the treatment of slaves:

> ...And the LORD said to Moses, "Thus you shall say to the people of Israel:... Now these are the ordinances which you shall set before them...

> When you buy a Hebrew slave, he shall serve six years, and in the seventh he shall go out free, for nothing. If he comes in single, he shall go out single; if he comes in married, then his wife shall go out with him. If his master gives him a wife and she bears him sons or daughters, the wife and her children shall be her master's and he shall go out alone. But if the slave plainly says, `I love my master, my wife, and my children; I will not go out free,' then his master shall bring him to God, and he shall bring him to the door or the doorpost; and his master shall bore his ear through with an awl; and he shall serve him for life....

> When a man strikes his slave, male or female, with a rod and the slave dies under his hand, he shall be punished. But if the slave survives a day or two, he is not to be punished; for the slave is his money.
>
> – Exodus 20:22 through 21:21 (RSV)

Don't trust me; read the original to verify that these are instructions said to have been given by God, from the cloud atop Sinai, to Moses, as Law. (The Bible is readily available on the internet; see (Web Bible))

10. From the Catholic Encyclopedia: "Exegesis is the branch of theology which investigates and expresses the true sense of Sacred Scripture." A lengthy article explains how the exegete identifies the literal sense of the scripture (what it actually says); and from that the derivative sense (what can be inferred from the literal sense); and thence the typical sense (the symbolic or allegorical sense). When these are insufficient, the exegete launches into *hermeneutics*, that is, creative interpretation of the Divine intent, as opposed to the actual words. The techniques of exegesis are not for everyone to use: "In its human character, the Bible is subject to the same rules of interpretation as profane books; but in its Divine character, it is given into the custody of the Church to be kept and explained..." (Web Catholic Enc.)

11. Kabbalism consists of a set of methods developed in the 12th and 13th centuries for extracting mystical meanings from the Hebrew Scriptures. The general idea was to find hidden, or encoded, meanings by manipulating the text of the Scripture. In the technique of *gematria*, letters are assigned numerical values. The scholar forms numerical sums of words and phrases and interprets them to yield new meanings. Using *notaricon*, the scholar discovers new words by forming acronyms from initial letters of sentences. Using *temura*, the scholar systematically transposes and otherwise rearranges letters. Other techniques systematically substitute letters for other letters, in effect decrypting the scriptural text as if it were a message in a substitution code.

Manipulations of this sort are more productive in Hebrew than they might be in English because written Hebrew consists only of consonants, with vowels implied. Michael Drosnin (*The Bible Code*) is a modern-day descendant of the medieval Kabbalists.

12. (Paine 1794).

13. (Clarke 1999).

14. (Feynman 1999).

15. You could start by getting a copy of the National Academy of Science's pamphlet *Science and Creationism: A View from the National Academy of Sciences, Second Edition*, available from (Web NAS 1). Then explore the NAS's special website on Creationism (Web NAS 2). To get a better personal understanding of the depth, applicability, and indeed sheer elegance of the evolutionary concept, read books

such as (Miller 1999), (Dennet 1996) or any book by Richard
Dawkins or Steven J. Gould.

3: Finding Community

1. (Maslow 1971).

2. (Cohen et. al. 1997).

3. (Williams 1999).

4. (Resnick et. al. 1997).

5. (Rodin and Langer 1977).

6. (Smyth et.al. 1999).

7. (Matthews et. al. 1998).

8. (Hallowell 1999).

9. You might not be aware that genealogy is a popular hobby with a
legion of enthusiastic practitioners. For a quick introduction, see
(Web Genealogy).

10. (Fulghum 1995).

4: Practicing Contemplation and Tranquility

1. From a web page devoted to the practice of Centering Prayer (a
modern contemplative practice), instructions in contemplative
prayer from a Fourth-century church father:

> Everyone who seeks for continual recollection of God uses
> this formula for meditation, intent upon driving every other
> sort of thought from his heart. You cannot keep the formula
> before you unless you are free from all bodily cares... The
> formula is this: 'O God, come to my assistance; O Lord, make
> haste to help me.'

2. This and other bits of the history of religion can be found in (Smart 1976), which mentions statuettes of deities in yogic posture. The fact that *all* Indus Valley figures believed to represent deities are in the same heels-together posture comes from (Kenoyer 1999).

3. This is an incident described in (Kalupahana 1992), in the appendix "History of the Lankavatara." Sri Lanka saw considerable conflict in the third century C.E. as the newer, Mahayana, school of Buddhism threatened to displace the older, Mahavihara, tradition. As each school in turn gained influence with the political leadership of the country, there were closures of monasteries and expulsions of monks of the other school. A monk named Sanghamitra was especially influential in spreading the Mahayana doctrine. Kalupahana writes that, during a resurgence of the older school, "One of the king's favorite wives, who was bitter about the suffering of the Mahavihara monks, got a carpenter to kill Sanghamitra." Clearly this was a time of great upheaval, and no doubt many people died or were made homeless in these doctrinal and social upheavals. However, I have read of no other incidents of the kind. One of the most remarkable things about modern Buddhism is the amity and tolerance between its schools. The doctrinal differences between Sri Lankan Buddhists, Tibetan Buddhists, and Japanese Buddhists are as wide or wider than the differences between, say, Roman Catholics, Anglicans, and Methodists. Yet tolerance and good will appear to reign on all sides.

4. One clear demonstration of the efficacy of meditation in a medical context is the success of the Stress Reduction Clinic at the University of Massachusetts Medical Center, where meditation is central to the treatment of stress of all types. For a narrative description of the program, its methods and results, as well as detailed instruction in meditative techniques for stress and pain relief, see (Kabat-Zinn 1990). Since the publication of that book, meditation for pain and stress has been taken up as a mainstay of "alternative medicine" clinics at a number of hospitals.

5. For a more detailed discussion of vipassana meditation and much common-sense advice for dealing with common difficulties, see (Gunaratana 1993).

6. The need for patience and non-striving is repeated in many Buddhist-oriented books on meditation, but writings in the Christian contemplative tradition call for the same attitude:

> Fight always with your thoughts and call them back when they wander away. God does not demand of those under obedience that their thoughts be totally undistracted when they pray. And do not lose heart when your thoughts are stolen away. Just remain calm, and constantly call your mind back. (Climacus 1982)

7. Hypnogogic hallucinations are that visions that appear to some people on the threshold of sleep. Freud summarized them as follows in the first chapter of *The Interpretation of Dreams*:

> ...hypnogogic hallucinations... are those very vivid and changeable pictures which with many people occur constantly during the period of falling asleep, and which may linger for a while even after the eyes have been opened. ...Not only pictures, but auditory hallucinations of words, names, etc., may also occur hypnogogically, and then repeat themselves in the dream, like an overture announcing the principal motif of the opera which is to follow. (Web Freud)

Most people who have hypnogogic visions see static images: faces, scenes. Others (including myself) see only abstract textures or patterns, or washes of light. However, a few people report vivid, detailed, and emotion-laden hallucinations in the hypnogogic state. When hypnogogic visions are combined with sleep paralysis, the result can be the kind of terrifying experiences that gave rise to legends of succubi and demon possession. Experiences of that intensity seem unlikely during basic mindfulness meditation, if only because sleep paralysis seems unlikely in the erect meditative posture.

8. In everyday speech, "meditation" and "contemplation" are near-synonyms. In this essay "meditation" means a physical, nonverbal focus, and "contemplation" a focus that includes words or ideas. This is based on present-day Western practice, rooted in Asian traditions, in which meditation is a state in which inner speech is avoided:

> There are literally hundreds of practices which can be listed under the heading of "meditation." All of these have in common the ability to bring about a special kind of free-

floating attention where rational thought is bypassed and words are of far less importance than in everyday life. (Carrington 1977)

Be aware that in books centered on Christian mystical tradition, like (Underhill 1915), "contemplation" is used for nonverbal worship and "meditation" for verbal prayer — just the reverse of the labels I'm using. The key point is that there is a spectrum of practices which vary in the amount of verbal content permitted, and that different practices have different effects.

9. (Benson 1975) was an early trend-setting paper on meditation, and introduced the term "relaxation response" for a cluster of physical relaxation symptoms that meditation seemed to induce.

10. For a sampling of the many contemplation-based self-help systems available, perform a subject search at the Amazon.com web site for books with the subject words "self-help meditation." *Caveat emptor.*

11. The four sublime states to be cultivated as part of Buddhist practice are *metta*, loving-kindness; *karuna*, compassion; *mudita*, appreciative joy; and *upekkha*, equanimity.

12. The Buddha taught for 40 years around 400 B.C.E., a time when a teacher's words were preserved by verbal transmission from teacher to student. Around 200 B.C.E., Buddhists held a conference and wrote down all they could remember of these teachings. They wrote in Pali, a linguistic relative of Sanskrit. Those writings, modified by the errors, omissions, and interpolations of 80-odd generations of scribes and translators, survive today as the Pali Canon, a work that is similar in age and in method of transmission (manual copying by devoted scholars) to two other important traditional documents: the Hebrew scriptures and the Dialogues of Socrates. The Pali Canon is more like Plato's record of Socrates' teachings, in that it aims to convey the teachings of one man. We cannot be sure we have an accurate account of the words of either Socrates or the Buddha, but we can guess when the Canon claims the Buddha taught such-and-such, and especially when the same idea turns up several times using the similar terms and images, that it is fairly sure that the historical Buddha actually said something pretty much like that.

English translations of major parts of the Pali Canon are available online; see (Web Pali Canon).

13. (Williams 1989).

14. Here's how I first learned the benefits of organizing one's account of a problem. Thirty years ago, I was a beginning service representative for IBM, repairing business machines in customers' offices. Often, I would run up against a problem that was beyond me. It is dreadful to be sitting on the floor in someone's office, surrounded by the bits of a disassembled machine, and not have a clue as to what to do next! In these situations I could telephone IBM's regional technical rep, a brilliant but somewhat irascible chap named Gene. When I called him, he would ask a series of crisp, incisive questions that stripped the problem to the bone, and my ego along with it. "Did you try this? Why not? Well, you better try it, hadn't you?" After a few of these sessions, I found myself sitting with my hand on the phone, trying to anticipate the questions Gene would ask so I would have my answers ready. And discovered that, when I did that, I often didn't have to make the call. Just preparing the problem and organizing it so that Gene would have no questions to ask me, was sufficient to show me what I should do next! I joked about how merely *thinking* about calling Gene was enough to get an answer. But what I had learned was that preparing a clear, concise, and above all a detached description of a problem is often enough to make the solution plain. At the least, it reveals the things you haven't tried and should.

15. Yet another benefit of prayer, for believers, is that it fosters detachment. After praying about a problem, the believer can "leave it on the altar," let the problem rest, at least for a while, because it has been handed off to a higher power. (Politicians get a similar relief from commissioning a study.) In Chapter 11 we look at detachment as one of the basic stratagems of happiness ("Using detachment" on page 191). One difference is that detachment as a deliberate practice does not have to put the problem out of mind; it continues to investigate and comprehend the problem.

5: Using Ritual

1. From the classic *Spirits, Stars and Spells* (de Camp and de Camp 1966), now sadly out of print.

2. You think you don't believe in sympathetic magic? OK, here's a test. Take a photograph of someone you care about. Make a copy of

it on the office copier. Now, in private, defile that copy: scribble on it, smear it, tear it up, grind your heel on it.

Go on, I dare you.

If you can actually do this — treat a picture of a loved person like the piece of paper it undoubtedly is — without any qualms, you really do not have any of the sympathetic magician in you. But if the idea of doing violence to a picture of a loved one does give you serious qualms, or if you just couldn't do it — excuse me, if you decided in a mature way not to do it — then welcome to the human condition!

3. On a tour of Turkey our group was allowed to visit several mosques, not only the awesome Blue Mosque in Istanbul but also tiny neighborhood mosques in an ancient village. At each of these places, we were asked to remove our shoes before entering the ritual space, as Moslem worshippers do. Moslems provide neat wooden shoe-shelves just outside the door of the mosque, and convenient benches or steps where you can sit to untie and retie your laces. While tying laces, I could not help but think about the Buddhist meditation group we sometimes attend back home. Here also, we all remove our shoes before entering the modest room where we "sit." It amused me to recall, in Turkey, how the Californians do not provide so well for the practicalities of their ritual space: there are no racks, no benches; and at the end of a sitting, the tiny lobby is a mass of people trying to find their shoes among the dozens of pairs on the floor, and put them on while standing up.

4. (Fulghum 1995).

5. In my imagination I hear groans from readers who are appalled at such pandering to the primitive. But look: for all our pretensions, we are not wholly rational beings. We *aspire* to rationality (I yield to none in the sincerity of that aspiration) but we look up at that shining goal from a brain that is firmly embedded in the body of a primate. One miracle of our rationality is that we can use it to comprehend ourselves and recognize just how ancient are the foundations of our minds! So: down in the sub-basement of our minds there is some ancient hardware that is not entirely clear on the difference between *wishing* and *doing*. It would be irrational to deny that. In fact, the rational thing to do is to *use* those parts of ourselves: put them to work to further the aims of the cerebral cortex!

6. For a start try (Web Holidays).

7. Apologies here to any reader South of the equator, where the dates are the same but the amounts of sunlight are reversed.

8. I speculate that this is just why so many rituals center on eating, snacking, or drinking. The varied actions of filling plates and glasses, sipping and nibbling, wiping the lips on a napkin, passing things to other people, and so on, provide a wealth of things you can do in place of really interacting with other people. The food and drink provide simple topics of conversation. They give ways in which you can symbolically serve and groom other people without having to make an emotional commitment. They give excuses to avoid, interrupt, or divert an uncomfortable conversational trend. In other words, food is part of so many rituals not because the sharing of food has great Jungian significance in our collective unconscious, but because the mechanics of sharing food and drink give us such a convenient set of "displacement activities" we can use to buffer the intensity of personal interaction.

9. (Kluger-Bell 1998).

10. (Fein 1997).

11. (Biziou 1999).

12. (Kato 1998).

13. (Beck and Metrick 1990).

6: *Pursuing Bliss*

1. (Bucke 1901).

2. (Laski 1962).

3. (Maslow 1964).

4. (Coxhead 1985).

5. I found useful first-person accounts of the Bliss experience in these books, listed in order of publication date: (James 1902), (Johnson 1959), (Laski 1962), (Cohen and Phipps 1979), (Hardy 1979), (Hay 1982), (Coxhead 1985), (Burnham 1997); and online in

(Web TASTE) and (Web EHE). The books, except for Sophy Burnham's and William James's, are out of print. I found most of them in a university library; many turn up in a search of the used-book vendors on the internet (Web Book Search).

If you would like to read first-person Bliss accounts for yourself, I recommend (Cohen and Phipps 1979) and (Coxhead 1985) for thoroughness and balanced tone. Online, see (Web TASTE), especially reports number 1, 3, 4, and 19.

6. Laski made the first attempt to survey for the frequency of Bliss (Laski 1962). However, her sample was very small and ungeneral. Sir Alister Hardy's Religious Experience Research Unit, set up in 1968 at Manchester College, collected thousands of responses to the question quoted in the text, and published a summary in (Hardy 1979). The Research unit is now sited at Westminster College, Oxford (Web RERC).

7. David Hay got the quoted question inserted into a national opinion survey in Britain, then compared those responses to several American surveys (Hay and Morisy 1978). Gallup asked similar questions of Americans in surveys from 1976 to 1985 and in (Gallup 1989) reported that "One American in three — 33 percent — claims to have had a religious experience, a particularly powerful religious insight or awakening."

8. (Hay 1982).

9. (Hardy 1979).

10. The only way to get better data would be through searching the archives of the Religious Experience Research Centre, a privilege granted to few and only on-site, in Oxford.

11. (Web TASTE).

12. (Thomas and Cooper 1980).

13. Coxhead (Coxhead 1985), Laski (Laski 1962), and Maslow (Maslow 1971) all make lists of the factors that preceded different people's experiences and try to categorize them. Austin (Austin 1998) also lists what he thinks are the "destabilizing influences" that might lead to experiences. In my opinion, all these lists end up including so much that they are not useful, either for prediction beforehand or for analysis afterward.

Maslow remarks rather flippantly, "the two easiest ways of getting peak experiences (in terms of simple statistics in empirical reports) are through music and sex." (Maslow 1971). Laski found a cluster of reports that were triggered by the childbirth experience. None of these writers mentioned physical illness as a trigger, but I noticed that a quite a few of the first-person accounts mention being ill or convalescent at the time of the experience.

14. (Hay and Morisy 1978).

15. (Gallup 1989).

16. (Hay and Morisy 1978) p 259-260.

17. (Gallup 1989) p 68.

18. It is commonly assumed that religions are founded by visionaries and mystics. This may be true, but I am aware of historical evidence for only two such foundings. George Fox, founder of the Quakers, had a number of colorful, compelling visions that he recorded in a diary; some are quoted in (James 1902). And the Buddha was nobody until he sat around the clock in meditation and received a transcendent experience that clarified and organized his thought. It is impossible to say now what the Buddha experienced, because his original account has been filtered through too many generations of pious reporters, all of whom knew his mature teaching in full. The account in the Pali Canon (see Note 12 on page 211) claims he realized the entire *dhamma*, or teaching, one part in each watch of the night. It is more likely that a good deal of it had been prepared by study and practice in the years before, and some details might well have been worked out in later years. Be that as it may, there are parts of the account of the Buddha's enlightenment experience that seem to echo the kind of spontaneous Bliss experience described in this chapter, especially the sensation of grasping vast, cosmic knowledge.

> I recollected my manifold past lives, i.e., one birth, two ... five, ten ... fifty, a hundred, a thousand, a hundred thousand, many eons of cosmic contraction, many eons of cosmic expansion, many eons of cosmic contraction & expansion...
>
> I saw — by means of the divine eye, purified & surpassing the human — beings passing away & re-appearing, and I

discerned how they are inferior & superior, beautiful & ugly, fortunate & unfortunate in accordance with their kamma...
– Majjhima Nikaya 19 (Web Pali Canon)

19. For an interesting survey of mysticism in different religious traditions, see (Web Mysticism).

20. (Cohen and Phipps 1979).

21. (Bucke 1901).

22. (James 1902).

23. The criticisms in this paragraph are summarized from (Forman 1999).

24. in (Forman 1999).

25. (Batchelor 1998).

26. "Epistemology" is the science of knowledge, that is, the study of what are the valid sources of knowledge. Forman is proposing to extend standard epistemology with a new category, knowledge that arises only from awareness of awareness. This parallels Buddhist epistemology, which admits only sensory experience plus meditative insights (Kalupahana 1992).

27. This recalls that the Buddha was emphatic that the ultimate goal, *nibbana* or Unbinding, is beyond language, only to be perceived and never to be cast in conceptual terms:

Directly knowing Unbinding as Unbinding, [the enlightened one] does not conceive things about Unbinding, does not conceive things in Unbinding, does not conceive things coming out of Unbinding...
– Majjhima Nikaya 1 (Web Pali Canon)

28. (Watts 1960). Alan Watts experimented at length with LSD, and wrote many essays about the insights he brought back from these trips. However, the experience quoted here was a spontaneous one that came early in his life, before he had even heard of LSD.

29. I have elaborated these paragraphs from an old Buddhist teaching that I first met in (Nhat Hanh 1975).

30. Granted, that phrase "in some measure" covers up some vanishingly small relationships. The causative effect of your kitchen

table on tomorrow's Dow Jones Average is pretty weak. But hey: this is philosophy, not engineering.

31. And, did you notice? Out of the unitive insight of the Bliss experience falls a basis for a moral system.

32. In this paragraph I am summarizing comments from (Merkur 1999) and (Coxhead 1985).

33. For example, (Gopnik et al 1999) describes how babies are born recognizing faces, and knowing that faces represent other people.

34. (Maslow 1968), emphasis added.

35. See the appendix to (Maslow 1964), or chapter 6 of (Maslow 1968).

36. (Austin 1998).

37. (Austin 1998) p 18.

38. (Austin 1998) p 394.

39. (d'Aquili and Newberg 1999), later extended with more research results in (d'Aquili and Newberg 2000).

40. For a clear survey and typology of the major systems of mystical training, see (Goleman 1972).

41. (Underhill 1915).

42. Austin, in his informative chapters on the use of koans, says "a koan in itself has no literal meaning. It is an artificial concentration device...a *procedure* for exploring life's deepest existential issues."

43. For a detailed account of what happens when one pursues this type of training at length and in depth, see (Walsh 1977). When I first heard of the idea that one could observe one's own thoughts as they happened, I protested to the teacher, "But when I have a thought, the thought occupies my mind. There's no margin to stand on and think about the thought." The teacher assured me that it was possible with practice. Walsh describes what it feels like. It seems to me that this ability, if it could be verified, would be just as upsetting to constructivist and phenomenological philosophy as the ability to be aware with no subject (see "Synthesis: Awareness preceding construction" on page 88).

44. (Nhat Hanh 1975).

45. In my teens I wrote the following poem, demonstrating that I was as little into Buddhist mindfulness then as I am forty years later:

> I scrubbed the place; my mind meanwhile
> Some turgid fancy wove.
> The dishes done, the skillet still
> Sat greasy on the stove.

46. (James 1902) Lectures XI, XII, XIII.

7: Inspiring Self-Transcendence

1. (Maslow 1968).

2. (Campbell 1968).

3. (Web Carlyle)

4. (Allen 1999). In these paragraphs I am not quarrelling with Marjorie N. Allen, whose excellent book I recommend to you. Her passing comment on fallible heroes was a well-phrased version of a common attitude.

5. Linda Barnett, private communication.

6. Carew played in the Major Leagues for 18 seasons: from 1967 to 1978 with the Minnesota Twins, then the Anaheim Angels 1979-1985. He batted above .300 in fifteen seasons, and retired with a lifetime batting average of .328.

For the benefit of readers who do not know baseball well, the contest between batter and defense is so designed that it is quite difficult to hit safely. Getting a hit every four trips to the plate (.250 average) generally secures a player's job. Dropping to one hit in five tries (.200 or worse) gives a player cold sweats at night. A player who can be counted on to get a hit every third time to the plate is unusual. At midpoint of the season during which I write, of about 150 American League players having 100 at-bats or more, only 31 are batting at .300 or higher. To do it year after year, as Carew did, is phenomenal.

7. (Pirsig 1974).

8. (Pirsig 1995).

9. See (Web Pirsig) for a gateway to the many on-line Pirsig fan sites.

10. The Buddhist description of human perception agrees. (Pirsig, of course, is familiar with Buddhist thinking.) In Buddhist philosophy, the body, including the sense organs, along with everything else in the world, is categorized as "form." When forms of the environment impact on the forms of the sense organs, however, the instant result is sense-impression. Sense-impression gives rise first to feelings (emotions), second, to perception. "Mental formations," which include what modern philosophers call "intentionality," then arise based on feeling and perception. Consciousness arises last in sequence, out of the totality of mental formations. Thus the Buddha's analysis of perception also places feelings earlier in time than intentionality and conscious appreciation.

11. (Maslow 1968).

12. (Maslow 1971).

13. (Web AHP).

14. (Ellis 1989).

15. For the latest on this fast-growing field, do a web search on the phrase "philosophical counseling."

16. Well, Fabian (a pop star of my youth) comes to mind, and the Monkees. It does happen. But even those people had looks and personal style. Even the most cynical promoter couldn't make a pop star out of just anybody.

17. (Allen 1999).

8: Articulating Your Ethics

1. (Dalai Lama 1999).

2. Here's the logical argument. If I do not grant the right to seek happiness to all other beings at the same time that I claim it for myself, I open a can of worms, philosophically speaking. If I do not agree that "the right to avoid suffering and seek happiness extends to all beings," my only alternative is to assert that "the set of beings that have this right is smaller than the set of all beings." And

immediately I have to define that set; in other words, I have to specify who I think has this right and who does not. And none of the possible answers is acceptable.

One answer is "none have it, the set of beings having a right to avoid suffering is empty." That basically denies the concept of a right, and ends this discussion and the use of this ethical basis. Another answer is to say "only me, of all beings, has the right." But that is the claim of solipsism, the claim that I am the only meaningful being in the world, and Solipsism is easily discredited. (See (Web Philosophy) for an article on Solipsism with its refutations).

You can concoct an infinity of other possible answers by defining the set of privileged beings on the basis of some characteristic such as gender, color, or national origin; but of course this is exactly what is meant by bigotry. Isn't that what bigots do, define a narrow set of people who can validly avoid suffering and seek happiness, and rule that all others lack the right? The evils that arise when people define other groups as unworthy are well-known.

So if I am to claim "the pursuit of happiness" as a right for myself, the only logically acceptable position is to grant the right at least to all other human beings at the same time. The question of whether I need to extend the right to sentient beings besides humans — to all mammals? to all animals? to all non-plants? — needs a separate argument.

3. (Hicks 1925).

4. For the complete history of the 4-Way Test, see (Web Rotary).

5. (Asimov 1992).

6. *Metaphysics of Morals*, as online at (Web Kant).

7. (Sartre 1995).

8. If you don't have a Bible handy, you can read it online, see (Web Bible).

9. For example, (Cimino and Lattin 1998) quote a survey showing that only 3 in 10 "boomers" had been to church in the past week in 1996, down from 5 in 10 in 1991. A number of citations at (Web Adherents) show that from 39% to 45% of American adults will answer "yes" to the question "Have you attended a religious service

in the past week?" (The percentages are much lower in other
countries). This should not be taken to mean that this many adults
really do attend church every week. However, it does establish a
firm upper limit. Even if every person polled tells the literal truth,
less than half of Americans attend religious services weekly.

10. Does the Ninth Commandment (Exodus 20:16) refer to perjury,
or to lying in general? Anyone can be a biblical scholar with the help
of the Internet. Using the Blue Letter Bible (Web Bible) you can
display the Hebrew text of the verse, and from that display a word-
by-word translation from Strong's Concordance. The key word is
"`ed "which means "testimony, witness of people or things." This
commandment is not a general precept "tell the truth"; it says
"don't testify falsely." You can look it up.

11. (Singer 1995).

12. The idea that following the Precepts is a way of giving the gift of
safety to others is of course not my original expression; it's from the
Buddha:

> A noble disciple, abandoning the taking of life, abstains from
> taking life.
> In doing so, he gives freedom from danger,
> > freedom from animosity,
> > freedom from oppression
> to limitless numbers of beings [and]
> he gains a share in limitless freedom from danger,
> > freedom from animosity,
> > freedom from oppression.
> This is the first gift, the first great gift...
> > – Anguttara Nikaya VIII.39

The same formula is repeated for each of the precepts: by adopting
each one, the disciple gives "freedom from danger, freedom from
animosity, freedom from oppression to limitless numbers of
beings," and gains a share in the same.

9: Dancing With Mister D.

1. There is some change: books on death, dying, grief, and
bereavement have multiplied greatly in the latest decade. After I
had drafted most of this chapter, Public Broadcasting began airing
Bill Moyers' series of programs on death and end-of-life care.

American culture is paying more, and more sophisticated, attention to death as we "boomers" begin to feel the edge of death's shadow.

2. (Duda 1987).

3. Timothy Leary suggested that society encourages fear of death as a handle for political manipulation:

> Throughout history "fear of dying" has been used by priests, police, politicians and physicians to undermine individualistic thinking, to increase our dependence on authority, and to glorify victimization ... If your life was dedicated to dutifully serving the reigning religious and political authorities on behalf of the gene pool, then logically your death is the final, crowning sacrifice of your individuality. Monotheists and Marxists would all agree. (Leary 1997)

4. I met this idea (that being dead is the same state as being unborn) in Michael Shermer's fine book (Shermer 1999), although later I found that Lucretius articulated it at least two millennia earlier:

> Look back: Nothing to us was
> all forepassed eld of time the eternal,
> ere we had a birth.
> And Nature holds this like a mirror up
> of time-to-be when we are dead and gone.
> And what in there so horrible appears?
> Now what is there so sad about it all?
>
> – (Web Lucretius)

Timothy Leary, as usual, had an original slant on the same idea:

> You are alive only where your viewpoint is. What's it like, phenomenologically, to be dead? Well, it's easy to evoke an accurate sensation of this. Where are you physically, now? Let's presume for the sake of argument that you're not in Algiers. Fine, then you are, right now, dead in Algiers. You experience no input or output from there, you affect nothing. People and things there are unaware of you. You don't exist there. ... You are dead most places in the universe at this moment.
>
> – (Leary 1997)

5. Epicurus, *Letter to Monoeceus*; see (Web Epicurus). Epicurus wrote in the third century BCE. His very sensible position has been

challenged by several modern philosophers. For a sample of the arguments pro and con, see essays by Rosenberg, Nagel, and others in (Fischer 1993). The most complete analysis of Epicurus that I have seen is in (Feldman 1992). These essays, in my opinion, demonstrate how dismally far modern philosophy has drifted from any meaningful concerns of life.

Feldman and the other anti-Epicureans do not argue that a dead person feels regret or pain (or anything else); they only argue the abstract point of whether death should be considered to be bad or not; in other words, whether Epicurus was correct to say "Death, therefore, ... is nothing to us." Feldman constructs an elegant, abstruse argument showing that for a person X, a hypothetical world in which X is not dead will usually have greater value than a world in which X is dead, and therefore most Xs, in dying, lose something of value, and hence death must be bad for most Xs.

Somehow this debate is allowed to ignore the issue that X, when alive, cannot know when she will die, and so cannot form any useful concept of this loss of value; and yet when dead, X is permanently incapable of calculating the loss or regretting it. In short, it ignores Epicurus's precise point, crisply expressed as "when we are, death is not come, and when death is come, we are not." But the whole value and comfort of Epicurus's doctrine, for ordinary people's lives and well-being, lies exactly in this.

6. Most of the writers who report on NDEs emphasize positive emotions, even ecstasies, according to the survey in (Siegel 1980). However, in a more recent summary of the literature in (d'Aquili and Newberg 1999), there is mention that in recent years some investigators have begun reporting "terrifying or hellish NDEs." Even in these cases, the terror was associated with visions of an unpleasant afterlife, not with the person's physical trauma or the body's process of dying.

7. (Kluger-Bell 1998).

8. In this summary I am echoing ideas gleaned from (Parkes 1993) and, to a lesser degree, from (Epstein 1993).

9. (Parkes 1993).

10. (Shuchter and Zisook 1993).

11. (Gonda and Ruark 1984).

12. (Stearns 1984).

13. (Menten 1991).

14. In these paragraphs I am summarizing ideas that I took primarily from (Bluebond-Langner 1978), and in part from (Despelder and Strickland 1983) and (Kluger-Bell 1998).

15. (Bluebond-Langner 1978).

16. (Despelder and Strickland 1983).

17. (Field and Cassel 1997).

18. If you need to explore the option of dying at home or in hospice, see (Sankar 1999), (Duda 1987); or perform one of the following searches on the Amazon.com search page:

- Search using the two words *dying home* in the Title Words field for a list of more than 20 books including the two cited.
- Search on the title word *hospice* for books on hospice care.
- Search on the title word *caregiving* for books on caring for the sick at home.

For more immediate information on dying alternatives see the links under (Web Dying).

19. (Markin 1999).

20. Such as *The Affordable Funeral*, (Markin 1999).

21. For starting points, see (Web Funerals).

22. No matter how much you know, you will leave a funeral director's office with the drafty feeling of a shorn lamb. Each of my parents asked for, and got, the simplest possible handling: cremation with no viewing. Hence there was no coffin, no embalming, no rental for a parlor or chapel, no hearse, no procession. Both were buried in a cemetery plot that the family already owned, and burial and memorial services were arranged separately, not through the funeral home. Even so, the bill each time was nearly $2,000 (5 and 10 years ago, respectively). There was a transportation fee for collecting the body — the same that an ambulance would charge to transport a live person the same distance. And a fee for receiving a body through the mortuary doors. And a fee for preparing the body for cremation. And a fee for

the cardboard box in which the body enters the furnace. And a fee for the cremation itself, and one for the container for the ashes, and one for putting the ashes into the container. A fee for filing papers with the county and a fee for extra copies of the death certificate. And a fee that was, as near as I could tell, for nothing more than the pleasure of doing business with that company.

23. (Web Dhammapada).

24. (Clifford 1999).

25. A power of attorney is a document that gives another a person the right to act for you, for example, to sign contracts in your name. A normal power of attorney is not valid when you are unconscious, because the law assumes that if you could speak, you might want to revoke it. A "durable" power of attorney remains in force even if you are incapacitated. An elderly person who wants to pass control of financial affairs to a trusted younger relative would execute a durable power of attorney for financial affairs, so the younger person can pay bills and so forth even if the older one becomes demented. The durable power of attorney for health care, sometimes called a "medical proxy," is specifically designed to delegate the power to act for you in medical matters.

26. My father died in San Jose, California, and his body was cremated there. However, his ashes were to be buried in the family plot a thousand miles away. I obsessed a bit about how to transport the ashes on the airline trip. I felt I had to hand-carry them; the idea of sending my father in the luggage, and possibly having the luggage go missing, was not attractive. I prepared myself with copies of the death certificate and an official form giving permission to transport human remains out of the state. I carried the papers in a shoulder bag with the ashes. The ashes were in a plain bronze box in a red velvet sack.

Came the moment when I had to place the bag on the belt of the X-ray machine at the airport. Of course, the metal box produced an opaque black image on the screen, and the security guards asked to inspect the bag. I exposed the red velvet bag and the bronze box, and began to unfold the papers, saying something about "...death certificate right here..." I shan't forget the look of shock that came over the head guard's face when he realized that he was handling a cremation urn. He couldn't get my bag zipped up fast enough; he might have been handling radioactive waste. "Sorry, sorry, go right ahead," and he breathlessly shooed me out of the security zone.

On the plane ride I thought about this. The guard's attitude toward death and human remains had led him into a shocking breach of airport security. There could have been two kilos of anything in that metal box, heroin, a gun, explosives. The guard should have inspected the documentation carefully, perhaps even called the mortuary. But he let his fear of death stampede him into a bad decision.

27. I and my wife have contracted with a California organization, the Neptune Society. A single contract for each of us provides for collecting the body, cremating it, and scattering the ashes at sea. The survivors only need to make one phone call, and will never deal with a funeral home. Similar organizations exist in other states.

28. (Leary 1997).

29. For example, (Clifford 1999).

30. Available from, for example, (Web Nolo).

31. My wife and I went through the work of setting up a probate-avoiding Living Trust in 1998, along with all the other documents mentioned in this section. The whole business took roughly thirty hours of work spread over a month. One time-consuming part was making two trips to the county courthouse to change the deed of our home from ourselves as joint tenants to our Trust. Other time was spent in locating records, making trips to a lawyer's office, and so on.

10: Being Happy

1. My introduction to the research on happiness was the clear summary in chapter 9 of (Baumeister 1991). Baumeister's thorough bibliography guided my subsequent reading. David Myers's readable, entertaining survey (Myers 1992) added detail and discussion. Seligman concentrates on the issues of optimism and personal control in (Seligman 1990). These writers agree in the interpretation of the research that I've summarized in the first part of this chapter. Freedman's earlier work (Freedman 1978), although it did not use the same rigorous random selection of other studies, came to generally similar conclusions.

2. (Ayton 2000).

3. (Myers 1992).

4. (Bradburn 1969).

5. (Costa and McCrae 1980).

6. (Brickman and Coates 1978).

7. (Costa et. al. 1987).

8. (Campbell 1981).

9. (Myers 1992).

10. (Seligman 1990).

11. Both I and my wife took Seligman's test and we produced very similar scores. However, our scores revealed a personality type that Seligman does not discuss in his book (Seligman 1990). It seems that we are both realists on both sides of the coin. We tend to see *all* events, good ones and bad ones alike, as temporary, limited, and external. This makes us, by Seligman's measurement, optimists regarding bad events, but strong pessimists as regards good ones. We can be resilient in adversity, but we do not have much faith in the outcome of our efforts.

12. (Freedman 1978). Although Freeman sounds very certain of his conclusions, there are later studies that contradict him. A recent survey says "Many studies have shown that religiously committed people tend to report greater subjective well-being" (Bergin and Richards 2000). Perhaps different questions were asked; for example, there may be a difference between one survey's definition of "religiously committed" and another's "beliefs regarding the existence of God." Problems of definition are rife in this area of research.

13. (Myers 1992).

14. It's worth noting that there are severe traumas that have lasting effects. Adaptation level theory applies to incremental changes within normal ranges. Just as looking at the sun can permanently scar the retina, or too loud a noise causes deafness, we don't "adapt" to the experience of rape, or combat, or a concentration camp.

15. (Brickman and Campbell 1971).

16. You can do your own comparisons of national happiness using the online database at (Web Happiness). The numbers from national surveys are available for downloading free.

17. (Campbell 1981).

18. (Myers 1992).

19. These suggestions are selected from among suggestions in the following sources: (Myers 1992), (Myers 1993), (Psychology 1994), (Seligman 1990) and (Silver 1967). For more suggestions, or for a different explanation of their benefits, refer to these sources, which should be in any library.

20. Studying and collecting is a route that many young people take toward self-esteem. At a certain point in adolescence, many people become almost driven to make themselves expert in something. In the first part of the last century it was train-spotting, obsessively collecting sightings of every type of locomotive. For many males it is collecting sports statistics, especially baseball statistics. Mastery of the world of details embodied in role-playing games or the strategies of video games does it for some. Others make themselves expert about a particular performer or group. Like many boys of the 1950s, I made myself an expert in automobile technology, and could explain in tedious detail what it meant that an engine was ported, stroked, or relieved. Such knowledge really has no value in itself, and the collectors might even admit as much if you have the bad taste to pin them down on the subject. What matters is being able to collect a lot of data and hold it in mind, and how that mastery makes you feel about yourself.

21. See Seligman's book (Seligman 1990) for a self-test and an introduction to a do-it-yourself approach to cognitive therapy. See (Web Cognitive Therapy) for online links.

22. (Nhat Hanh 1998).

23. From *Walden* (Web Thoreau).

24. If you can tolerate the inherent contradiction of researching "simplicity" with your computer, you can gain quick access to these allies from the sources listed under (Web Simplicity).

25. (Butler 1999).

11: Being Content

1. (Bergin and Richards 2000).

2. I swear, I wrote most of the following paragraphs before reading Epictetus or Epicurus. But since it hews so close to the Epicurean line, I daren't take credit for original thought. I absorbed these ideas from many sources.

3. (Web Epictetus).

4. Professional sports also base their popularity on getting people emotionally involved in contests that they cannot personally influence. Being a fan of a losing team is quite painful, and clearly demonstrates the negative power of attachment. Think about it: a large, wealthy, and powerful industry — the whole apparatus of professional and collegiate sports promotion, and the advertisers who use sports as a medium — is founded on the idea of getting you to abandon detachment and commit yourself to caring about their product.

5. I had a chance to test this in practice when, on the morning of September 11, 2001 I sat in my bathrobe and watched all the events of that day unfold on TV. One of the many thoughts that passed through my mind that morning was, "Well, here's a perfect example of an event that is out of my control." Knowing that made it possible to recognize what was going on, I think, with less of that common, shell-shocked reaction, "I can't believe it's really happening."

6. Recently there has been research to support this claim. (It's wonderful when modern research supports ancient philosophy.) Richards and Gross showed emotionally unpleasant pictures to two groups of people. One group was told to suppress any display of emotions while they watched. The other group was told to "view these slides with the detached interest of a medical professional." Not only did the detached group report less emotional distress afterward, they also retained better verbal and nonverbal recall of the experience than did the group who were trying only to suppress their emotions (Richards and Gross 2000).

7. Results summarized from the research abstracts at (Web Forgiveness). Luskin has also published a book (Luskin 2001).

References

Recommended Books

I heartily recommend the following books as ways to go deeper into subjects that I've barely scratched. In order by chapter:

1. Benefits of a Religious Practice.

   Varieties of Religious Experience (James 1902) is essential to anyone who wants to understand the range of meanings that religion can have; it is full of first-person experiences as well as wise commentary by James. The full text is online as (Web James). *How We Believe* (Shermer 1999) is a modern exploration of why belief is so powerful.

   Thought Contagion (Lynch 1996) is a wide-ranging review of the possible applications of the concept of the meme. Packed full of intriguing ideas, many highly debatable.

2. Finding Validity.

   The Sacred Depths of Nature (Goodenough 1998) and *The Fermenting Universe* (Malville 1981) are two well-written, readable, sometimes lyrical reflections on the depth and wonder to be found in the world through science.

   Finding Darwin's God (Miller 1999) has detailed arguments against Creationism in all its various forms. *Darwin's Dangerous Idea* (Dennet 1996) is an intellectual's tour of the breadth of the idea so simply expressed as "evolution by natural selection" — a phrase that rivals $E=MC^2$ for the compression of the greatest meaning into the fewest symbols.

   Age of Reason (Paine 1794) is a mordant critique of organized religion and an exposition of Deism by one of the greatest writers in an age of great writers. Gain heart from reading Paine's thunderous prose, preferably aloud.

3. Finding Community.

   Connect (Hallowell 1999) is a therapist's eloquent explanation of why human connections are so important to mental and physical health. For an enthusiastic popular treatment of the research on health and human connections, with many citations, see Dean Ornish's *Love & Survival* (Ornish 1998).

4. Practicing Contemplation and Tranquility.

Mindfulness in Plain English (Gunaratana 1993) is a detailed, practical introduction to mindfulness meditation, without any trace of supernaturalism. An earlier edition can be read online at (Web Gunaratana).

Full Catastrophe Living (Kabat-Zinn 1990) describes the use of meditation in a clinical setting, for pain and stress relief, with examples and exercises.

A Heart as Wide as the World (Salzberg 1997) goes in detail into the methods and benefits of metta practice.

5. Using Ritual.

New Traditions (Lieberman 1991) is a wonderful compilation of the experiences of real people who invented traditions to serve the needs of singles, families, single parents and neighborhoods. *From Beginning to End* (Fulghum 1995) is a warm and folksy read, and very good on wedding rituals. *The Joy of Ritual* (Biziou 1999), despite some some new-age flakiness, has good ideas for designing rituals.

6. Pursuing Bliss.

The Mystical Mind (d'Aquili and Newberg 1999) presents a detailed, credible model for how the Bliss experience might work, based in neuroanatomy.

Zen and the Brain (Austin 1998) contains several good books interwoven: One is a detailed, well-written tour of the brain and what is known of the function of each of its parts; another is a layman's study of Zen meditative practices; a third is a doctor's survey of different methods of Bliss induction, with special attention to the use of mind-altering drugs.

Cosmic Consciousness (Bucke 1901) is *not* recommended. Although a citation to this pioneering work is obligatory in any work on mysticism, the book has no modern relevance. The text reveals Dr. Bucke as an eccentric, a naive racist, and charmingly innocent of any concept of statistical rigor.

7. Inspiring Self-Transcendence.

What Are Little Girls Made Of? (Allen 1999) has capsule reviews of many current and classic children's books provide a useful resource for any parent who wants to build up a stock of hero material.

Immigrant American Women Role Models (Reynolds 1997) has short biographies of fifteen interesting women, clearly written in matter-of-fact style.

Shambhala (Trungpa 1988) is an inspiring, poetic, yet purely secular invocation to reach for the best you can find within yourself. It calls you to be a "warrior," not in an aggressive sense but in the sense of one who fears nothing and acts with decision and forethought.

8. Articulating Your Ethics.

Ethics for the New Millennium (Dalai Lama 1999) contains an eloquent argument for the need of a secular ethical system that can be respected world-wide. It explores the practical reasons why one needs to rid oneself of anger and replace it with compassion.

9. Dancing With Mister D.

Living Through Personal Crisis (Stearns 1984) is a deservedly popular manual on the experience of bereavement. But don't give a copy to a bereaved person; the bereaved lack the patience to read. Read it yourself in order to get insight and practical knowledge on how to be genuinely helpful.

Dying at Home (Sankar 1999) is a comprehensive guidebook for home care of the dying.

The Affordable Funeral (Markin 1999) is a detailed consumer's guide to purchasing funerary services. Markin explains industry jargon and reveals the marketing tricks in a style that is crisp, bordering on irascible.

Estate Planning Basics (Clifford 1999) explains in lucid and reassuring style the options of preserving and passing on an estate.

10. Being Happy.

The Pursuit of Happiness (Myers 1992) is a readable, entertaining survey of the research on happiness.

Learned Optimism (Seligman 1990) goes at length into the many effects of cognitive style (optimistic versus pessimistic) on every part of life. *A Guide to Personal Happiness* (Ellis and Becker 1986) is a brisk introduction to Rational Emotive Behavior Therapy.

In addition to these, the online resources listed under (Web Bible) and (Web Pali Canon) are endlessly useful as well as entertaining.

Print References

Allen 1999

Allen, Marjorie N. *What Are Little Girls Made Of? A Guide to Female Role Models in Children's Books*. Facts On File, 1999 (ISBN 0-8160-3673-X).

Anderson 1991

Anderson, Patricia. *Affairs in Order: A complete resource guide to death and dying*. Macmillan Publishing Company, 1991 (ISBN 0-02-501991-0).

d'Aquili and Newberg 1999

d'Aquili, Eugene G. and Andrew B. Newberg. *The Mystical Mind: Probing the Biology of Religious Experience*. Fortress Press, 1999 (ISBN 0-8006-3163-3).

d'Aquili and Newberg 2000

d'Aquili, Eugene G. and Andrew B. Newberg. Why God Won't Go Away: Brain science and the biology of belief.Ballantine Books, 2001 (ISBN 0345440331).

Asimov 1992

Asimov, Isaac. *Asimov's Guide to the Bible: The Old and New Testaments*. Wings Books 1992 (ISBN 051734582X).

Asimov 1994

Asimov, Isaac. *I. Asimov: A Memoir*. Bantam Books, 1994 (ISBN 055356997).

Austin 1998

James H. Austin, MD. *Zen and the Brain: Toward an Understanding of Meditation and Consciousness*. The MIT Press, 1998 (ISBN 0-262-0116406).

Ayton 2000

Ayton, Peter. "If you're happy and you know it..." *New Scientist* 9/2/2000 p45.

Banerjee 1975

Banerjee, Nikunja Bihari. The Spirit of Indian Philosophy. Curzon Press,1975 (no ISBN).

Batchelor 1998

Batchelor, Stephen. "Toward a Culture of Awakening." Talk given for the Sati Center in Berkeley, California, 5/13/1998.

Baumeister 1991

Baumeister, Roy F. *Meanings of Life*. The Guildford Press, 1991 (ISBN 0-89862-531-9).

Beck and Metrick   Beck, Renee and Sydney Barbara Metrick. *The Art of*
1990   *Ritual: A Guide to Creating and Performing Your Own*
                    Rituals for Growth and Change. Celestial Arts, 1990
                    (ISBN 0-89087-582-0).

Benson 1975   Benson, Dr. Herbert. *The Relaxation Response.* Reissued
                    by HARPE, 1990 (ISBN 0380006766).

Bergin and   Bergin, Allen E. and P. Scott Richards. "Religious
Richards 2000   Values and Mental Health" in *Encyclopedia of*
                    Psychology vol 7 p59-62. Oxford University Press, 2000
                    (ISBN 1-55798-187-6).

Berlin and   Berlin, Isaiah and Ramn Jahanbegloo. *Conversations*
Jahanbegloo 1992   *With Isaiah Berlin.* P. Halban, 1992 (no ISBN).

Biziou 1999   Biziou, Barbara. *The Joy of Ritual: Spiritual Recipes to*
                    Celebrate Milestones, Ease Transitions, and Make Every
                    Day Sacred. Golden Books Publishg Co, 1999 (ISBN 1-
                    58348-001-5).

Blackmore and   Blackmore, Susan and Richard Dawkins. *The Meme*
Dawkins 1999   *Machine.* Oxford University Press, 1999 (ISBN
                    0198503652).

Bluebond-   Bluebond-Langner, Myra. *The Private Worlds of Dying*
Langner 1978   *Children.* Princeton University Press, 1978 (ISBN
                    0691028206).

Bradburn 1969   Bradburn, Norman M. *The structure of Psychological*
                    Wellbeing. Aldine Publishing Co., 1969 (no ISBN).

Brickman and   Brickman, Philip and Donald T. Campbell. "Hedonic
Campbell 1971   relativism and the good society" in: Appley, M.H.
                    (ed). *Adaptation-Level Theory: A symposium.* Academic
                    Press, 1971 (no ISBN).

Brickman and   Brickman, Philip and Dan Coates. "Lottery winners
Coates 1978   and accident victims: is happiness relative?" *Journal of*
                    Personality and Social Psychology vol 36 no 8 p917-927.

Bucke 1901   Bucke, Richard Maurice, M.D. *Cosmic Consciousness: A*
                    Study in the Evolution of the Human Mind. E. P. Dutton
                    and Co., 1901, 1923 (no ISBN).

Burnham 1997   Burnham, Sophy. *The Ecstatic Journey.* Ballantine
                    Books, 1997 (ISBN 0-345-42479-4).

Butler 1999   Butler, Katy. "The Great Boomer Bust." Essay read
                    during the program "Giving Thanks," produced by
                    Minnesota Public Radio, broadcast on National Public
                    Radio Thanksgiving Day, 1999.

de Camp and de
Camp 1966

de Camp, L. Sprague and Catherine de Camp. *Spirits Stars and Spells: the Profits and Perils of Magic.* Canaveral Press, 1966 (no ISBN), out of print. Republished by Owlswick Press, 1981 (ISBN 0913896179), also out of print.

Campbell 1968

Campbell, Joseph. *The Hero with a Thousand Faces* (2nd ed). Princeton University Press,1968 (ISBN 0-691-09743-7).

Campbell 1981

Campbell, Angus. *The Sense of Well-Being in America.* McGraw-Hill, 1981 (ISBN 0-07-009683-X).

Camus 1955

Camus, Albert. "The Myth of Sisyphus" in: O'Brien, Justin (tr). *The Myth of Sisyphus and other essays.* Vintage Books, 1991 (ISBN 0-679-73373-6).

Carrington 1977

Carrington, Patricia, Ph.D. *Freedom in Meditation.* Anchor Press/Doubleday, 1977 (ISBN 0-385-11392-7).

Cimino and
Lattin 1998

Cimino, Richard P. and Don Lattin. *Shopping for Faith: American religion in the new millennium.* Jossey-Bass Inc., 1998 (ISBN 0-7879-4170-0).

Clarke 1999

Clarke, Arthur C. *Greetings, Carbon-Based Bipeds! Collected Essays 1934-1998.* St. Martin's Press, 1999 (ISBN 0312267452).

Clifford 1999

Clifford, Attorney Denis. *Estate Planning Basics: What you need to know and nothing more.* Nolo Press, 1999 (ISBN 0-87337-535-1).

Climacus 1982

Climacus, St. John. *The Ladder of Divine Ascent.* Colm Luibheid and Norman Russell (trs). Paulist Press, 1982 (ISBN 0809123304).

Cohen and
Phipps 1979

Cohen, John M. and John-Francis Phipps. *The Common Experience.* St. Martin's Press, 1979 (ISBN 0-312-15271-X).

Cohen et. al. 1997

Cohen, et. al. "Social ties and susceptibility to the common cold." JAMA, vol 277 no 24.

Costa et. al. 1987

Costa, P., R. McCrae and A. Zonderman. "Environmental and dispositional influences on well-being: Longitudinal follow-up of an American national sample." *British Journal of Psychology* vol 78 p299-306.

Costa and
McCrae 1980

Costa, P. and R. McCrae. "Influence of extraversion and neuroticism on subjective well-being: happy and unhappy people." *Journal of Personality and Social Psychology* vol 38 no 4 p668-678.

Coxhead 1985	Coxhead, Nona. *The Relevance of Bliss: A Contemporary Exploration of Mystic Experience*. St. Martin's Press, 1985 (ISBN 0-312-67055-9).
Dalai Lama 1999	His Holiness the Dalai Lama. *Ethics for the New Millenium*. Riverhead Books, 1999 (ISBN 1-57322-025-6).
Dawkins 1976	Dawkins, Richard. *The Selfish Gene*. Oxford University Press, 1990 (ISBN 0192860925).
Dennet 1996	Dennet, Daniel. *Darwin's Dangerous Idea*. Touchstone Books, 1996 (ISBN 068482471X).
Despelder and Strickland 1983	DeSpelder, Lynne Ann and Albert Lee Strickland. *The Last Dance: Encountering death and dying*. Mayfield Publishing Company, 1983 (ISBN 0-887484-535-1).
Duda 1987	Duda, Deborah. *Coming Home: a guide to dying at home and with dignity*. Aurora Press, 1987 (ISBN 0-943358-31-0).
Ellis and Becker 1986	Ellis, Albert and Irving Becker. *A Guide to Personal Happiness*. Wilshire Book Company, 1986 (ISBN 0879803959).
Ellis 1989	Ellis, Albert. *Why Some Therapies Don't Work: The Dangers of Transpersonal Psychology*. Prometheus Books, 1989 (ISBN 0879754710).
Epstein 1993	Epstein, Seymour. "Bereavement from the perspective of cognitive-experiential self-theory" in: (Stroebe et al 1993).
Fein 1997	Fein, Esther B. "For lost pregnancies, new rites of mourning." *New York Times* 1/25/97.
Feynman 1999	Feynman, Richard P. *The Pleasure of Finding Things Out*. (ed. Jeffrey Robbins) Perseus Publishing, 1999 (ISBN 0-7382-0349-1).
Feldman 1992	Feldman, Fred. *Confrontations with the Reaper: A philosophical study of the nature and value of death*. Oxford University Press, 1992 (ISBN 0-19-508928-6).
Field and Cassel 1997	Field, Marilyn J. and Christine K. Cassel (eds). *Approaching Death: improving care at the end of life* (report by the Committee on Care at the End of Life, Division of Health Care Services, Institute of Medicine). National Academy Press, 1997 (ISBN 0-309-06372-8).

Fischer 1993   Fischer, John Martin, ed. *The Metaphysics of Death.*
                    Stanford University Press, 1993 (ISBN 0-8047-2046-0).

Forman 1999   Forman, Robert K. C. *Mysticism, Mind, Consciousness.*
                    State University of New York Press, 1999 (ISBN 0-
                    7914-4169-5).

Freedman 1978   Freedman, Jonathan L. *Happy People: What happiness is,
                    who has it, and why.* Harcourt Brace Jovanovich, 1978
                    (ISBN 0-15-138476-2).

Fulghum 1995   Fulghum, Robert. *From Beginning to End: The Rituals of
                    Our Lives.* Ivy Books, 1995 (ISBN 0-8041-1114-6).

Gallup 1989   Gallup, George Jr. and Jim Castelli. *The People's
                    Religion: American Faith in the 90's.* Macmillan
                    Publishing Company, 1989 (ISBN 0-02-542381-9).

Gardner 1996   Gardner, Martin. "The Mystery of Free Will" in: *The
                    Night Is Large: Collected Essays 1938-1995.* St. Martin's
                    Press ,1996 (ISBN 0312-169949-3).

Gardner 1997   Gardner, Martin. "Notes of a Fringe-Watcher."
                    Skeptical Inquirer Nov-Dec 1997.

Goleman 1972   Goleman, Daniel. "The Buddha on meditation and
                    states of consciousness, Part II: A typology of
                    meditation techniques." *Journal of Transpersonal
                    Psychology* vol 4 no 2.

Gonda and Ruark   Gonda, Thomas Andrew M.D. and John Edward
1984   Ruark, M.D. *Dying Dignified: The health professional's
                    guide to care.* Addison-Wesley Publishing Company,
                    1984 (ISBN 0-201-10603-5).

Goodenough   Goodenough, Ursula. *The Sacred Depths of Nature.*
1998   Oxford Univ Press, 1998 (ISBN 0195126130).

Goodstein 1999   Goodstein, Laurie. "Sense of resignation as horror
                    wears off." copyright NY Times, printed in the *San
                    Jose Mercury News* 9/18/1999.

Gopnik et al 1999   Gopnik, Alison, Andrew Meltzoff, and Patricia Kuhl.
                    *The Scientist in the Crib: Minds, brains, and how children
                    learn.* William Morrow & Co, 1999 (ISBN 0688159885).

Gunaratana 1993   Gunaratana, the Venerable Henepola. *Mindfulness in
                    Plain English.* Wisdom Publications, 1993 (ISBN
                    0861710649).

Hallowell 1999   Hallowell, Edward M. M.D. *Connect: 12 vital ties that
                    open your heart, lengthen your life, and deepen your soul.*
                    Pantheon Books, 1999 (ISBN 0-375-40357-4).

Hardy 1979   Hardy, Alister Clavering. *The Spiritual Nature of Man: A Study of Contemporary Religious Experience.* Clarendon Press, 1979 (ISBN 019-824618-3).

Hay 1982   Hay, David. *Exploring Inner Space; Scientists and Religious Experience.* Penguin Books, 1982 (no ISBN).

Hay and Morisy   Hay, David and Ann Morisy. "Reports of esctatic (*sic*),
1978   paranormal, or religious experience in Great Britain and the United States — a comparison of trends." *Journal for the Scientific Study of Religion* vol 17 p255-268.

Heinrich 1994   Heinrich, Bernd. *A Year in the Maine Woods.* Perseus Books, 1994 (ISBN 0-201-48939-2).

Hicks 1925   Hicks, R. D. M.A. (tr). *Diogenes Laertius: Lives of the Eminent Philosophers.* Harvard University Press 1925, 1980 (ISBN 0-674-99203-2)

Hofstadter 1998   Hofstadter, Douglas R. *Le Ton Beau De Marot: In Praise of the Music of Language.* Basic Books, 1998 (ISBN 0465086454).

James 1902   James, William. *The Varieties of Religious Experience: a Study in Human Nature.* Modern Library, 1994 (ISBN 0679600752).

Johnson 1959   Johnson, Raynor C. *Watcher on the Hills: A study of some mystical experiences of ordinary people.* Harper & Brothers Publishers, 1959 (no ISBN).

Kabat-Zinn 1990   Kabat-Zinn, John. *Full Catastrophe Living.* Bantam Doubleday Dell, 1990 (ISBN 0-385-30312-2).

Kalupahana 1992   Kalupahana, David J. *A History of Buddhist Philosophy.* University of Hawaii Press, 1992 (ISBN 0824813847).

Kato 1998   Kato, Donna. "Rites of passage celebrating and demystifying menstruation — a biological milestone for girls." *San Jose Mercury News* 4/28/1998.

Kenoyer 1999   Kenoyer, Jonathan Mark (Director of the Harappa Archeological Research Project). "The Origins and Decline of the Indus Valley Civilization." Talk presented at Stanford University, broadcast on the Stanford University cable channel 8/30/1999.

Kluger-Bell 1998 Kluger-Bell, Kim. *Unspeakable Losses: understanding the experience of pregnancy loss, miscarriage, and abortion.* W.W. Norton & Company Inc., 1998 (ISBN 0-393-14572-2).

Laski 1962   Laski, Marghanita. *EAcstacy: A Study of some Secular and Religious Experiences.* Indiana University Press, 1962 (No ISBN).

Leary 1997   Leary, Timothy, with R.U. Sirius. *Design for Dying.* HarperCollins, 1997 (ISBN 0-06-018700-X).

Lieberman 1991   Lieberman, Susan Abel. *New Traditions: Redefining Celebrations for Today's Family.* Farrar, Straus and Giroux, 1991 (ISBN 0374522626).

Luskin 2001   Luskin, Frederic, PhD. *Forgive for Good.* HarperSanFrancisco 2001; ISBN 0062517201.

Lynch 1996   Lynch, Aaron. *Thought Contagion.* Basic Books, 1996 (ISBN 0-465-08466-4).

Malville 1981   Malville, J.McKim. *The Fermenting Universe: Myths of Eternal Change.* The Seabury Press, NY 1981; ISBN 0-8064-2345-8.

Markin 1999   Markin, R. E. *The Affordable Funeral: Going in style, not in debt* (2nd ed). F. Hooker Press, 1999 (ISBN 0961522348). See (Web Funerals) for the URL of an online version.

Maslow 1964   Maslow, Abraham H. *Religions, Values, and Peak-Experiences.* Ohio State University Press, 1964 (no ISBN). (Currently reprinted by Viking Press as ISBN 0140194878)

Maslow 1968   Maslow, Abraham H. *Toward a Psychology of Being, 2nd Edn.* D. Van Nostrand Company 1968 (no ISBN). (Third edn. currently in print by John Wiley & Sons as ISBN 0471293091).

Maslow 1971   Maslow, Abraham H. *The Farther Reaches of Human Nature.* The Viking Press, 1971 (no ISBN). (Currently in print by Peter Smith Publisher as ISBN 0844660698).

Matthews et. al.   Matthews et. al. "Religious Commitment and Health
1998   Status: A Review of the Research and Implications for Family Medicine." *Archives of Family Medicine* vol 7 no 2 (March/April 1998).

Menten 1991   Menten, Ted. *Gentle Closings: How to say goodby to someone you love.* Running Press, 1991 (ISBN 1-56138-004-0).

Merkur 1999   Merkur, Dan. *Mystical Moments and Unitive Thinking.*
                   State University of New York Press, 1999 (ISBN 0-
                   7914-4064-8).

Miller 1999   Miller, Kenneth R. *Finding Darwin's God: A scientist's
                   search for common ground between God and evolution.*
                   HarperCollins, 1999 (ISBN 0060175931).

Myers 1992   Myers, David G. Ph.D. *The Pursuit of Happiness: Who is
                   happy—and why.*
                   William Morrow and Company, Inc., 1992 (ISBN 0-
                   688-10550-5).

Myers 1993   Myers, David G. Ph.D. "Pursuing happiness: where to
                   look, where not to look." *Psychology Today* vol 26 no 4.

Nhat Hanh 1975   Nhat Hanh, Thich. *The Miracle of Mindfulness* (revised
                   edn). Beacon Press, 1975 (ISBN 0807012017).

Nhat Hanh 1998   Nhat Hanh, Thich. The Heart of the Buddha's
                   Teaching. Broadway Books, 1998 (ISBN 0-7679-0369-
                   2).

Ornish 1998   Ornish, Dean, M.D. *Love & Survival: The scientific basis
                   for the healing power of intimacy.* Harpercollins, 1998
                   (ISBN 0060930209).

Paine 1794   Paine, Thomas. *Age of Reason.* Available in editions
                   from several publishers, e.g. Prometheus Books (ISBN
                   0879752734).

Parkes 1993   Parkes, Colin Murray. "Bereavement as a psychosocial
                   transition: Processes of adaptation to change." In:
                   (Stroebe et al 1993).

Pirsig 1974   Pirsig, Robert M. *Zen and the Art of Motorcycle
                   Maintenance: An inquiry into values.* William Morrow &
                   Co., 1974 (ISBN 0688002307).

Pirsig 1995   Pirsig, Robert M. "Subjects, Objects, Data and Values."
                   Presented to the Einstein Meets Magritte Conference,
                   Brussels, 5/1995. Full text available from (Web Pirsig).

Psychology 1994   (no byline) "The road to happiness." *Psychology Today*
                   vol 27 no 4.

Resnick et. al.   Resnick et. al. "Protecting adolescents from harm:
1997   findings from the National Longitudinal Study on
                   Adolescent Health." *Journal of the American Medical
                   Association* vol 278 no 10.

Reynolds 1997   Reynolds, Moira Davison. *Immigrant American Women Role Models: Fifteen Inspiring Biographies 1850-1950.* McFarland & Company, 1997 (ISBN 0786404094).

Richards and   Richards, Jane M. and James J. Gross. "Emotion
Gross 2000   Regulation and Memory: the cognitive costs of keeping one's cool." Journal of Personality and Social Psychology vol 79 no 3 p410-424. (Also at *www.apa.org/journals/psp/psp793410.html*)

Rodin and   Rodin, J. and E. Langer. "Long-term effects of a
Langer 1977   control-relevant intervention with the institutionalized aged." *Journal of Personality and Social Psychology,* vol 35 p897-902. Summarized in (Kabat-Zinn 1990).

Rokeach 1960   Rokeach, Milton. *The Open and Closed Mind.* Basic Books, 1960 (no ISBN).

Sagan 1996   Sagan, Carl. "In the valley of the shadow." *Parade* magazine, 3/10/1996.

Salzberg 1997   Salzberg, Sharon. *A Heart As Wide As the World : Living with mindfulness, wisdom, and compassion.* Shambhala Publications, 1997 (ISBN 1570623406).

Sankar 1999   Sankar, Andrea. *Dying at Home: A family guide for caregiving.* Johns Hopkins University Press, 1999 (ISBN 0-8018-6203-5).

Sartre 1995   Sartre, Jean-Paul. "Existentialism" in: Frechtman, Bernard (tr). *Existentialism and Human Emotions,* Carol Publishing Group, 1995 (ISBN 0-8065-0902-3).

Shermer 1999   Shermer, Michael. *How We Believe: The search for god in the age of science.* W. H. Freeman and Company, 1999 (ISBN 0-7167-3561-X).

Seligman 1990   Seligman, Martin E. P. *Learned optimism.* Alfred A. Knopf, 1990 (ISBN 0-394-57915-1).

Shuchter and   Shuchter, Stephen R. and Signey Zisook. "The course
Zisook 1993   of normal grief." In (Stroebe et al 1993)

Siegel 1980   Ronald K. Siegel. "The psychology of life after death." *American Psychologist*, vol 35 no 10 p911-925.

Silver 1967   Silver, Rabbi Samuel M. *How to enjoy this moment.* Trident Press, 1967 (no ISBN).

Singer 1995   Singer, Peter. *How Are We to Live? Ethics in an age of self-interest.* Prometheus Books, 1995 (ISBN 0-87975-966-6).

Smart 1976	Smart, Ninian. *The Religious Experience of Mankind.* Charles Scribner's Sons, 1976 (ISBN 0684146479).
Smyth et.al. 1999	Smyth, J.M., et.al. "Effects of writing about stressful experience on symptom reduction in patients with asthma and rheumatoid arthritis." *Journal of the American Medical Association* vol 281 p1304-1309. Summarized in *Mind/Body Health Newsletter*, vol VIII no 3.
Stearns 1984	Stearns, Ann Kaiser. *Living Through Personal Crisis.* Ballantine Books, 1984 (ISBN 0-3445-32293-2).
Stroebe et al 1993	Stroebe, Margaret S., Wolfgang Stroebe and Robert O. Hansson. *Handbook of Bereavement.* Cambridge University Press, 1993 (ISBN 0-521-39315-9).
Thomas and Cooper 1980	Thomas, L. Eugene and Pamela E. Cooper. "Incidence and psychological correlates of intense spiritual experiences." *Journal of Transpersonal Psychology* vol 12 no 1 p75.
Trungpa 1988	Trungpa, Chogyam. *Shambhala: The Sacred Path of the Warrior.* Shambhala Publications, Inc., 1988 (ISBN 0-87773-264-7).
Underhill 1915	Underhill, Evelyn. *Practical Mysticism.* E.P. Dutton, 1915 (no ISBN). (Currently in print by Dover Publications as ISBN 0486409597).
Walsh 1977	Walsh, Roger. "Initial meditative experiences, Part I." *Journal of Transpersonal Psychology* vol 9 no 2 p 151
Watts 1960	Watts, Alan. *This is IT and other essays.* Pantheon Books, 1960 (no ISBN). (Currently in print by Random House as ISBN 0394719042).
Williams 1989	Williams, Redford. "The trusting heart." *Psychology Today* vol 23 no 1.
Williams 1999	Williams, Redford. "Social Ties and Health." *Harvard Mental Health Letter* vol 15 no 10.
Williams and Marshall 1976	Williams, Allen and William Marshall. *The Man Who Gave the Beatles Away.* Ballantine Books, 1975 (ISBN 0345-27074-6).

Internet Resources

As any internet user knows, web addresses change all the time. These were checked just before press time, but see this book's home page at *www.tassos-oak.com* for the latest, and for additional links of interest.

Web Adherents   A rich compendium of statistics on religious membership and attendance, covering most countries and all religions, assembled by Preston Hunter:
http://www.adherents.com/

Web AHP   The web presence of the Association for Humanistic Psychology, containing historical and philosophical overview papers, a list of practitioners, and an annotated bibliography:
http://ahpweb.org/

Web Bible   The complete text of the Bible is available at several sites. One of the most useful is the Blue Letter Bible, which provides word-by-word translation to Greek and Hebrew as well as various commentaries.
http://www.blueletterbible.org/
The Bible Browser provided by the Scholarly Technology Group at Brown University offers an advanced search engine for access to the Bible in several translations:
http://www.stg.brown.edu/webs/bible_browser/

Web Book Search   There are several used-book search engines, but BookFinder is a meta-search engine that interrogates several others:
http://www.bookfinder.com

Web Carlyle   Carlyle, Thomas P. *Heroes and Hero Worship*. Quotes taken from the online text of the *Complete Works* available from Project Gutenburg:
http://www.gutenberg.net/index.html

Web Catholic Enc.   The Catholic Encyclopedia is online at:
http://www.knight.org/advent/cathen/

Web Cognitive Therapy   The International Association for Cognitive Psychotherapy:
http://iacp.asu.edu
The Albert Ellis Institute supports Rational Emotive Behavior Therapy with online articles and a catalog of books and tapes at:
http://www.rebt.org/

Web Dhammapada	The *Dhammapada*, an ancient collection of poetic aphorisms illuminating aspects of the Buddha's teachings, is available at: *http://www.accesstoinsight.org/canon/khuddaka/dhp/index.html*
Web Dostoevsky	The text of the Constance Garnett translation of Dostoevsky's *Brothers Karamazov* can be found at the English Server at the University of Washington: *http://www.eserver.org/fiction*
Web Dying	A good starting point for an Internet exploration of dying, with many useful articles and links, is: *http://dying.about.com/health/dying/* Other useful starting points include: *http://www.nlm.nih.gov/medlineplus/deathanddying.html* *http://dir.yahoo.com/Society_and_Culture/Death_and_Dying/* *http://www.death-dying.com/* *http://www.aarp.org/indexes/life.html*
Web EHE	The Exceptional Human Experience network is an earnest attempt to collect and document a variety of experiences, including unitive or mystical ones: *http://www.ehe.org/*
Web Epictetus	Epictetus. *Enchiridion*. Elizabeth Carter (tr). Available on the MIT Internet Classics Archive, *http://classics.mit.edu/Epictetus/epicench.html*
Web Epicurus	Epicurus. *Letter to Monoeceus*. Robert Drew Hicks (tr). Available on the MIT Internet Classics Archive, *http://classics.mit.edu/Epicurus/menoec.html*
Web Forgiveness	Luskin's Forgiveness research is documented at *www.learningtoforgive.com*
Web Freud	The text of *On the Interpretation of Dreams* (1900) is online at: *http://www.yorku.ca/dept/psych/classics/Freud/Dreams/index.htm*
Web Funerals	The Federal Trade Commission's Consumer Guide to Funerals is at *http://www.ftc.gov/bcp/conline/pubs/services/funeral.htm* The American Association of Retired Persons (AARP) publishes a guide to funeral costs and options at *http://www.aarp.org/confacts/money/funeral.html* A condensed version of (Markin 1999) is online at *http://www.dragonet.com/funeral/*

Web Genealogy   Amateur genealogists are everywhere on the internet; start with
                   http://dir.yahoo.com/Arts/Humanities/History/Genealogy/
                   http://genealogy.about.com/hobbies/genealogy/index.htm

Web Gunaratana   The text of the first edition of (Gunaratana 1993):
                   http://www.enabling.org/ia/vipassana/Archive/G/
                   Gunaratana/MindfulnessIPE/index.html.

Web Happiness   A comprehensive bibliography and database of multinational happiness research is maintained for free access by the Erasmus University Rotterdam:
                   http://www.eur.nl/fsw/research/happiness/index.htm

Web Holidays   Suggestions for secular seasonal holidays are at:
                   http://www.secularseasons.com/
                   Tips for frugal and noncommercial celebrations:
                   http://www.frugalitynetwork.com/holidays.html

Web James   The text of (James 1902):
                   http://www.csp.org/experience/james-varieties/james-varieties.html.

Web Kant   The works of Kant are available online at the English Server sponsored by the University of Washington:
                   http://eserver.org/philosophy
                   The Categorical Imperative is covered in his *Metaphysics of Morals,*
                   http://eserver.org/philosophy/kant/metaphys-of-morals.txt

Web Lucretius   Lucretius, Titus Carus. "Folly of the fear of death." in *On the Nature of Things, Book III.* William Ellery Leonard (tr). On the Project Gutenberg system:
                   http://www.gutenberg.net/index.html

Web Mysticism   A well-organized collection of quotations about mysticism and the mystical experience, drawn from the literatures of six world religions:
                   http://www.digiserve.com/mystic/

Web NAS 1   The pamphlet "Science and Creationism":
                   http://www.nap.edu/catalog/6024.html

Web NAS 2   The National Academies' website on Creationism:
                   http://www4.nas.edu/opus/evolve.nsf

Web NASA   Images of the planets from all NASA/JPL missions:
                   http://photojournal.jpl.nasa.gov/

Web Nolo	Nolo Press offers articles on estate planning and other legal topics, as well as selling highly-regarded self-help legal books and software, at: *http://www.nolo.com*
Web Pali Canon	The English text of large parts of the Pali Canon can be read at Access to Insight, along with a number of interpretive books and papers: *http://www.accesstoinsight.org/*
Web Philosophy	A useful, brief encyclopedia of philosophical topics (which includes explanations of most philosophical schools and biographies of most philosophers) is at *http://www.utm.edu/research/iep/*
Web Pirsig	Home page of the Metaphysics of Quality organization has many resources related to Pirsig's philosophy: *http://www.moq.org* The paper "Subjects, Objects, and Data Values" can be read at *http://www.moq.org/forum/emm.html*
Web Quran	The complete text of the Quran is available at several sites. The Quran Browser provided by the Scholarly Technology Group at Brown University contains an excellent search engine with access to texts of three translations: *http://www.stg.brown.edu/webs/quran_browser/* *pqeasy.shtml*
Web RERC	The home page of the Alister Hardy Trust, sponsoring society of the Religious Experience Research Centre at Westminster College, Oxford, is *http://www.charitynet.org/~RERC/index.html*
Web Rotary	The internet presence of Rotary International is *http://www.rotary.org/* The story of Herbert J. Taylor and the Four-Way Test originally appeared in The Rotarian, vol 175 no 4 and is now online at: *http://www.rotary.org/pubs/rotarian/1999/9910/* *page05.htm*

Web Simplicity   Two internet entry points to the subject of voluntary
                     simplicity are:
                         http://dmoz.org/Society/Lifestyle_Choices/
                                 Voluntary_Simplicity/
                         http://dir.yahoo.com/Society_and_Culture/
                         Cultures_and_Groups/Voluntary_Simplicity/
                     Many books on the subject are revealed by a search at
                     Amazon.com using the subject keyword "simplicity."
                     You can cause the books to be sorted with the most
                     popular first, and thus discover which are most-read.

Web TASTE   TASTE is an online journal devoted to anonymous,
                     first-person accounts of transcendental experiences of
                     scientists. It is found at:
                                 http://www.issc-taste.org/

Web Thoreau   Information about Henry David Thoreau, as well as
                     the complete texts of *Walden* and other works, is
                     available at several sites online, including
                                 http://www.walden.org/thoreau/

Subject Index

Index to Cited Authors

Space for notes